Why Daddy, Why?

Sandra

God Bless You

Emelia Hardy

Why Daddy, Why?

by Emelia Dion Hardy

Writers Club Press
San Jose New York Lincoln Shanghai

Why Daddy, Why?

Writers Club Press
an imprint of iUniverse, Inc.

For information address:
iUniverse, Inc.
5220 S. 16th St., Suite 200
Lincoln, NE 68512
www.iuniverse.com

ISBN: 0-595-21498-3

Printed in the United States of America

I dedicate this book to the memory of my brother Jerry.

Also, to mama—for all the pain she's been through and has kept inside all these years.

And

To anyone who suffered pain because of Daddy and his mother Mommie.
To them I say I'm sorry.

Blessed are the meek, for they shall inherit the earth.
—Matt.5:5

Foreword

This book about extreme cruelty by a daddy for his children and his loving wife is written simply and from the heart, much of it from the point of view of the little girl Emelia who suffered unimaginable torture at the hands of her abusive, alcoholic father. "I wrote this book simply, like a little girl but with the heart of a woman," the author says. "You will find no words that you can't pronounce or understand. What you will find is the open heart of a little girl, then of the woman she became." The author goes on to give a vivid and heartfelt account of the abuse the same little girl suffered at the hands of nuns, supposedly the agents of God's love and mercy, behind the closed doors of a convent; thereafter she reveals how she found herself in a life–threatening situation, brought about by her own hand at fifteen, as a result of an unfeeling husband who raped and beat her. The picture she paints is made all the more poignant by the loss of the one true love whose memory will never die, by the loss of a devoted brother who couldn't stay because God wanted him more, and by the unconditional love of a mother prepared to sacrifice anything for her children.

The book shows how the shadow of a father's cruelty can be cast over the whole life of a child—a child who, in this instance, never failed to turn the other cheek, or return love for cruelty and abuse, who manifested, in the end, the overriding power and strength of Christ who advocated love above all things. The book is a protest against domestic violence and institutionalised cruelty, and will hopefully stand as a beacon and warning against the violations suffered by so many Emelias whose heartfelt cries go unheard behind the closed or locked doors of our apparently respectable western civilization.

CHM

Acknowledgements

I want to thank my husband Bob and my son Shaun for putting up with me during this emotional roller–coaster ride I've been on while writing this book.

I thank my brothers, Albert, Leo and Paul for their support.

I thank my sister Cecile not only for her support but also for her input.

I thank my step dad for being there for all of us when it counted.

I thank mama for reliving this terrible nightmare with me. She truly has been my inspiration.

Most of all, I thank God for his guidance in my life.

1

I took a long ride today and now I'm sitting on a park bench right on Main Street in Berlin, New Hampshire. There's grass under my feet and a cool breeze on my face. You'd think that would put a smile on my face, but it doesn't.

The Columbia Hotel once stood in this small grassy spot before it burnt down. It was a tall building with twenty rooms and living quarters where the owner lived. The owner—Gerard Dion—was my dad, a very handsome man of average build, brown hair and blue eyes. There was also a restaurant on the bottom floor that he owned.

I thought that if I sat on the park bench I'd forget all the bad things that took place here. I thought that when I saw the building had *really* gone—that it no longer stood in its prominent position before me—that all the pain, the bad old memories, would vanish with it.

But instead the pain floods back. The memories of those days are as strong as ever, as though they happened yesterday.

◆　　◆　　◆

I heard a noise outside the door of our living quarters.

It scared me! I remembered just a month before how I had heard the same noise and I opened the door. My uncle Archie was standing there holding a pillow against his face. He was bleeding from his nose and mouth and the pillow was red with his blood. I was so scared I couldn't move. I started calling, "Mama, mama!" She came running. Just as she got to the door, my uncle fell. Mama caught him in her arms and he died right there. I was only five and ever since the sound of a knock at the door would bring back the memory, the terrible sight of seeing someone bleed and die right in front of me! Uncle Archie had cancer and he hemorrhaged from the mouth and nose, and the memory was so scary I got so I didn't want to open that door anymore.

I heard some keys jingle and in my mind I could see uncle standing there again, covered with blood! But I steeled myself and opened the door, and there he was! But it wasn't uncle Archie this time, it was my daddy—tall, handsome, but his blue eyes burned with a fire that took my breath away.

"Are… are you drunk again, daddy?" I asked nervously.

The fire in his eyes flared and he reached out for me. I broke free and ran just as fast as my five–year–old legs would take me. He chased me all around the house. I ran into my room and jumped up on my bed.

But he was right behind me! I looked up at him. All I could see was his fist coming at me.

This was the first time I saw his fist. Normally he used his army belt. He would hit me so hard he would leave welts all over my backside. Mama would always nurse me back, of course. She would put cold washcloths on my back, legs and bottom, too. She would tell me to always close my eyes. "Don't look at him, honey," she would say. "He won't stop if you keep looking at him."

Mama knew that—because that's what *she* would do.

I closed my eyes and the fist hit. I could hear the sound. I heard his fist hit hard but I felt no pain. Why couldn't I feel the pain? When he hit me with the belt it hurt—but it didn't hurt this time.

I could feel pressure up against me. He must be looking at me. Could he tell that it didn't hurt? But I mustn't look! If I did he'd know and he might hit me again—and then it might really hurt. I'll just wait, I thought, and maybe he'd go away.

I think I heard him cough but it sounded like it was far away. I could still feel the pressure up against me, so he must have still been there. There was that cough again! I just *knew* it was him, but it sounded like it was coming from another room.

I *had* to open my eyes but I couldn't move my legs—there was something heavy on them.

"Mama! It's *you!*"

I managed to crawl out from under her. I whispered in her ear, "Mama it's okay—you can open your eyes now. Daddy's gone into the living room." I sat up to look at her. "Oh mama!" I gasped. "Your face is all bloody! I'll get a tissue and wipe your face." But it wouldn't wipe off—it was all sticky. "It's okay, mama, I'll get a washcloth and take care of you, just like you always take care of me."

But I couldn't wash all the blood off. "Mama, *please* open your eyes, he's gone!"

Mama looked up at me and took me into her arms. She held me just as tight as could be.

The next morning when I woke up, mama was gone.

I could smell food cooking and thought I'd better get up before daddy got mad like he always did. I went into the kitchen and everyone was sitting there quiet as could be—Albert in his high chair and Leo sitting on the booster chair that used to be mine. Cecile was sitting next to daddy, where she always sat. I think daddy liked her best. Jerry, being the oldest, was busy putting the coals in the furnace that heated the hotel.

I didn't look at daddy. I was afraid he would want to hit me where he had hit mama the night before. Mama jumped in front of me and daddy's fist hit her instead of me. Mama always did things like that to protect us.

She was over by the stove but I knew I couldn't go and look at her because that would make daddy mad. So I sat down at the table.

When mama came to sit, Jerry was back from his chore. Her face was all swollen. I looked over at daddy and he told us mama had hurt herself when she was moving things in the overhead cupboard. Some things had fallen on her.

"Isn't that right, Emelia?" daddy asked.

I didn't know what to say. I knew that wasn't true. My heart was pounding so hard, I thought the others would see me shake.

"Isn't that true, Emelia?" daddy asked again.

I knew that if I agreed with him he would beat me later for telling a lie—just as he did when he helped me with my catechism: we never made it past the first question.

"Who made you?" he would ask

"God made me," I would answer.

"No!" said daddy. "*I* made you."

"No daddy, in the book it says that God made me."

Then the belt would show up out of nowhere. It hurt!

"Please, daddy, don't!" I would cry. "Please, daddy, it hurts!"

Then I would remember what mama told me about not looking at him: don't say anything to him—only then it would stop.

When the next time came and he wanted to ask me my catechism question I thought I would be smarter and tell him what he wanted to hear.

"Who made you?" he asked.

"*You* did daddy. You did!"

But it was no good. The belt would show up again because I had lied to him.

I was so glad when mama spoke up. "I don't think she was in the room when it happened, Jerry," said mama.

That was daddy's name too—just like big brother.

After mama spoke up, daddy didn't say any more about it.

But later on that night mama looked like she was hurting more than she did in the morning. Daddy had punched her a couple more times for protecting me.

◆　　◆　　◆

I could hear Albert crying. His crib was at the foot of daddy's and mama's bed. It wouldn't last long. Daddy would throw a pillow on top of his head. He didn't like it when Albert cried.

If any of us got hurt we would hide so daddy wouldn't hit us for crying. He would keep hitting us to teach us to be able to stand the pain and not cry any more. Sometimes he did it for no reason. The one that got it the worst was Jerry because he was the oldest. He was the best older brother anyone could ever have. He looked just like daddy, there was no denying that, even though he was only nine. He had brown hair and blue eyes, and a separation between his front teeth that suited him.

I always thought he was the oldest until I found out about Paul. He was the first–born but we never got to know him at that time. When mama and daddy first got married, she got pregnant with Paul. Daddy was still in the service.

Mama was working and living at the orphanage in Manchester, N.H., when daddy got out of the service. Paul was four months old. Daddy went to live in Berlin, N.H., and took mama with him. Daddy made mama leave Paul behind just until they got settled. He said he would take her back to get him.

Paul was six months old when mama went with daddy to pick him up, but when they got there daddy still wouldn't let mama take him home because she was pregnant with Jerry—and he said it would be too much for her. So she would have to wait just a little while longer. How she longed for her little boy! She kept asking daddy if he would take her to get him. The day finally came when Paul was a year old.

Mama was so excited! When she got there she was so overwhelmed with joy when she saw him. It had been six months since she had seen him and he had grown so much! She paid so much attention to Paul that daddy became angry. He was clearly jealous of him.

"Lets go!" daddy said. "We're leaving."

Mama reached for Paul.

"No!" daddy said emphatically. "He stays here!"

"But Jerry!" mama protested, "you *said* we could take him home now! I have his room all ready. He won't be any trouble. I'll keep him out of your way. I'll still have time to get everything done that you want me to do. Please Jerry, *please* let me take our son home!"

"He's *not* my son!"

"Jerry, what are you *saying*?" Mama was aghast. "He *is* your son."

"No." Daddy shook his head. "He's not. You must have gotten pregnant while I was in the service."

"Jerry!" She couldn't believe her ears. "How can you *say* that? I haven't been with anyone else! You *know* that."

But daddy was unmoved. "Furthermore," he announced coldly, "Jerry's not my son either."

"I can't believe what I'm hearing!" said mama.

"It doesn't matter what you believe. Paul is *not* coming home and that's the end of it. Grab your purse and let's go. You'll never see him again. I'll see to it!"

A couple of days later mama called the orphanage. They told her Paul was no longer there. "Your husband came in and signed all the papers," the woman said brightly. "He said it was too hard for you to do so and he would take care of the matter for you."

"Where is Paul?" asked mama, her heart in her mouth.

"You'll be happy to know he's already been adopted!"

Mama was crushed. Her little boy was gone and she would never see him again.

What a cruel thing for daddy to do to mama! It was much, much worse than the beating he gave her when they got home from the orphanage.

2

"**M**om," said Jerry. "There's a Walt Disney movie playing at the Princess Theater. Do you think that maybe I might be able to go? I'll take Cecile and Emelia with me."

"I'll have to let you know later, Jerry," mama smiled. "In the meantime make sure all your chores are done—and you two girls do the same."

"Okay, mom." Jerry turned to us. "Come on, girls! Let's make sure, like mom said."

It was dinnertime and daddy came home to eat. He was already sitting at the table when we went in and took our seats.

"Your mother tells me you kids want to go to the movies," he said gruffly.

"Yes, dad," Jerry smiled tentatively.

"You'll have to earn your 15¢." Daddy gave Jerry a sour look. "I have a truckload of wood coming in. In fact, the truck's here now. The guys are unloading it. They're throwing it down the cellar stairs. If you and your two sisters want to stack it all up against the wall that I'll show you, I'll give each of you 15¢ to go to the movies."

"That would be great!" beamed Jerry.

"You'll have to hurry if you want to get it done in time to go." He gave Jerry a grudging smile that failed to include his eyes.

It was 12 noon. The last movie of the day was at 5 p.m. Daddy said that even though we couldn't be out that late, he would make an exception this time.

We were so excited! Not only were we going to the movies, we were going to be able to stay out until 7 p.m., for that was when the movie finished. Wow! That would be the nicest thing daddy had ever done for us. Mama was so pleased. She could see the smiles on our faces that brightened up the whole room. It was nice to see mama smile too. It was the first time in a long time I could remember seeing a smile on her face.

"Well, let's go!" said Jerry.

"You just wait one minute!" said mama. "You have to eat some dinner first."

"That's what I like to see," daddy said approvingly. "Kids anxious to go to work! Let them go, Irene."

Mama wanted us to have something in our bellies so she gave us each a banana and a piece of bread and butter folded in half.

"Leave the peels here," said daddy. "I don't want them in the cellar. Now make a start!"

We stood outside looking at the cellar door. We couldn't believe our eyes! There was so much wood thrown down the cellar stairs that there was no way to get in.

"Come with me," said daddy.

We went into the restaurant and in the kitchen there was a trapdoor that he lifted, revealing stairs that led down to the cellar. He pointed to the wall where he wanted the wood stacked.

"Only on that wall!" he said. "It should all fit. Jerry, you'll have to stack it high in order to get it all in."

"Okay, dad," said Jerry. Then daddy disappeared.

We all walked over to the woodpile and just stood there looking up at it—perfectly cut two–foot logs and so many of them!

"Let's get started," said Jerry. He was in charge and that was all right with Cecile and me.

"Emelia," said Jerry. "You take one at a time and bring it over to the wall and lay it on the floor." He turned to Cecile. "Can you carry two at a time?"

"I don't know. Let me see." Cecile struggled, but lifted a log. "Yep, I can."

Jerry picked up three logs at once. "Okay, lets get moving," he said.

We worked so hard. Sometimes Jerry would carry only two and Cecile would only take one. Sometimes I had to drag mine. It was 3 p.m. when mama showed up with three glasses of sarsaparilla. Oh! how I loved sarsaparilla! I liked Bubble Up too, but daddy wouldn't let us kids have the soda because it was for paying customers only.

"It's okay," said mama. "I paid for it with my tip money."

We all knew about mama's tip money—except for daddy.

One day daddy told mama, "Get dressed—we're going out tonight with my buddies." Mama hated going out with them. It was just one big drinking party with daddy as the center of attention. Mama wasn't allowed to talk to anyone, especially the men, unless daddy was in hearing distance. Mama never wanted to, anyway, because she knew it would only make daddy jealous and he would accuse her after they got home of one of them being the father of one of us kids.

Daddy wanted to make sure mama didn't say anything bad about him. The last thing he wanted was for his friends to find out how he treated his family.

Mama asked him if she could have $1.25 to buy a pair of nylons. Daddy did what he always did—he took out a $1.00 bill and threw it on the floor, making her pick it up and then telling her to make do. He never gave her enough and mama worked so hard for him.

Jerry had a little piggy bank. "Here, mom, I have 25¢. You can put it towards your nylons."

"Thanks, Jerry," she said, accepting the money. "I'll pay you back someday."

One time Jerry wasn't around but I had 10¢ and Cecile had 15¢, so we were able to help mama instead.

"That's the last time he will ever do that to me," mama assured us this time. When daddy threw the money on the floor his friends laughed at mama. "I'll have my own money so I'll never have to ask him again!"

So mama started hiding some of her tip money. She made a little hole way back on top of the counter in the kitchen of the restaurant. She would drop some of her change into that little hole and it would drop into a box under the counter. No one ever saw it. Every time she needed money, she would go into her little hiding place and get what she needed.

When daddy wasn't around, mama would give us each enough money to go across the street and buy a candy bar and a soda. What a treat that was! Mama was so nice. Why couldn't daddy be like that?

"Emelia, are you going to finish your drink so we can get back to work?" Jerry asked. "We don't have much time left!"

"Okay, Jerry." I said "I'm done."

"Thanks for the cold drinks, mom," said Jerry.

"You kids are doing a great job," said mama. "Your father should be real happy with this. I'm so proud of all of you. Hurry now!"

"We will!" said Jerry.

I was able to pick up my wood again, Cecile was back to carrying two and Jerry was able to handle three. Thanks to mama bringing us nice cold drinks and taking a break we were back to full speed again.

"Look, girls, we only have a little time left," said Jerry. "It's 4:15. We can do it. Work faster!"

We worked as fast as we could.

"We did it!" Jerry exclaimed, breathless with excitement. "How about that! We did it! And it's only 4:45. We have 15 minutes before the movie starts. I'm going to get dad!"

Cecile and I were so happy! We were holding hands and swinging around and around. Then we heard daddy coming.

"Look, dad!" Jerry said proudly. "We're all done! We even swept the floor so it would be nice and clean when you saw it. It's 4:50, dad. We've just enough time to get to the movies before it starts."

Daddy looked around. He looked at the woodpile, then looked at us with a sour expression. He shouted and his words were like a thunderclap.

"YOU STACKED IT AGAINST THE WRONG WALL!" He glared at us. "NOW MOVE IT ALL OVER TO *THAT* WALL... OVER *THERE*!" He took a breath. "I want it done before any of you go to bed tonight! That means you won't have time for supper—so don't plan on it."

Daddy turned and walked away. We all just stood there. We couldn't speak right away.

"I can't believe he did that," said Cecile in a choked voice.

"I can," Jerry said bitterly. "I should have known it was too easy to have him agree that we would work to earn money to go to the movies." He shook his head. "Dad had already made up his mind that we were going to do this job anyway. Why pay when you can get the job done for nothing."

Jerry, Cecile and I started to move the wood again. I could see great big tears in Jerry's eyes. That put tears in my eyes, too. We could hear daddy yelling at mama upstairs. Then we could hear banging. We all knew that mama must have said something to daddy and now he was beating her again.

"Someday I'm going to be big enough...," said Jerry

Every time daddy beat mama, Jerry always said that to her. "Someday, mom, I'm going to be big enough!" And mama would say, "Yes Jerry, someday you *will* be big enough."

It's a good thing that mama made us eat that buttered bread and banana. I was so hungry, but I knew that if I hadn't had that banana, I would have been a lot hungrier. It was 10 p.m. and we were exhausted.

"Okay, it's done," Jerry said at last. "Lets get upstairs and get cleaned up."

Mama wasn't allowed to come downstairs to see us, but she was waiting for us when we got upstairs. Her face was all red where daddy had slapped her around. She looked at us and the tears started to flow.

Mama felt so bad for us and we felt bad for her, for what she had to go through every time she tried to help us. She loved us so much, she would have taken our place for a beating anytime she could—and she did, many times.

Jerry and Cecile went and got washed up. Mama gave me a sponge bath, sitting me on the edge of the counter near the sink. We were told that we could have no supper; but mama made us a snack and put it in our rooms so we would have something to eat.

"Don't tell," said mama

I would never tell on mama, never.

Daddy walked into the room where mama was getting me cleaned up. "Did you give them supper after I told you not to?" he demanded.

"No," said mama. "I did not give them any supper."

Satisfied, daddy walked away.

"I gave them a snack—not supper," she whispered to me.

Off to bed we went. I lay there with thoughts of what mama had done for us. I sure was hungry before that snack and felt a lot better now. I liked the way mama got the better of daddy and never told a lie! I couldn't help but smile as I went to sleep.

The next morning I woke to daddy yelling at Jerry. What could Jerry have done wrong this early in the morning? I crept up to the door. Daddy grabbed Jerry right out of bed! He had overslept because of the late night we all had moving wood. Normally Jerry was up by 5 a.m. One of his chores was to put coal in the furnace and he didn't wake up in time. It was now 6 a.m. and daddy was mad. The hotel had cooled off just a little, but that didn't matter to daddy. He had Jerry by his hair, dragging him down the hall and out of sight. I ran to get mama but she already knew it. She told me to stay out of sight—but I just *had* to check on Jerry.

'I'll just tiptoe and he won't hear me,' I thought. Cecile told me about that once. I asked her how come she didn't get beaten all the time like Jerry and I, or like mama, too. She told me she tiptoed around and he never saw her. I asked her if she would teach me how to do that—I didn't like getting the belt all the time. She said I had to practice to get good at it.

I ran down the hallway and down the stairs, then I moved real slow so he wouldn't see me. Daddy was shaking Jerry, then started punching him on his arms. One time Jerry fell down to the floor and when he tried to stand up, daddy kicked him on his bottom. Daddy grabbed Jerry by the neck and was pushing his head towards the open door of the furnace. I couldn't look any more. It hurt so bad inside, I hid my face.

"Jerry!" mama yelled.

It made me jump. It made daddy jump, too. He let go of Jerry and he got away.

"That's the last time you're going to protect one of those kids!" daddy yelled.

"Jerry, I don't know what you're so upset about," mama said quickly. "You asked me to make you a nice hot cup of coffee with a shot of whiskey in it. I fixed it right up for you. I thought you would want it before it got cold. I was only trying to get your attention. Would you like me to bring it back upstairs for you?"

"No," daddy said grumpily. "Give it to me now. What about the rest of my breakfast?"

"I'll go right now and fix it for you," said mama.

Mama couldn't get back upstairs fast enough. She wanted to check on Jerry before daddy came back upstairs.

So big brother got through another one of daddy's beatings. Sometimes I wondered just how many more times daddy would do this to Jerry before he killed him.

Now I knew why mama went right to the kitchen when I went to find her to tell her about Jerry. She knew she would have a better chance of getting Jerry free from daddy if she showed up with something daddy would want—and that would be the whiskey.

Daddy had his breakfast, then left. Mama went down to the cellar and filled the furnace with coal so Jerry wouldn't have to.

I went into Jerry's room. He was just lying there on his bed.

"Are you okay?" I asked.

"I hurt all over," said Jerry, "but I'll be all right. Were you down there when he beat me?"

"Yes, I was. It was awful. I thought daddy was going to put you in the furnace! I was so glad when mama showed up."

"I was too," Jerry sighed. "You know, *you* could have gotten caught and dad would have beat you too."

"I was hiding. I had to go just in case there was something I could do to help you—but I wasn't much help, was I?"

"That's okay, Emelia." He smiled. "Thanks for trying anyway."

"I love you Jerry," I said, trying to swallow the lump in my throat.

"I love you too, Emelia," said Jerry.

3

Cecile used to love to eat canned tomatoes. She would heat them up, then add salt, pepper and butter. That was daddy's favorite too—which is where Cecile got her taste for it in the first place. When she was little daddy would give her bites of his.

One day Cecile thought she would fix herself up a can. When she started to open the can our cousin ran into the room and warned her: "Your father's coming!" Cecile hurriedly put the can of tomatoes back. She slid the half–opened can onto the top shelf of the cupboard, then ran out of the room.

No way was I going to stay there! I ran off, too, before he got there.

It was a couple of weeks later when daddy decided to have a can of tomatoes. I walked into the kitchen just as he reached for the can. As he pulled it down off the shelf, he tipped it so the juice poured over his face. He was so angry that he reached out for *me!* He dragged me into the room where the belt was and beat me with it.

I was so sick of that belt! Here was I, seven years old, and this punishment just kept going on and on. Would it *ever* stop? I asked myself the question because I knew I could never ask him. Why did Cecile put that open can back into the cupboard? Why did daddy always blame *me?*

Cecile just stood there and watched daddy give me a beating for something *she* had done. It hurt so much! Daddy liked to hit bare skin, so down came my panties every time he felt like beating me. What hurt even more was that my big sister never tried to stop him. When he was all done giving me the belt I went to my bedroom. Cecile followed me.

"Why didn't you tell him I was the one that opened the can?" asked Cecile.

"Why didn't you tell him *you* were the one that did it?" I answered. "Besides, you knew that if I opened my mouth and said it was you that did it, he would have hit me that much harder—and it already hurt enough! He thinks you don't do *anything* wrong!" I said, the tears running down my cheeks. "And you know how to tiptoe, remember? I still haven't learned how."

"I'm sorry that happened to you," Cecile said softly.

"Then why don't you go *tell* him it was you that did it and not me!" I wailed.

"I *said* I was sorry—not *crazy!*" said Cecile. "That's the last thing I'd do."

"Well," I said, wiping my eyes, "I'm just going to stay out of his way today. He doesn't seem to be in a very good mood. Not that he ever is, anyway."

Mr. Frank came into the restaurant for his dinner. He took all his meals there since he was one of our full-time boarders. Daddy had already come and gone.

"Irene," Mr. Frank said to mama, "I like these kids of yours. You and Jerry have been kind to me over the years, so I took it upon myself to buy your son Jerry a bicycle. Every boy should have a bike." He smiled. "I hope you don't mind."

Jerry was so excited when he saw it! He never had anything so shiny and new before and it was all his. Daddy didn't believe in wasting money on kids—or mama.

"I also picked out a watch for each of the girls," Mr. Frank said.

"Mr. Frank!" exclaimed mama. "You didn't have to do that!"

"I know," Mr. Frank smiled, "but I wanted to."

"Oh mama! Can we keep them?" Cecile and I chorused.

Mama smiled and nodded her head yes.

"*Thank* you Mr. Frank, it's beautiful!" I said.

"Come on, Emelia," said Cecile, "I'll show you how to use it."

"*Would* you, Cecile?" I asked.

"Thank you, Mr. Frank," said Cecile as we walked off.

Mr. Frank nodded. "Leo and Albert are too small right now, but I'll get them something a little later down the road." He looked at mama and held out some dollar notes. "Oh, before I forget, I want you to have this money to buy yourself a couple of dresses."

Mama was taken aback. "I can't take that money from you!" she said. "I wouldn't feel right about that, Mr. Frank. Besides, I don't have the time to go shopping."

"Now, don't give me that for an excuse!" Mr. Frank's smile broadened. "There's a store right across the street. I really would like to do this. I have no family, you see. You and your husband have always made me feel like I was part of yours. So please allow me to do this."

"Okay." Mama hesitated, then took the notes. "As long as you're *sure*."

"Yes, I'm quite sure," said Mr. Frank.

"Than I say thank you, Mr. Frank"

"You are very welcome."

The truth is mama was excited, for she hadn't bought herself anything for a long time. She was able to take a break right away, so she ran across the street and it only took her twenty minutes to buy what she wanted. No matter what mama did, it never took her very long to do it. She got used to being around daddy. If she didn't move fast enough he would kick her—and he always made sure it was where it didn't show. He didn't want anyone asking questions. There were times when he messed up by punching her in the face, but even then he made sure mama had plenty of makeup to be able to cover up the marks.

There were times that mama had marks on her when we went to visit *memere* and *pepere*. They were mama's parents. Daddy made sure that mama had her story straight, like something fell on her, or she ran into something, or she banged into a door; or Albert, being a baby and having his diaper changed, accidentally kicked her in the face—and so on and on.

Right after mama would explain her bruises, daddy would sit back in his chair with his hands clasped together behind his head and say, "Now Irene, tell the truth—I beat you up!" Everyone would laugh, of course. They had already believed what mama had said and thought daddy was only kidding. That's how he fooled a lot of people.

Daddy came home when it was time for supper. He saw the red bike sitting outside when he came in.

"Whose bike's outside the door?" he asked.

"It belongs to Jerry," said mama. "Let me tell you why." Then she told him everything Mr. Frank said, about him feeling like family and all. But daddy was far from happy.

"The only way Jerry can keep that bike is to tell everyone *I* bought it for him!" he said. "And that goes for the girls too. Do you hear me?"

"Yes, Jerry," mama said with downcast eyes, "I hear you."

"What about the dresses?" he went on, yelling. "What does Frank think? That I can't afford to buy any of you anything?" He pursed his lips. "We're not a charity case! If I wanted to I could have gotten those things myself!"

I bet I knew what mama was thinking. 'If *you* can afford it,' she would say, 'then why don't you do it? You never buy your kids anything!' But I didn't blame her for not saying it. I hate to think what would have happened to her if she had.

The next day mama was explaining to Jerry that the only way he would be able to keep his bike was to tell everyone that his father had bought it for him.

"Why, mom?" he asked. "Dad didn't buy it for me! I already told my friends that Mr. Frank bought it."

"I spoke to Mr. Frank," said mama. "He said it was all right with him."

Jerry shook his head. "That's not right, mom."

"No, it's not, Jerry." Mama smiled sadly. "But you know your father. He'll take it away from you."

Jerry was insistent. "I don't think dad has the right to make me say something that's not true."

"You're right, Jerry," mama agreed. "Your father doesn't have the right to make any of you kids say something that's not true."

What mama and Jerry didn't know was that daddy was listening outside the door. He was outraged! He stormed outside and took Jerry's bike and threw it in the back of his truck. He drove furiously to the pawnbroker and sold it to him. He came back home and never said a word. When Jerry noticed his bike was gone, he somehow knew that it was his dad that took it. Shortly afterwards mama got a phone call from a friend who told her that she saw daddy put the bike in the back of his truck. Mama had to tell Jerry—but he already knew. "Only dad can be mean enough to do something like that," Jerry said to mama.

Cecile came and found me to tell me that Mr. Olsen's door was open.

"You know what that means, don't you?" asked Cecile.

"I sure do," I said. "That means we can go and make some cookies!"

We ran down the hall where Mr. Olsen was waiting for us. He was the nicest man ever. He taught us how to make sugar cookies. He was also one of our full–time boarders and he had a stove in his room. That's how we made the cookies.

Mr. Olsen was very old, but when he was younger he made doll-house furniture. He made Cecile a table and chair set and it was beautiful! It took him a long time to make it because his hands didn't move so good anymore. He said that someday he would make me a set too, but it would be different. He said it would be the best he would ever make because it would be the last one that he would make. His hands were hurting him now and he could no longer do it. So, being the last one, it would have to be a very special one—and he was making it for me!

I waited a long time for my table set but one day he had it all done. It was so beautiful! The legs of the chairs and the table legs were all carved just like a real dining room set, with big bumps and little bumps and they were all perfect. The set was dark brown wood that was made shiny. The top of the table was like nothing I had ever seen before. He carved the Roman numeral clock right on the face of the whole table.

"You take care of this now," Mr. Olsen had said. "You'll never see another one like it. I made this special, just for you." It was the most wonderful thing I ever had. So now I had two wonderful things—the watch from Mr. Frank, and my table set from Mr. Olsen!

"Hi, Mr. Olsen! How are you today?" I asked. "I haven't seen you for a long time now."

"I saw your door was open so I went and got Emelia," said Cecile.

"Come in girls, come in," Mr. Olsen said cheerfully. "I miss seeing you two." He smiled warmly. "Have you come to make cookies?"

"Oh yes, we did!" I said. "Are you going to help us, Mr. Olsen?"

"Not today girls." He shook his head, still smiling. "But you two go right ahead. I have everything ready for you."

Cecile did most of the work but I didn't care. I liked eating the cookies!

"Have some, Mr. Olsen?" asked Cecile.

"Oh, I will, don't you worry," Mr.Olsen beamed, "but not right now. I'll save mine for later. It sure was nice having you two girls visit me today."

"The pleasure was all ours," said Cecile.

She had some really neat words like that. Maybe I'll be able to talk like that someday, I thought as we were leaving Mr. Olsen's room.

That was the last visit Cecile and I ever had with Mr. Olsen, for he died a little while after that day. I sure did miss him.

Later I was sitting on my bed looking at my wonderful watch that Mr. Frank gave me and I thought about Jerry losing his bike. "That wasn't very nice of daddy, taking Jerry's bike away," I said aloud, the sadness welling out of me. "Why does he do things like that? Poor

Jerry, I feel bad for him. It was *such* a nice red bicycle." Then I sensed someone was near and I turned round.

"Daddy!"

I was so surprised. He was standing in the doorway of my bedroom.

"Who gave you that watch?" daddy demanded.

"Mr. Frank did, daddy," I said, my heart beating wildly.

"Didn't *I* give it to you?" he asked, sneering.

"No daddy," I said.

Daddy held out his hand. I just looked at him. Then he pointed to my watch and held out his hand again. I could feel the tears welling up into my eyes. I handed him the watch. He walked over to Cecile's dresser and picked up her watch that she had put there. I held back the tears—I could hardly stand it! Daddy started to walk out of my room but he stopped and looked over to my shelf. He reached over and picked up my little table and chair set that Mr. Olsen had made for me. My heart went to my throat. "No, daddy, *please!* Not my table set! It's one of a kind. *Please* daddy!" my insides were screaming out. "That was made special for me, daddy."

"Where did you get this?" he asked coldly.

"From Mr. Olsen. He made it for me, daddy."

"Did *I* give this to you?" he asked.

"No daddy, you didn't," I said, my voice breaking.

Daddy took it with one hand and, keeping his eyes on me with a smile that didn't touch his eyes, he crushed it into little pieces. He threw the pieces onto my bed. He was still smiling at me.

Oh daddy! If it was all right to hate you I would, but it's not so. I can't, because mama says it's wrong to hate anyone. But if it was okay to hate one person, it would be you. I couldn't stop the tears that welled up and ran down my cheeks. I couldn't stop myself from crying any longer. I didn't care if daddy heard me cry. He couldn't make me hurt any more than I already did.

After daddy left my room he went looking for mama. He found her looking at her pretty new dresses. She was in her bedroom getting ready to hang them up so they wouldn't wrinkle.

I could hear daddy yelling at her.

"You think more of those dresses than you do me!" he shouted. "Why did Frank buy them for you? I want to know right now! Is he the father of one of those kids? What about Paul? Is he the father of him?"

There was that name again. *Who is Paul?* I asked myself.

"Give me those dresses!" daddy demanded. He went into the kitchen to get a pair of scissors.

"Jerry!" mama begged. "Look, I could always take them back to the store and give Frank his money back. Please don't cut them up!"

But it was too late. Daddy cut mama's dresses up into little pieces.

Daddy wouldn't let mama take them back because his sister and brother–in–law were the one's that owned the store, and he didn't want them to know what he was really like.

Daddy landed a backhand across mama's head. She went flying a good five feet before she lost her balance and fell to the floor. He walked up to her. "Don't *ever* talk back to me again! Next time I won't let you off so easy."

I walked up to mama after I heard daddy go out the door. She was still sitting on the kitchen floor crying. We never saw mama cry much. She didn't because if daddy saw her, he would make her cry more. He would say, "You want to cry? *I'll* give you something to cry about!" Then he would kick her as hard as he could.

I knelt down beside her. "Mama, please don't cry."

Mama looked up at me. She cried even more.

"Mama," I said, "Please don't cry, please mama! Someday you can get some more pretty dresses. We'll hide them so daddy won't cut them up again. It will be okay, mama."

But mama wasn't crying because of her dresses. She held up my hand and saw all the small broken pieces of my table set that Mr. Olsen had made for me. Mama's heart went out to me. She knew how much my table and chairs meant to me and it broke her heart to think that my daddy would do that to me.

She didn't care about her loss. She was used to it. Mama knew I would never have another table set because Mr. Olsen was gone now and it was the last one he ever made—and he had made it for her little girl. That was such a compliment he gave to mama—that he thought that much of her daughter.

I saw mama looking at my hand and I realized why she was crying. "It's okay mama," I said. "I got to have it for a little while before he broke it." But then I broke down and it was my turn to cry. "Oh mama! I'm not as strong as you are. I'm sorry. It hurts so much inside!"

Mama sat me on her lap and hugged me and we cried together.

The next day, Jerry, Cecile and I were sitting at one of the restaurant tables. Mr. Frank came over to our table.

"Can I sit down?" he asked.

"Yes," said Jerry.

"I'm sorry about what happened," he said. "You kids wouldn't be feeling so bad right now if it weren't for me. I should have asked permission from your father before I went and bought those things. Then he probably wouldn't have gotten so angry and you would still have your things. Jerry, can you—and you two ladies—ever forgive me?" He looked at me. "And I hear that you lost your precious table set that Mr. Olsen made for you, Emelia. I am so sorry."

"That's okay, Mr. Frank," I said. "It wasn't your fault. Daddy would have seen it sooner or later and break it anyway."

"You know something, Mr.Frank?" said Jerry. "Losing my bicycle is bad—but it's what he wanted me to do. That was worse. Dad wanted me to lie about it. He wanted me to tell everyone that *he* bought it for me."

"Yeah," agreed Cecile. "He wanted me to do the same thing."

"Me too," I said.

"Mama always teaches us not to lie," said Jerry. "Why does dad want us to lie for him? Not only that, but dad sold everything and kept the money. That's not right either, is it? It's just not right. That money belonged to you, Mr. Frank. Not dad."

4

"**G**et up," mama said, "daddy's waiting for you. It's dump time again."

Jerry jumped out of bed. There's no keeping daddy waiting—Cecile and I were ready to go. The three of us left with daddy. We went to the dump first, where we got to watch daddy pick through it—anything he thought he could use one of us would take to the truck. He even picked up pieces of wood that had rusty nails in it. The three of us had to pull out the nails with our hammers, then straighten them out. That took a lot of practice but we were all able to do it. Daddy never had to buy any nails. Every once in a while he would come across a nail that would bend when he used it. That would make him so wild he would kick the closest one of us that was near him. "You didn't straighten this one out right!" he would yell.

Our next stop would be to the back of the other restaurants in Berlin and Goram to pick up the swill they saved for him to feed his pigs. Sometimes daddy would say, "This head of lettuce don't look too bad. I think I'll take this one home and you kids can eat it." He did that a lot. What he didn't know was when he wasn't around, mama would throw it away—just like it had been in the first place.

Then, off to the farm where the pigs and the chickens were, we had to gather the eggs while he fed the pigs. There were times that we had to watch him kill some of the chickens and bring them home to mama so she could clean out the insides and pluck the feathers. That was a nasty job. I sometimes helped mama do that. I didn't like it much, but it had to be done. We would also go to the train station and climb into the boxcars. The cars that weren't cleaned out all the way had grain still left in them. We would fill grain bags with what was left. With any luck at all, we would make it back home in one piece without too many bruises.

We would be so tired and hungry when we got home. Daddy got to drink his beer all day, but us kids didn't even have a drink of water.

Mama would have supper all ready for us. We all got cleaned up and sat down to eat.

Jerry took a bite of his supper. "This fork tastes like soap," he said.

"*What* did you say!" daddy yelled.

Right away Jerry knew he was in trouble. He also knew that daddy heard exactly what he said so he didn't dare change one word.

"I asked you what you said, Jerry," daddy repeated.

"I… I said that this fork tastes like soap."

Daddy flew out of his chair and grabbed the silverware that was on the table. He looked at Jerry. "Lap it, every piece!" he yelled. "Lap it. Does it taste like soap?"

Daddy went over to the silverware and pulled out the whole draw and dumped it in front of Jerry.

"Lap it! Take another one. Lap it! Keep going! Keep lapping. Does it taste like soap? Does it?"

Then daddy grabbed Jerry and brought him down to the restaurant, sat him at a table and made him lap every piece of silverware in the restaurant.

"Does it taste like soap? Does it? Now you wash every piece—now!"

When Jerry got done washing every piece of silverware, daddy said, "Now you're going to lap them again! We want to make sure that there's no soap taste! Now lap, keep lapping! Don't stop. Oh no, you don't—you lap both sides of that knife!"

This went on for two hours.

"Now you wash *every* piece of silverware in this restaurant and put them away! When you're done you go upstairs and wash everything there too! You got that?"

"Yes dad," Jerry said.

"Louder! I can't hear you! And you refer to me as *sir*, do you understand?"

"Yes sir," Jerry said.

I ran back upstairs before daddy saw me. Mama had already cleaned the silverware upstairs. She hid some food in Jerry's room because she knew that after all that, daddy wouldn't let Jerry have any supper, and us kids had already missed out on lunch. Cecile and I hurried up and ate our supper before daddy got back upstairs.

Jerry had a sore tongue for a few days. Mama tried giving him ice to put on it, to make it feel better.

"One of these days, mama," Jerry said, "I'll be big enough. Dad won't hurt any of us any more. Not you, not Cecile, not Emelia—and I won't let him get to Albert and Leo. He doesn't do anything to Albert and Leo yet—they're still too small; but I'll find a way, mom, I will. You just wait and see! You just wait and see!"

You wouldn't believe how daddy was if his dinner wasn't ready when he was. The meals had to be at a certain temperature, not too hot, not too cold—mama had it down to a science! If daddy didn't get his meal on time then someone would get an awful beating! The problem was getting the dinner exactly right on Sundays when, being a conscientious mother, she wanted to take as many of her children as she could manage to church. Sunday morning came around again and it was Jerry's turn to stay home. Cecile and Jerry would take turns to stay home and watch the dinner. Daddy had to have his dinner at a certain time and not a minute later. The only way that mom could attend church was to set a time on a clock that didn't work to the time that the potatoes had to be turned on, for Jerry and Cecile had not yet learnt to tell the time. They would watch the clock that did work and when it matched the one that didn't work they would turn the stove burner on under the potatoes.

Mama told Jerry that if his father did come home early, just to tell him that his dinner would be ready on time—and that she had gone to church with the rest of the kids and would be right back.

It just so happened that daddy came home early this time and he was far from happy when he found out where mama was.

"How long has this been going on?" he yelled.

"Cecile and I take turns each Sunday staying home to make sure the potatoes get turned on—so mama can make sure your dinner is ready, dad," said Jerry.

"It *better* be ready on time—that's all I can say!" said daddy.

Jerry couldn't believe it! Daddy didn't beat him this time. But the day wasn't over with yet.

Daddy was waiting for mama when she got home. "Why have you been leaving the house? You know you don't have time to go to church!"

"I thought I should take the kids to church," mama said meekly.

"I don't care what you think!" daddy shouted. "You're not to take them again! You have better things to do than go to church! And these kids have plenty of chores."

"I always make sure that their chores are done before we go," mama said softly.

"I guess you're not hearing me too good! I said you are not *ever* to take them again. I couldn't care less about church. As far as I'm concerned, the four corners of the sky can fall down—and God can fall into shit!"

I couldn't believe my ears! I couldn't believe daddy had just said that to mama. What an awful thing to say!

I went to mama afterwards to talk to her about it.

"Mama, why did daddy say such a terrible thing? Why would he say something bad about God?"

Mama told me that daddy said it all the time. He had just never said it in front of anyone before. "I wish you never heard that, Emelia," said mama. "It's something that never should be said. I hate it when he says that—it puts cold shivers right through me every time."

Mama gave daddy his dinner and never said another word—and neither did he.

Jerry had gone out for a walk. When he was walking on the other side of the road, he noticed a shoebox full of heart–fund envelopes that had been thrown out into the trash. He thought it would be a neat thing to play with. He took it home and was opening the envelope when, in one of them, he found a $1.00 bill inside. He went to daddy to show him. Daddy grabbed him and slammed him up against the wall.

"You didn't find that—you stole it out of my wallet!" he shouted. "How dare you steal from me! You don't ever want to steal from me!"

Jerry kept trying to tell daddy that he didn't take it from him—that he really *did* find it in the envelope. But daddy wouldn't listen to him.

Mama held the envelope up to daddy's face. "He's telling the truth!" she said.

But daddy was too busy pounding Jerry to hear what mama was saying to him.

Then mama took the whole shoebox full of the envelopes and threw them at daddy. He finally realized that Jerry was telling the truth.

"Where did you find these?" Daddy asked.

"Across the street, dad," Jerry replied with big tears in his eyes.

"Do I see you crying, Jerry?"

"No daddy," Jerry said quickly.

"You better not be! Now go through the rest of these and see if there's any more money in them!"

"I already did, dad, and there wasn't any."

"I don't care if you already checked! Do it again!"

While Jerry was doing that, daddy called the police station to tell them. The police came to the house and daddy played the big shot. He was so good at that. He made a big deal over that $1.00 bill. He never gave Jerry any credit for anything.

Mama went to Jerry and told him how proud she was of him.

"Why can't dad ever be proud of me, mom?" Jerry wiped the tears from his eyes. "I thought I was going to make him so happy when I found that money. I never thought dad would think *I* stole from him! I should have known it was too good to be true when I didn't get beat this morning when daddy came home and everyone was at church. It seems like there's never a day that goes by that dad doesn't find some kind of reason to beat on me!"

What Jerry didn't know was that when he was born, daddy tried to make mama do something real bad. Daddy was always looking to find a way to make money. Easy money, he would call it. There was a young man that liked mama when she was in high school. In fact, he had bought mama a compact. That was before mama even knew daddy. Nothing came of it, because mama just wasn't interested in going out with him. He still wanted mama to keep the compact and if she ever changed her mind, he would be there.

Daddy knew about this person because some of mama's friends would tease her when daddy was around. "You're going to make so and so jealous if he finds out that you have an eye on Jerry here." Daddy was just starting to date mama at that time.

Daddy asked mama, "Who are they talking about, Irene?"

"Oh, just someone who wanted to go out with me some time back," mama smiled.

"I think he was more interested than that!" laughed her friends. "He bought her a fancy compact, and we're pretty sure he wanted to marry her some time!"

"Oh, cut it out!" mama said. "That's not true and you know it. He liked me and wanted to date, that's all."

A few years later—just after Jerry was born—daddy decided he could make some money if mama were to accuse her former admirer of being the father of Jerry.

"*No way!*" mama said, shocked. "You and I have been married for some time now. What in the world is the matter with you?"

"I think it's a good idea," daddy shrugged. "This way he'll have to pay child support. We can make some money out of this guy!"

The jealousy that daddy had for mama was unbelievable. He couldn't stand the thought that there was someone out there that had feelings for mama, even though this man was now happily married and had a family of his own. It's like daddy wanted to punish this man for caring for mama way back when they were in high school together.

"I will do no such thing!" mama stated. "And there is no way that you're going to make me do this!"

"Is that right, Irene?" daddy smirked. "You *will* do it—or I'll kill you."

Then daddy pulled out some papers he kept in his drawer. He put them down on the table and made mama sit down in front of them.

"Sign these papers," he said.

"What are they for?" mama asked with wide eyes.

"Just sign the papers!" daddy yelled.

Mama started to read them. They were for a lawsuit against the man they were just talking about—for child support!

"Jerry, I said that there was *no way* I would do something like this to a man that has done nothing to me!" insisted mama.

Daddy took mama by the hair in one hand and held a gun to her head with the other. "SIGN THE PAPERS *NOW*—or you're dead!" he shouted.

Mama could hear daddy pulling the trigger back. 'He really *is* going to kill me, he really will!' mama thought to herself. 'What will happen to Jerry! I know he'll kill him too! He'll probably find Paul, too, and do the same to him. He always said he would kill me first—then kill the kids. I know that he'll do it!'

"Sign the papers, Irene," daddy persisted. "If you don't, first you—then the kids, understand? And you *know* I will!"

It was true—mama knew he was capable of carrying out his threat.

Daddy yelled one more time. "This is your last chance, Irene!" He pulled mama's hair even harder and pushed the gun just as hard as he could into her head.

Mama picked up the pen and signed the paper.

"There—that wasn't so bad now, was it?" daddy grinned.

Mama was made to bring this man to court. What daddy didn't know was, when mama had a chance—when daddy wasn't around—she was able to talk to this man's lawyer. She told him every-thing that had happened and that this man was innocent. The only problem, she told the lawyer, was that daddy would kill her now for sure. The lawyer said he would give it some thought and maybe he could come up with something that would work out. "Just keep it under your hat for now," he said to mama.

Court was about to start and it was proven that if this man was the father of Jerry, it would mean mama had been carrying the unborn child for eleven months.

After daddy realized what the lawyer was saying, he felt really dumb. He never brought it up again. That was the end of the case for child support.

The man's lawyer spoke to mama and said, "If you hadn't told me the truth when you did, he would have had to pay it. He wants me to tell you, thank you—and he is really sorry that you had to go through this. But he promised to keep his mouth shut and not tell anyone about your husband; but he also said that in the future if you're ever in any trouble with your husband, that he and his wife would be there to help you." Mama replied, "Please tell him thank you but not to worry." She was so happy it was all over with.

This is one of the reasons why daddy was always beating Jerry. It's as though he believed his own lie. He also missed out on eighteen years of child support, so he never got his easy money. He took it out on Jerry and mama. Sometimes, I thought, he took it out on me too. Daddy would slap Cecile around if she didn't get his beer fast enough, or if he wanted his feet washed. There was a time that daddy wanted me to wash his feet and I didn't want to—and Cecile spoke up for me and said, "Let me, daddy. Emelia is too small. She won't do a good job. Let me do it for you instead."

Oh, thank you Cecile, I thought. I would have hated to have to do that. I just knew I would do something wrong and he would let me have it, and my bottom couldn't take any more belts.

"Okay, then," daddy said to Cecile. "You do it."

Oh, I was so glad.

Mama wished she could tell Jerry that story about what daddy wanted her to do. But she couldn't—for two reasons. First, she didn't want it to slip out from Jerry and get daddy worked up all over again, so it was better left alone. The second reason, more important, was that she never wanted Jerry to know how his daddy didn't want to claim him for his own son. That would have hurt Jerry real bad, for he was always trying to make daddy proud of him.

It's too bad that he wasn't proud of him. *You missed out on a lot, daddy.*

5

I could hear daddy talking to mama. "She's going—and that's final!" Who was he talking about? Was it me? And if it was, where was I going?

Then I heard daddy say: "If I don't do what she *says,* she'll cut me out of her will. You know how my mother is—she means it, and there's no way I'm losing out on her money when *she's* dead." Then I heard Cecile's name. Daddy's mother, our grandmother, we called mommie; and daddy's father was called poppie. She wanted Cecile sent to the convent in Gorham. She said that Cecile was a stubborn child and needed to be taught how to act like a lady.

At first I felt relieved, then I felt bad for Cecile; then I was happy for her because she wouldn't get slapped anymore for not moving fast enough when daddy told her to do something. But then I was sad because she wouldn't be with me anymore.

"I don't want you telling Cecile anything," said daddy. "I'll tell her myself, and I don't want you to ever talk about it when she comes home for a visit—*if* she comes home for a visit."

"What do you mean?" asked mama. "*If* she comes home? What are you saying? You're not going to take another child away from me!"

"I'll do what I want!" daddy yelled as he backhanded mama on the mouth. "You just keep your mouth shut or I'll send her away for good!"

Mama didn't say another word. She knew daddy meant what he said and she didn't want to lose Cecile too.

Daddy called out: "Cecile, Cecile—come here!"

"I'm coming, dad."

Then he called me.

"Emelia!"

35

"Yes, daddy?" I said meekly, full of foreboding.

"Come here," daddy said.

Why was he calling me, I thought—it was Cecile that he was going to tell about the convent.

"You two go get in the truck. We're going for a run—you know the routine."

The booze was already in the truck when Cecile and I got there.

So off we went. Daddy had to be careful and kept a watchful eye out for the cops. What he was doing was wrong and we knew it, but we had no choice but to keep quiet. When daddy was being chased, he had a place where he could drive to and had time to unload the booze into the ground, cover it and be back on the road before the police caught up with him. Daddy never got caught.

"Going kind of fast, weren't you, Dion?" The police always called daddy by his last name. "Okay if we check your truck?" the officer would say.

"Okay with me," daddy would reply. "You're not going to find anything. You don't think I would take these two little girls with me if I were doing what you thought I was, do you?" Daddy would smile.

"Is that so?" the policeman would grudgingly accept his excuse, and add, "Well, take it easy, Dion—as you say, you have kids in the truck."

There was one time that daddy got a speeding ticket and I can't remember if mama or Jerry ended up with the beating. Oh, it was mama—because we were her kids, and if it weren't for us, he never would have got caught!

On the way home daddy told Cecile that she was going to have to go to the convent. Cecile couldn't believe it.

"Dad, *why?* What did I do wrong for you to send me to the convent?"

"*I'm* not sending you to the convent," daddy said. "Your mother is. She can't handle you anymore. She says you're too stubborn. She wants you to learn how to be a lady!"

"*Please*, dad, don't let mom send me there! *Please* dad, please," pleaded Cecile.

I couldn't believe what I just heard! Daddy was telling Cecile that *mama* wanted her to go to the convent! I thought to myself: 'That's not true, daddy, that's not true! Why are you telling her that? It's mommie that wants her to go—and you're sending her so you won't lose her money!'—but I didn't have the courage to say it.

"I don't want to go there, dad. *Please* don't let mom send me!"

"There's nothing I can do about it—the arrangements have been made," daddy said implacably.

"I hate her for doing this to me, I *hate* her!" Cecile cried.

Oh, Cecile, I thought—it's not mama that did this! I wish I could tell you but I can't. Daddy doesn't know that I heard him. I don't want him to send you away for good like he told mama. I will tell mama when daddy's not around. Mama should know what daddy did. Oh, Cecile, don't hate mama! My insides were yelling these thoughts but I never made a sound.

"Cecile," said daddy, "I don't want you to say a word to your mother about this. Then maybe I can get you out of there. So keep your mouth shut for now."

And that's exactly what he told mama—keep your mouth shut.

Why did you lie, daddy? Why do you want Cecile to hate mama? Do you hate mama that much that you would want my sister to hate her too? I wished I could say these things out loud but I knew what would happen if I did.

"I won't say anything," agreed Cecile. "I won't say a word, just like you said, dad. But please hurry and get me out. Okay, dad?"

"Okay," daddy said.

We were almost home when the truck caught on fire. Daddy grabbed me and Cecile and threw us out of the truck and he jumped out. When we got home, daddy called up his cousin Burt. I could hear him. I think everyone could hear him. "Did you set the timer in the truck to go off *today*? You fool! I *told* you to set it for *tomorrow*. I was in that truck when the timer went off and it caught on fire! I could have been killed...." He paused, listening, then continued: "Yeah, you're right, it will look better for the insurance company, I agree. When they find out there was two kids in the car, they'll pay off faster. What? Yeah, I meant to say truck. Okay—but next time we set this up, let me know the right day so I won't be in it! Once is enough for me!"

Daddy noticed we were all standing there hearing what he just said.

"Don't anyone of you open your mouth to anyone about this!" he warned.

We all knew better. Daddy didn't have to say a word to us. We found out a long time ago not to talk about daddy to anyone.

Two days later the call came in for Cecile to be brought down to the convert.

Mama tried to give Cecile a hug but she didn't want to. Mama said, "I love you, Cecile," but Cecile never answered a word. Mama held back the tears. She knew why Cecile was acting the way she was because I told mama exactly what daddy had said to her—and she knew that if she were to say anything to Cecile about it, she would never see her again—just like Paul.

I couldn't say goodbye to big sister. I didn't want to. If I said goodbye, I might not ever see her again; so I hid—but I could still see her when she went out the door. I didn't want anyone to see my tears. They were private. Sometimes Cecile was mean to me, but she was nice to me more often than mean.

"I love you, Cecile," I whispered. Then she was gone.

Jerry and I had more chores to do then, with Cecile gone. Leo tried to help out but he was still a little too small; but there was one thing he learned how to do and that was staying out of daddy's way. Albert still didn't have to worry about daddy; but just like the rest of us, his day would come.

I'm glad there was no more room to put any wood down in the cellar. The last time we had to stack wood, Cecile was still home and I fell asleep in the wheelbarrow. Jerry and Cecile heard daddy coming, so Jerry grabbed me and pulled me out and stood me up, and Cecile put a piece of wood in my hands. I had no idea what was going on, but thanks to their quick thinking I didn't get a beating. Not that time, anyway.

I missed mama having her tip money. It was so nice when mama would send us to the store across the street and we would have our treats, all bought with her own money.

Daddy began to wonder why mama never asked him for money anymore. One day he saw some money on one of the tables in the restaurant. It was tip money that someone had given mama and she hadn't picked it up yet. There were two quarters. What mama would do is put half of her tips in a can that later daddy would pick up and keep for himself. The other half she would put in her secret hiding place. Daddy decided to wait it out and see what she did with the money.

Mama didn't know that daddy had already seen the money that was left on the table. She picked it up and daddy pretended he didn't see her. She walked out into the kitchen where she dropped one of her quarters into her hiding place, then walked over to the can under the counter. But just as she was about to open her hand, daddy grabbed it. Mama jumped. She didn't know daddy was right behind her. As far as she knew he was still talking to a customer as he was leaving.

"Open your hand," daddy said coldly. Mama opened it. "What do you think you're doing?" he demanded.

"Doing? I'm putting my tip money in the can," mama said, turning pale.

"How much do you have in your hand?" daddy asked.

"A quarter," mama said.

"Really? What did you do with the other one?"

"What do you mean?" mama said.

"You know what I'm talking about—don't play stupid with me!" daddy said, beginning to lose patience. "I want to know where the other quarter is!"

Mama looked at him, wide–eyed and lost for words.

"Never mind," he said icily. "I'll find it myself. I saw the two quarters on the table before you went over there to pick them up." When he still received no answer his temper flared. "Get out of my way!" he yelled, shoving mama roughly out of his path. "I'll find it! I saw you walk over here by this counter!"

He swept what was on the counter onto the floor. He didn't see the small hole in the counter top. He opened up the lower cupboards and emptied everything out. The more he threw on the floor, the madder he got. He grabbed mama by the neck.

"Tell me where you put that quarter!" he roared. "I want to know *now!*" As he said it, he hit the counter top with his fist. He heard some change jingle. He let go of mama and banged the counter again. Then he saw the small hole.

"So—what's this!"

He started tearing the counter apart and he finally found mama's money she had been hiding. There was so much change! Daddy grabbed mama by the neck again. He took her face and stuffed it into the change box. "What's this?" he yelled. "You've been stealing from me, have you? No wonder your kids steal—they learn how from you!"

"My kids don't steal!" mama replied furiously, "and I didn't steal from you, either! This is *my* tip money—and it's only half of it!"

"So where's the rest of it?" daddy shouted.

"I put the other half of it right in that can." Mama pointed to it. "That's the money you've been taking. You've been getting half of all my tips."

"You had no right to hide this money from me! *I* buy you what you need."

Mama broke free and drew herself up to her full height. Her green eyes flashed with indignation. A beautiful woman, she was even more so when she was angry. "You threw money on the floor for me to pick up, remember? And you never give me the full amount of what something cost! You always tell me to make do. Well, I *did* make do. I never asked you for any more money, did I? I made do!"

"Don't you raise your voice at *me!* Have you forgotten who you're talking to? *I'm* the one who says whether you live or die—and don't you ever forget it!"

Daddy grabbed mama again by the neck and stuck her face in the change box. "You see that money right there! It's mine! Everything you see is mine! You're just along for the ride. Don't you *ever* think about hiding anything from me again!" He took mama, still hanging on to the back of her neck, and made her fall down to her knees; then he kicked her just as hard as he could on her bottom. When she yelled, he kicked her again. "Now you clean up this mess!" he shouted.

Daddy went back to the moneybox and brought it out to one of the tables and counted it. Mama had over $200.00 in change in her tip box and daddy kept it all.

Mama couldn't walk very well the next day. Jerry and I tried to help her as much as we could so mama wouldn't have to bend down. I always think about how hard daddy hit mama but he never broke any bones. He always made sure that she could do her work. This was the day that all the beds had to be changed in the hotel. Mama always made sure that all her full-time boarders had nice clean rooms. I went with mama to help make beds, and dust. We used to do it pretty fast, but that day mama had to move slower.

When daddy was hurting mama he would call her all kinds of nasty words. Some of them I never heard before. I didn't know what they meant, but I did know that it couldn't be too good because he was always yelling when he said them. He called us kids some bad words too, but mama would never tell what they meant.

"You don't need to know," she would say. "No matter what they are, they're not true, anyway."

I wondered how Cecile was doing. I hadn't seen her or heard from her since she left. Daddy wouldn't take mama to visit her and Cecile hadn't been home to visit at all.

I hope you're happy, mommie, I thought to myself. *You wanted Cecile gone and she is. It's all your fault that I don't see my big sister anymore. Daddy keeps telling Cecile that he still can't get her out. That's such a lie! If I ever see Cecile again, I'm going to tell her the truth about daddy and that what he said to her was a lie. I wonder if she's still at the convent? Daddy says she is, but he said that he wouldn't take me to see her. Daddy said if I was to go there, that they might keep me there. I have to stay with mama. I have to be here to take care of her when daddy hurts her.*

6

Daddy walked into the restaurant and saw mama talking to a male customer. He became outraged. She didn't see him coming up behind her as she walked back into the kitchen.

The man wanted to know if mama could make him a sandwich to take with him. Daddy was right behind her. He swung her around, one hand on her shoulder and the other on her throat, and pushed her up against the steam pipe. She made a sound like something had just taken her breath away.

He kept pushing her against the pipe, yelling at her. "Who is that man! Is *he* the father of Paul? Who is he?"

Daddy had never seen him before. Mama squeaked out the words, "He's just passing through Berlin... had a long ride ahead of him... wanted to know if I would make him a sandwich to take with him... I said I would."

"You're lying!" daddy shouted. "If he's not the father of Paul, then maybe he's the father of one of the other kids—Jerry, Cecile, Emelia, Leo, Albert—which one's his kid? Tell me!"

Daddy was so mad, he kept holding her there. I could smell her uniform; it smelt like when she ironed it after the laundry was done. I used to like that smell but it was getting stronger, now. It smelt awful.

Someone called him from the dining room—"Jerry!" Daddy let mama go and she fell to the floor.

"Don't move!" daddy said to her. "I'll be back."

It was Mr. Tony. He wanted to pay the bill for his coffee and eggs that mama cooked for him.

Mama did all the cooking in the restaurant plus the cleaning, and she also took care of running the Hotel. Daddy never had a job. He picked the dump, took care of the pigs and chickens, and made his own beer that he sold. His mother made other kinds of alcohol that he also sold. Between daddy and mommie, they made a tidy sum doing that.

I was named after mommie and I hated it—she was such a mean person, just like daddy. He must have gotten his meanness from her. Poppie was so nice and he treated mama nice too.

I saw mama lying on the floor from my hiding place. As soon as I heard daddy yelling, I went and hid. I saw all the awful things that daddy had done to mama. I came out to see her but as soon as she spotted me she said, "Go hide, Emelia! Don't let your father see you! Run!"

So I went back to my hiding place and a good thing too. Daddy was right back there again. When he walked back into the kitchen, he kicked mama on her thigh. Jerry wasn't so lucky as I was. He walked into the room and saw mama on the floor. He looked up at daddy but before he had a chance to say anything, daddy told Jerry, "Your mother tripped and fell! Go and help her get up!"

Jerry couldn't believe his eyes. Daddy spoke up and said, "She hit the steam pipe when she tripped and fell."

"Dad," Jerry said. "Her uniform is all melted—and her back has bumps all over it. Look, dad! Her back has blood on it too!"

"Are you deaf!" daddy yelled. "I told you to help your mother up off the floor!"

Jerry did as he was told. "Are you all right?" he asked her as he helped to lift her. "Does it hurt real bad?"

It was more than daddy could take. He lunged and grabbed Jerry by his hair and pounded his head up against the wall. He kept pounding and pounding it, bang, bang, bang!

From my little hiding space I could see everything. I shook all over. I was so scared. I wanted to scream at him: *Why do you hate all of us so much, daddy! Why, daddy why? Stop, daddy, please stop!*

Mama reached for daddy's arm and held it just long enough for Jerry to free himself from daddy's grip. Mama yelled: "Run, Jerry, run! Go hide Jerry! Go, run fast!"

Daddy grabbed mama by the neck and hurled her to the floor; then he kicked her three times on the back. He made it bleed more than ever.

Mama wasn't moving anymore. Daddy went to the refrigerator, took out a cold beer and drank it down in two gulps. Then he was gone. He just left mama lying senseless on the floor. Jerry and I went running to mama. She was a mess. I went and got a cold washcloth for her face.

Jerry helped mama to stand. I gave her the cloth and she wiped it over her face. "I'm sorry, mom, that dad beats on you like that! Someone should beat him up so he can feel the pain he gives to all of us. Most of all you, mom."

"If I could find a way to leave him, Jerry, I would." Her voice was so soft we could hardly hear it. "But he would find me and all of you kids and kill all of us. Believe me, he would!"

Jerry and I helped mama get up the stairs to our living quarters of the hotel.

Jerry knew he had to get something to put on mama's back. She gave him a telephone number to call. It was a doctor that knew the family for years. She would take us to him after daddy gave us a beating—when our injuries were too severe for her to make better. She would only do that on condition the doctor didn't tell anyone. If he didn't promise mama, then she wouldn't take us. He helped us all he could. He knew that was the only way we kids would be able to seek medical attention.

Jerry called the doctor and he told Jerry to come right over.

I sat with mama and tried to help her take off her uniform. It was stuck to her. She got a basin of water and had me put a wet cloth on the material that was glued to her skin. It started to soften and I was able to peel what was left off her skin.

"Oh mama, your back is all burnt!"

"I know," said mama. "Don't worry, Emelia, it will get all better after a while. Jerry has gone to get some medicine to put on it."

Jerry got home. It felt like he was gone for hours, but it was only for fifteen minutes.

Mama sat down and I put the cream on her back. Poor mama! She sat just as still as she could but every time I touched her she would jump. She had tears in her eyes. I knew it was hurting her real bad.

"It's okay, Emelia. You keep putting it on—it has to be done."

I was so glad when the doctor showed up.

"What are you doing here?" mama asked. "If big Jerry comes back and you're here, it will be worse."

"Don't worry, Irene," the doctor said. "I saw him with his drinking buddies. He'll be out for the night." The doctor knew daddy liked to gamble.

We never got ahead because daddy would gamble away all the profits from the hotel and restaurant.

The doctor gave mama a shot for the pain. "You two kids did a good job taking care of your mother. She will sleep now. Jerry, after your mom gets up in the morning, I want you to ask her how she is. Then I want you to either call me or come to see me—either way, I want to know how she is, okay?"

"Okay," Jerry nodded.

"Emelia, you did a nice job putting the cream on your mother's back," the doctor smiled.

"Thank you," I said.

Next morning, mama's back was hurting bad, but she wouldn't say anything. Jerry and I could tell. Daddy wasn't around so Jerry phoned the doctor as he had told him to.

"Jerry," the doctor said, "Can you come back to the office? I want to give you some more cream for your mother's back. That tube won't last long. I didn't realize her burn covered so much area or I would have given you a bigger tube."

So Jerry left for the doctor's right away, before daddy showed up.

It was a quiet day for a change. Jerry and I helped mama with the breakfast crowd and we stayed around to help with the dinner people too. Mama was moving around a little better now, or she was doing a good job of hiding it from Jerry and I. "You kids have been very helpful to me," said mama. "The babysitter said she would stay with Leo and Albert for another hour, so if you two want to go out and play for awhile, it's okay."

"Really, mom?" said Jerry. "Okay, I'll take Emelia with me, mom. We'll be back to help you with the supper people."

We went across the street, up a few buildings. That's where Jerry's best friend, Clint, lived.

Jerry and Clint decided to go over where the kids used to cross over the water. There was an old bridge there, or what was left of it, and it was no longer in use. All that was left was the underneath of the bridge. The only way across was to hang from the pole and put hand over hand to make it to the other side. I never did it—it was only the big kids that were brave enough to do it. The water ran fast under the bridge and it was scary!

We were almost there when Jerry realized he had forgotten something. He asked Clint if he would watch me for a few minutes. He'd be right back, he said.

We continued to walk to the bridge. It wasn't far. We could see it from where we were standing.

When we got there, Clint asked me if I wanted to try just hanging from the pole.

"No!" I said. "I'm too scared."

"Come on!" A grin spread across his chunky fat face. He didn't share the good looks of most Italians. "I won't let you fall. Don't you want to see what it's like to be one of the big kids?"

"No–o," I hesitated.

"I'll just hold you there," he assured me. "You grab the post and than you'll be able to see how it feels. You don't have to worry. There isn't any water right at the beginning."

I started to walk towards the spot he was talking about and all of a sudden he picked me up and had me way up high. He said, "Grab the pole or I'll drop you!"

So I grabbed the pole and he let go of me. I was so scared! "Let me down!" I yelled. "Let me down."

"Not until I do what I want first," he smirked.

He put his hand up my leg, then inside my panties. I couldn't stop him. I couldn't let go of the pole. "Leave me *alone!* Leave me alone! Jerry, where are you? Please, Jerry! Come back!" I was too scared to move away because it would take me over above the water. I tried kicking him, but he wouldn't stop!

I was so scared, but what he was doing was so horrible that I started to put one hand over the other to get away from him. I finally got far enough away from him, over the rushing water, so he couldn't touch me anymore.

At last I saw Jerry coming. "Please, Jerry, hurry!" I shouted. "I can't hang on anymore! *Please—hurry!*"

Clint just stood there and laughed. "You better not tell anyone, you hear me?" he said. "If you do, I'll beat you the same way your father beats you! I'll beat you the same way your father beats your mother! You better not tell."

"What are you doing up there?" Jerry asked, then turned to Clint. "Did *you* put her up there?"

"Yes, I did!" Clint boasted. "She wanted to see what it was like being one of the big kids, so I showed her."

Jerry was up on the pole trying to talk me into putting one hand over the other to get to him so he could get me down. I was frozen right in that spot and couldn't move. Jerry kept talking to me. I finally got my hands to move. The water was up high. "Don't look down!"

Jerry said. "Just keep coming towards me." Jerry grabbed me and took me down from there.

"That wasn't too smart," he told Clint. "Emelia is much too small to be up there."

"I did what she wanted me to," Clint replied and looked at me. "Isn't that right, Emelia?"

"Will you take me home now?" I said.

"Emelia, I just got here!" Jerry said.

"*Please* Jerry. I need to go home."

Jerry didn't know what to say—he just stood there and looked at me. "That really scared you, didn't it?" he said. Then he turned to his friend. "You shouldn't have done that to her, even though she wanted to try it. You're older than her and you should have known better."

It made me feel better when my big brother stood up for me. I thought to myself: *I wish I could tell you, Jerry, I wish I could tell you what he did to me.* I started to walk off towards home. I was going, no matter what.

"Hold up, Emelia," Jerry said. "I'm coming with you." He looked at Clint. "Are you coming?"

"No, I'm going to hang around here for a while."

"Okay," Jerry said.

After that any time that Jerry asked me if I wanted to go with him to hang out with him and Clint, I always said no. I never spoke to that boy again. Jerry thought it was because I got so scared the last time I was with him, but that wasn't the reason. I couldn't tell him why, that his best friend had touched me, had put his fingers into my little crack where my pee–wee was, that his rough, crummy fingernails had scratched me, making me so sore that it burnt when I had to go pee. How I hated him for doing that to me.

If anyone found out about it, Clint would beat me—and daddy beat me enough as it was. I never told anyone.

It was time for the supper crowd so Jerry and I helped mama like we said we would.

"You're kind of quiet tonight, Emelia," said mama. "Do you feel okay?"

Jerry spoke up and told her what had happened at the bridge earlier and how it scared me. "I can see why," said mama kindly. "That would have scared me too. Are you okay now, Emelia?"

"Yes, mama, I'm okay now," I said in a small voice.

Daddy was home by now. He was sitting at the table. That was the first time any of us had seen him since he held mama against the steam pipe.

Mama had to get some things cooked up for the restaurant dinner for the next day. She had a big kettle that was at a full boil.

"Where's my supper?" daddy demanded.

"I'll get you some right now," mama said. She had some pork roast left over from the supper crowd. She heated it up and fixed up some potatoes and vegetables. She set it down in front of him. He took the plate and flung it right across the room. "I don't want pork roast! Cook me a steak!"

Mama went straight to the refrigerator, got a steak and went to the stove and started cooking it without saying one word. Jerry and I cleaned up the mess on the floor. We didn't want mama to have to bend over. We wanted everything to go right. Mama hurt too much to have daddy picking on her tonight. After mama was done getting daddy's supper ready, she continued with her boiling kettle of water.

Mama barely managed to pick up the kettle, it was so big and heavy. Daddy just sat there and watched her. As she was walking by he stuck out his foot and tripped her. She fell down and the boiling hot water landed on top of her. How she screamed when the hot water hit her burn!

Daddy sat there and laughed! It was a horrible shrieking scream that came out of mama's mouth. It made daddy laugh even louder. Jerry and I didn't know what to do. One thing was certain—we didn't move from our spot, frozen by terror. We watched as daddy got up from the table and walked away. We heard the door shut and he was gone.

"Mama, mama!" But she didn't move. "She's passed out!" Jerry said. He ran and called the doctor.

"Mama, wake up, please mama!" I called to her. "Open your eyes! Daddy's gone out, mama—wake up!"

Jerry came back. "The doctor is on his way," he said. "Go wait for him by the door. It's okay, Emelia, I'll stay with mom."

I ran to the door. It only took a few minutes and the doctor was there.

Mama was awake now. "We need to get her upstairs to her room," the doctor said. "Come on kids, give me a hand."

We got mama in her bed with the help of the doctor.

"It's okay, kids, your mother will be all right now. She passed out because of the pain. Your body will do that sometimes if the pain is too great." He looked down at mama with concern. "Irene, you need to get away from that man before he kills you or one of your kids." Then he gave her a shot so she could sleep.

7

Two weeks had gone by. Mama was doing much better. Jerry and I took turns getting beat from daddy so he would leave mama alone. It worked and it was worth it.

Mama was sad the whole time. She knew what we were up to but she didn't stop us because she was too weak to argue.

"No more," mama said. "You two kids have done enough. I'm better now, so I'll take over." And she did.

Daddy had just had his supper. "I'm going out for a while. When I get back, you and I are going to talk about who the father of these kids are!" He had already had quite a bit to drink.

Mama knew it would be really bad this time. She went through it enough times. When daddy got like that, he ended up beating all three of us—and Leo was just getting big enough to be included, for daddy was already starting to slap him around. It always started with slaps—then we graduated to beatings.

Mama was frantic. "Come on, we don't have much time. Jerry, Emelia, get yourselves each a pillowcase and pack it with a couple pairs of socks, underwear and some outside clothes. Make sure you dress warm now—it's cold outside. Hurry!"

Mama went and did the same for Leo, Albert and herself. "Hurry!" mama yelled.

So there we were, all dressed and ready to go. Jerry held Albert, I took Leo by the hand and mama took all the pillowcases that had been half filled with clothes.

We went outside. It was snowing, but it was light snow. Mama got the car going. Daddy never would let mama use the car or truck. They were his and nobody was to touch them.

"Oh, daddy's going to be *so* mad when he finds out the car's gone!" I said.

"Dad is going to be a lot madder when he finds out we are missing too," Jerry said.

Mama didn't say anything but we knew it was because she was scared, not only for taking the car but all of us too.

"What will daddy do to us when he finds us, mama?" I asked.

"I don't think I want to think about that right now," mama said.

The snowstorm was getting worse. Mama was nervous. She never said a word except for one time when we first started, when she asked if everyone was okay.

"Mama," Jerry said, "where are we going?"

"I thought we would go to *memere's* and *pepere's* house in Sanbornville."

"Won't dad find us there?"

"It depends on whether or not *memere* or *pepere* tell him," mama said.

"Can't we tell them not to tell?" Jerry asked.

"That will be up to them, Jerry," mama said.

"Are you scared, mama?" I asked.

"Yes, Emelia, I am—but don't worry, okay? We'll be all right. Now you two sit back, the road is very slippery and I have to concentrate. We're coming up on the Notches, so make sure you hang on."

Mama went around the bend. All at once the car spun out of control. It spun round and round, three times, before it stopped by the edge of the cliff. I could hear mama breathing. She was so shook up! Leo sat up and said, "Wow! Mommy, that was *fun!* Can we do it again?" That made everyone laugh.

"I sure am glad Leo said that!" mama said. "I was about to cry from fright!"

We were facing the wrong direction now, but mama very carefully turned the car around. None of us thought she would be able to do it but that's just like mama. She pulled a lot of things off and even she doesn't know how she managed—but she did.

"Listen kids," mama said, looking straight ahead as she edged the car into the driving snow, "I don't want any of you to tell *memere* or *pepere* about the beatings, okay?"

"It's okay, mom, we know dad always made you make up excuses to them about your bruises. We won't tell." Jerry was so grown up in the things he said. I guess he had to grow up fast.

It seemed forever, the snowflakes swirling out of the dark at us as the headlights caught them—it was like driving through a tunnel cut through the storm and the night. At length the road straightened into a familiar stretch.

"We made it, kids." There was relief in mama's voice. "Just one more mile and we're there. Jerry, Emelia—wake up the two boys."

We pulled up in front of the house. *Pepere* and *memere* had caught the sound of the engine and were waiting for us at the door.

"Hi, mom. Hello, dad," mama greeted them.

"What in the world are you doing here in a middle of a storm?" *pepere* quizzed, his eyebrows raised in surprise.

"Well, to tell you the truth, I left Jerry, and this was the only place I could think of to come." Mama confronted their amazement with a hesitant smile.

"You left your *husband?*" Pepere's eyes were wide with disbelief.

"Yes, dad, I did." Her voice was soft and calm.

"Why?" he asked.

"Come on, Joe," *memere* interjected. "Can't you see how tired they all are! Come on, Irene, I'll show you where you can lay the kids down. We can all talk later, okay Joe?"

"Okay," *pepere* agreed. "We'll talk later."

"Mom, please don't tell Jerry where I am," mama said to *memere*.

"I won't," she nodded, "but I can't speak for your father. You know how old–fashioned he is. Why did you leave?"

"Oh mom," mama sighed. "It's a long story. Can we talk about it tomorrow?"

"Sure we can. You get yourself a good night's sleep. I'll talk to your father about not telling Jerry where you are—at least for the time being."

"Thank you, mom, thanks for everything." She slumped down on the sofa. She looked worn out. I looked at her and my heart went out to her. She was doing this not just for herself, but for all of us.

Afterwards mama lay in bed thinking about all that had happened in just the short time from when she had gotten up that morning. 'I can't believe it,' she mused. 'I actually left him! Now what will tomorrow bring? What am I going to tell mom and dad?'

Mama was up early the next morning. *Pepere* was already sitting at the table.

"Would you like a cup of coffee, dad?" mama asked.

"Yes, that would be nice," said *pepere*.

Mama thought it was kind of strange that her father hadn't asked her any questions about her leaving home. Half an hour went by and still he hadn't said a word about it. She thought to herself: 'I wanted mom to ask him not to tell Jerry, but how come he's not asking me why? He did last night. Maybe he's waiting for me to say something to him.'

There was a knock at the door.

"Will you answer that, Irene?' *pepere* said.

Mama opened the door and jumped backwards. "Jerry!" she gasped.

Daddy reached out for her, but then put his hands on the doorknob and started to laugh. Mama thought he was going to belt her. "Irene, you look like you've seen a ghost!"

Mama couldn't believe it. She was thinking to herself, 'I didn't hear the phone ring and I listened for it all night long!'

"I called him last night, Irene," *pepere* said levelly, coming up from behind. "I know you didn't want him to know where you were—your mother told me. But as far as I'm concerned, a wife belongs with her husband."

"Oh, dad!" mama said, close to tears. "You have no idea what you've just done."

"What do you mean by that, Irene?" *pepere* asked.

Daddy walked over to mama and held her by the arm. "Like I told you last night, Joe, it was a misunderstanding. Irene is a little upset with me right now, but I'm sure we can get this all ironed out." Daddy was squeezing mama's arm. Mama knew she was in for a rough ride ahead and her heart sank into her shoes.

"You don't understand, dad! All the times I came here with bruises on me—well, *he* put them there!"

Daddy started laughing. "Your parents know I was only kidding when I told them I put them there, Irene. You're not starting to *believe* it, are you!" He was hurting mama with his grip.

"I'll show you the..." mama began, but daddy interrupted her, preventing her from saying another word. He gave us all a firm command:

"Come on kids!" he yelled. "Let's get your things back into the car! We're all going home. Right, Irene? We can work this out—but let's not do it in front of your parents, okay?"

Mama knew she didn't have a choice. Her father wasn't going to believe her. And daddy just made her look bad in front of him. Jerry looked like he wanted to say something on mama's behalf, but daddy caught his eyes and he knew that if he said anything it would make it worse for mama. I looked over at Jerry and he shook his head at me, so I didn't say anything either.

We got outside and there was only one car. How did daddy get there?

"Where are the keys, Irene?" daddy asked. Mama handed them to him.

"*Now get in!*" daddy said through clenched teeth. He was *very* angry!

Mama made sure all of us kids were sitting in the back seat. She didn't want any of us in harm's way.

As we drove off daddy said, "Okay, everybody, wave to *memere* and *pepere*—you too, Irene. I said, *you too*, Irene!"

So mama waved. We were about five miles down the road when daddy, without even taking his eyes off the road, lifted his fist and punched mama in her face without saying one word.

A few hours later we were home. Jerry carried Albert, I took Leo by the hand and daddy took the pillowcases of clothes. Up the stairs we went with mama not far behind us.

Daddy looked at mama. "I'm not done with you," he said under his breath. "I'll deal with you later."

Mama was relieved for the time being, but she knew daddy meant every word he said. He would deal with her later. She knew he wasn't finished with her. It's only just begun, she thought to herself: 'What have I done? Things can only get worse from here. Now what do I do?' Even her own father didn't believe her!

Mama kept thinking he would beat her any second. But he withheld the beating, keeping her on edge and scared all the time. Every time he would walk into the room she was in, she thought, this is it! Instead, he would walk away. He did this for about a week. Then mama couldn't stand it any more.

"If you're going to beat me, then *do* it—and get it over with!" mama shouted.

"You're not going to get away with it that easy, Irene," daddy smirked. "I'm not ready yet. There are things I have to take care of first." He was as cool as a cucumber.

Mama didn't know what to think. I had never seen daddy so cold before. Mean, yes, but the coldness was creepy.

One night mama came to kiss me goodnight.

"Mama?" I said.

"Yes, Emelia?"

"I don't want to go to sleep."

"Why?"

"Because I have a bad dream every night now."

"What are your dreams about, honey?" she asked, concerned.

"It's not dreams, mama, it's only one dream—and I have it every night."

"Do you want to tell me about your dream?"

"Yes, mama, I do."

Mama looked down at me, kindly, but the worry lines creased the corners of her eyes. Everyone used to say I reminded them of a little doll, I was so fragile, and for a moment I seemed to see myself through mama's eyes. "Tell me," she said softly. There were tears in her eyes.

"Every night the witch comes and gets me and brings me in the living room and ties me on the windowsill," I said.

"Is that all that happens in your dream?"

"No, after she takes me out of bed and ties me to the sill, she stands there and laughs at me. My back hurts because I'm leaning up against the blind that is open. I can't move. I holler to you and daddy. You don't hear me. I say, *mama, mama, look up at me! Can't you see me? I'm right here. Look at me, mama—please, mama. The witch has got me again! She won't let me go! Can't you see me?*"

Mama kissed me. "I *am* here, Emelia. Just remember that. I'm always here for you."

Then I drifted off to sleep.

I don't know how long I slept, but all at once someone grabbed my arm and stood me up. What was happening? Was I dreaming again? I looked up and it was daddy. Why did he take me out of bed?

"Put your shoes and coat on!" Daddy yelled at me.

"Why, daddy?"

"Do as I say! Don't ask any questions!"

His voice was fearful so I did as he said.

"Come with me!" he ordered.

I followed him. Mama was standing by the door to go outside. She had Albert in her arms. Jerry was coming down the hallway hanging on to Leo. 'What's going on?' I thought to myself. I looked at Jerry. He just looked back and never said a word.

I was by mama's side. We all walked to the car. Daddy opened the back door.

"Get in!" he said.

Jerry got in first and mama gave Albert to him. Then Leo climbed in. I helped him—his legs were a little too short. Then I got in. Daddy slammed the car door. Mama was already in the front seat. Daddy got in and we drove off.

I whispered to Jerry: "Where are we going? It's the middle of the night!"

Jerry put his finger up to his lips and said *shhhhhh* to me. I didn't know what to think. When Leo asked me why we had to get up, I said the same thing that Jerry said—*shhhhhh*. Daddy turned the corner and drove up a big hill. 'Where are we going?' I kept asking myself. Then I found out. Daddy drove into the cemetery! What in the world were we doing in the cemetery?

Daddy stopped the car and turned off the engine. It was so silent. Why were we there? No one made a sound.

Without even turning her head or saying a word, mama wound down her window. She continued to stare out the front windshield of the car. Then I saw it—a gun! *Daddy, why do you have a gun? What are you going to do with it?* He pointed the gun at mama's head. *No daddy, no daddy! Don't hurt mama!* I couldn't speak but the thoughts rushed through my head.

"You'll *never* leave me again, Irene," daddy said to mama. "Do you hear me? Say yes!"

Mama, say yes before he shoots you! My body was screaming that out. I was shaking all over. Jerry reached over and patted me on my arm, just like he knew something I didn't know.

"You will never leave me again, Irene, or I *will* kill you. I *will* kill you!"

Then he pointed the gun out of mama's window and he shot it right by her face. Mama never moved a muscle, or ever said a word. Daddy put the gun down and started the car and drove us all home. We got out of the car and went upstairs and we went back to bed. I snuck out of my room and went to Jerry's room. I wanted to know why he acted like he knew what was going to happen.

"Daddy's been doing this to mama once a week—ever since mama left him and went to *memere's* and *pepere's* house," Jerry explained. "I was surprised to see you, Emelia. He has made me go every time, but no one else."

"I wonder why he wanted to take me this time?" I said. "Did he ever take Leo and Albert before?"

"No," Jerry said. "I'm the only one that he's taken so far. I don't know why he included you or even Leo and Albert this time. Maybe it's just his way of keeping us in line, to use daddy's famous words."

"Boy!" I exclaimed. "He really wants to make sure that mama never leaves him again."

"It's not always for the same reason. Sometimes he brings her up there and asks her who the father of Paul is."

"*Who* is Paul?" My nose crinkled. "I've heard that name a lot."

"I don't know," said Jerry, "but whoever he is, it sure hurts mom every time dad brings up his name. There are times that he asks mom who *my* father is—and Cecile's."

"Yeah, I know, I heard him ask her about Leo, and Albert too," I said. "I've even heard him ask about *me*," I added.

"You better get back to your room before dad catches you here," Jerry said.

"Okay, Jerry," I replied.

"Be careful."

"I will be. I'm learning how to tiptoe. I'm getting a lot better at it. Goodnight, Jerry."

"Goodnight to you too, Emelia."

I made it back to my room and daddy didn't see me. *Thank you, Cecile, for teaching me how to tiptoe,* I thought to myself. *I miss you so much Cecile. It's been so long since I've seen you. I wish daddy would take me and mama to see you. I know that mama misses you so much. It hurts her real bad to know you think she's the one that put you there. Oh, I miss you, my big sister! Mommie, why—why did you do that? Daddy, why did you have to worry about money and take my sister away from me! Why daddy, Why!*

Poor mama. That must have been so *awful*, having that gun pointed at her head! And then to sit there while he shot his gun past her pretty face!

Oh mama, why does daddy have to be so mean?

I fell back to sleep again, hoping the witch wouldn't come back to get me.

8

It had been almost two months since I heard daddy telling mama that he planned to take a trip to Alaska. Just daddy and his cousin Burt were going, but mama knew better—that daddy's girlfriend would be with him too. I guess we all knew Pearl would be with him. She was his drinking buddy along with other things. When I saw her it was the first time I had ever seen anyone who drank more than daddy—and it was a woman! Daddy never brought her to the hotel or the restaurant, but I used to see her in his car riding around with him.

He didn't think that mama knew about her, but mama was getting calls from different people in Berlin letting her know all about it—like she really needed to know with all the other problems she had! Yet daddy still wouldn't let mama leave him, even if mama were to tell him that she knew. That would only have caused mama to get yet another beating.

Daddy got everything ready. He even put a canvas on the back of his truck and spray–painted big white letters on the side: BOUND FOR ALASKA. When he had everything ready, he called the newspaper company in Berlin to come and take a picture of him with his truck, and he told them all about the coming trip. The story was in the next morning edition. Daddy loved getting all that attention. Mama welcomed this because it meant he would be gone for a while and there would be no more beatings for any of us! We were all so excited. Daddy thought it was because his story hit the headlines—but what he didn't know wouldn't hurt him, mama said.

"You keep track of every meal you sell, Irene, and make sure you don't hide any money from me! You got that?" daddy yelled, adding as he drove off: "And that means your tip money too!" I could almost see the relief on mama's face when the truck turned a corner and went out of sight.

I felt guilty because I was hoping that wherever he was he would stay there for a very long time, and that when he got back he would be a nice daddy like mama was a nice mommy—but I guess that would be asking for an awful lot.

◆   ◆   ◆

"Oh! Look at the time!" I exclaimed. "Mama will be worried. I better get downstairs. Everyone should be gone now and the restaurant will be closed, so now we can sit and have our supper. Come on Leo, we're going downstairs to eat!"

"I'm coming," Leo replied. "Boy, am I hungry!"

"You're *always* hungry, Leo," I laughed.

"I know! I have to eat a lot so I can get bigger, like Jerry."

Everything was quiet in the restaurant, but it sure smelt good! Mama always made everything smell good. She was the best cook in the world.

Albert sat in his high chair with Jerry facing the wall.

"Mama, why is Jerry facing the wall?" I asked, surprised, as I walked into the room.

Leo went flying off the end of daddy's foot.

"*Daddy!*" I gasped.

Then I saw mama's face. It was bleeding. *Oh no!* I thought to myself, *not again, not again! You didn't change daddy, you're still the same!*

Jerry turned to look and daddy kicked him.

"You keep facing the wall!" daddy yelled, then turned to me. "And don't *you* dare move!"

Daddy grabbed me and swirled me around. I went flying into the wall. My head! It hurt! I landed over by Jerry. Then daddy went after mama.

"Where's all the money!" daddy yelled. "Where are the books I told you to keep while I was gone?"

"I *told* you they are upstairs in the safe, Jerry," mama said, exasperated.

Oh, I hated it that big brother has the same name as daddy! How could two people with the same name be so different?

Mama turned to us. "You kids sit down and eat your supper while I take daddy upstairs to give him what he wants out of the safe." She looked imploringly at daddy. "Is that all right with you, Jerry?"

"Yeah yeah," daddy said impatiently.

Jerry picked Leo up off the floor and put him in his booster seat. Leo never made a sound when he landed: he knew not to get daddy's attention, so he kept very quite. Though only three, he was no dummy when it came to daddy: he knew when not to cry, no matter how much it hurt.

"I'm going to check up on mom," Jerry said.

"You better eat some of your supper, Jerry," I said. "If daddy catches you, he'll beat on you, and you can forget about getting anything to eat after that."

"I'll be okay," Jerry said. "Watch over Leo and Albert and make sure they eat all their supper, okay?" Jerry looked at me. "And make sure you eat all of yours too, Emelia."

"I will," I said, still feeling very concerned for my brother's safety. "You be real careful, okay, Jerry?"

"I will—don't worry," said Jerry.

Jerry was gone for a long time. Albert and Leo ate all of their supper and I ate most of mine. I cleaned the table off best I could.

Eventually Jerry reappeared. "Emelia," he said. "The coast is clear. You take Leo and I'll take Albert. Let's go, hurry!"

We made it upstairs and got Leo and Albert to their rooms. I had already washed Leo and Albert when I was downstairs. Mama kept some diapers in one of the cupboards and she had shown me how to change Albert. I got Leo into his pj's and Jerry did the same for Albert.

"Jerry," I said. "I put some food in a bag for you. I knew you would be hungry."

"Thanks," Jerry said.

"Albert and Leo are already sleeping."

"I know. I checked on Leo to make sure he was all right where dad had kicked him—and it looked okay to me.

"How's mama?"

"I think she's okay. Dad did a lot of yelling at her after they got upstairs. I could hear him slap her a few times but you know mom, she didn't make a sound. He got the safe open and mom gave him something. I could see her through the crack of the door when she handed it to him. Everything seems to be quiet now."

We were so relieved to see mama when she joined us in Jerry's room. We were sitting on the floor and she stood leaning against the door, holding the handle to support herself.

"Are you kids okay?" Her voice was so soft we could hardly hear her.

Jerry clenched his teeth. "Some day, mom, I'm going to be big enough!"

"Yes, Jerry," she sighed. "Some day you will be big enough." She looked around. "Where is Albert and Leo?"

"They're in bed sleeping," Jerry reassured her.

"Did they eat their supper?"

"Yes, mama," I said. "They ate everything on their plate. I tried to clean up the table for you. And I changed Albert's diaper, and I washed them up, and Jerry came back and got me and we brought Leo and Albert up here and put them in there pj's and put them to bed." I took a deep breath. Had I left anything out? "Oh, and me and Jerry checked Leo to see if everything looked okay and it did."

"Dad kicked him pretty hard," Jerry said.

"I know." Mama came closer and sank down, sitting on the floor right there next to us. A strand of her hair had fallen across one eye and she looked deadbeat.

Why did he have to come back? Everything was going so good. Why is he so mean? Why does he hate all of us so much? He just got home after being away two months. You'd think he could be nice just for one day, or even just for a few hours. These thoughts went through my head and I was sure Jerry and Mama were thinking pretty much the same thing. The three of us just sat there on the floor in Jerry's room and not another word was said.

Next morning, sitting at the breakfast table, daddy told mama it was time for him to be admitted to the VA (Veteran Administration) hospital in Vermont. (Daddy was a veteran of the second–world war) He went there every so often to be checked out and stayed for five or six days. Mama always had to drive him there and when he was ready to come home, he would call her to come get him.

"I plan on going first thing tomorrow morning," he said. "Be ready to go."

"I'll have everything ready," mama said.

Daddy got up from the table and left. It was a nice day—at least, for a while. We could hear a siren blowing. There was a fire going on somewhere. It went on for some time. We stood outside to see if we could see any smoke, but couldn't see anything.

It was suppertime when daddy showed up. He never came home for dinner.

"We're going to watch some movies I took in Alaska," he said.

He had a camera that you cranked up and it took moving pictures with no sound—but daddy liked to talk the whole time to tell us everything that he saw. Sometimes he would stop the film so he could talk and talk about something that he was interested in but it would have to do with how brave he was. He showed us a fire that was going on in Alaska: it was a big fire and he had it on film. He was very taken with the fire. He talked about it for half an hour before the phone rang. I was glad when it did. I was falling asleep and that is one thing you should never do when daddy's talking about himself. He'd wake you up and it never felt too good when he did.

Daddy answered the phone. We could hear him talking.

"I can't see any reason why they would even suspect me!" daddy said. "I was very careful. I know that no one saw me there. The only time was when I showed up and was talking to the fire chief—and that was when it had already burnt down… No, everyone was very sympathetic towards me. They knew how hard I was working on building that house and I'm sure they'll never put it together that I was the one that burnt it down."

My blood froze. *Oh no*, I thought! Daddy's burnt the farmhouse we were going to move to when it was finished! All that wood we picked from the dump! All the wood that was given to daddy by people who cared about us—people who felt bad for mama because she had to work so hard in the restaurant and the hotel! Daddy had said that after we moved to the farmhouse mama wouldn't have to work so hard. I couldn't wait for that to happen. It was already taking too long to build. The trip to Alaska for two months stopped everything on the farmhouse, but that was okay because daddy being away was worth it. Oh, and to think of all the nails that Jerry, Cecile and me, had to straighten out for him! Everything was gone! And *he* was the one that did it! All those sirens we heard earlier—that was *our* house that was burning. Oh daddy, how *could* you!

Mama's eyes were wet. Tears were running down her face. She knew it was too good to be true when daddy told her this house would be for her and she wouldn't have to keep working as hard as she was. But it had been two years ago that he had told her that, so at least for all that time the dream of the house was something for her to hang on to, to keep her going—something to look forward to, even if it took two years or more to finish. Daddy worked very slowly. He had a lot of drinking buddies who would go to the house, and as long as daddy kept the beer coming, the men would work for nothing. That was for one day a week. That's why it was taking so long.

I ran and got mama some tissues to wipe her face before daddy came back into the room. We could still hear him talking on the phone.

"You got that right," he was saying. "I had plenty of insurance on it. I'll be at the VA hospital for a few days—so things should cool down before I get back... Okay Burt, I'll talk to you later—and you make sure you keep your mouth shut!"

The phone was hung up. Daddy walked back into the room where we where sitting waiting for him to return.

"I guess you heard me on the phone?" he asked gruffly.

Silence. No one wanted to answer him.

"Irene! I'm talking to you!"

"Yes," mama said meekly. "I heard you."

He nodded. "Then I don't have to tell any of you that you're not to say one word about this to anyone, right?"

"No, you don't have to worry about it, Jerry," mama said in a shaky voice. She had all she could do not to break down and cry. Daddy noticed and it made him furious.

"Did you really think I was having that house built for *you*?" daddy sneered. "Don't tell me you really thought you were going to get out of working that easy! There's *no way* that you'll get out of running the hotel and the restaurant." He sat down and lolled in his chair, regarding her with half–closed eyes, his face twisted into a sneer. "Hell, I wouldn't have a house built for *you*—or your kids! What do you think—I'm crazy? The only reason I was having it built was for the money. That's what it's all about, Irene—money! That's why I have you, to make money for me. If I can't have you making money for me, then what use are you? You keep that in mind!"

My blood froze again when he pulled out his gun. He waved it at mama. "If I have no use for you, no one else will either—because you won't exist! I'll make sure of it and you *know* I will." He turned his gaze to us and spoke with contempt. "If you kids want to keep your mother alive, then you better keep your mouths shut! Do I make myself clear?"

No one could speak but we managed to nod our heads up and down to indicate a 'yes' answer. Daddy stuck his gun back into his pocket and left.

Mama fell apart. I don't think I've ever heard mama cry so loud before.

"It's okay, mama, please don't cry. We won't tell anyone—that way daddy won't use his gun on you."

We knew, from the way he was waving his gun at mama as he spoke, that he would surely shoot her and kill her. And he had told mama he would shoot us too.

"I won't let anything happen to you kids," she sniffed. "That means I have to stay alive or he will do something bad to all of you, even Cecile. He told me she wanted to go to Alaska with him and stay there. She hates me! She still thinks *I* was the one that put her there. Oh Cecile, I wish you knew the truth!" She wiped the tears from her eyes. "I would *never* send you away!"

"Can't we go and see her, mama?" I asked.

"No," mama shook her head. "If I was to go there, he would find out. The nuns would tell him and he would send her away to some place else—and I would never see her again. So I *have* to stay away from her. At least she's safe where she is and… and it does my heart good to know that."

The newspaper people called up mama and wanted to know how she felt about daddy's trip and if she would comment on it. Mama told them she had nothing to say about it. Then they asked her if she would ever move to Alaska like daddy had told them during his interview when he got back.

"Why should I?" she asked them. "It would be no different in Alaska than it is in Berlin."

But they had no idea what she meant. We knew, of course. Dad would be the same anywhere.

9

Mama received a letter from the doctor that was seeing daddy at the VA hospital.

"I wonder what this is all about," mama said. "Your father has only been gone three days." She opened the letter and read:

> *Dear Mrs. Dion,*
>
> *This is difficult for me to say in a letter. I feel that you should know right away. I have done a mental evaluation of your husband and the outcome is not good. His anger has increased towards you and your children. As far as that goes, he has become a dangerous person. So dangerous, in fact, that he should be committed to a mental institution without delay. I have the necessary papers that you will need. All you have to do is sign them.*
>
> *Please call me at this number # as soon as you can so we can discuss this further. Don't delay.*

Mama was shocked! She knew daddy was crazy but she thought it to be only a saying. Daddy was mean but there was no way she could do *this*. She knew he would find a way to get out and then he would kill her for sure!

Mama called the doctor right away.

"You have no idea what you're asking me to do," she said. "I can't have him locked up! You think you know this man with all your tests, but let me tell you, no one knows him like I do. He is a mean, vicious man who gets his own way no matter what."

"All the more reason to have him locked up," said the doctor.

"You don't understand," she said. "This man will find a way to get out and he will come after me and my children and do away with us! If it was just me I wouldn't hesitate a bit, but I have five children to worry about. There's no way that I can do this."

"Then I have to tell you that if you value your life and the lives of your children, leave him now!" the doctor said. "The outcome is quite dubious!"

"Mama," Jerry asked after she had finished speaking to the doctor, "what are we going to do?"

"Nothing," mama said. "All I have to do is do everything he wants me to—and you kids do the same. We have to learn to stay out of his way. When he becomes angry, I want you kids to go and hide and make sure you have Leo and Albert with you, understand? We can make this work if we all work together."

"Okay, mama," Jerry said.

I just shook my head, for I was too scared to do anything else. We were already hiding every time daddy started yelling.

"We're going to have to show Leo how to hide with you, Emelia," Jerry said. "And I'll take Albert with me. But what about you, mom?"

"Don't worry about me—just make sure that all of you are safe, okay?"

"Okay, mom," Jerry conceded.

Mama was taking a practical attitude and accepted that she had to make the best of the way things were. "Your father still has about three more days before he calls me," she told Jerry, "so practice how you will hide with Albert and Leo, and make sure you don't say anything about this letter or the phone call that I had with the doctor."

"We won't, mom—will we, Emelia?"

"I won't say anything," I promised.

It was getting late so mama told us we should get ready for bed.

Mama let Jerry and me stay up for another hour after Albert and Leo were put to bed. It was so peaceful when daddy wasn't home.

"Okay, you two, off to bed with you," mama said. So we gave our kisses and off we went.

Mama went to her room. She sat at her vanity and read her letter over and over again. "What am I going to do," she asked herself. She left her letter there and went to bed.

I woke up, startled. What was that noise?

It was daddy! What was he doing home? Mama said he would be calling her to go pick him up in about three more days. But he was home and he was yelling at mama! Then I knew—he had found the letter! *That's* what he was yelling about! Oh no, poor mama. What was he going to *do* to her?

"How long have you had this!" daddy demanded.

"It just came in the mail today," mama said.

"Did you call him up like this letter asked you to?"

"I didn't believe the letter," mama said. "I was going to throw it away."

"You're *lying!*" daddy shouted. "If you were going to throw it away, then you would have done it right away!"

I could hear mama screaming. I could hear daddy hitting her. *No, daddy no! Stop hitting mama!* Everything was breaking. I could hear smashing sounds. I ran into Jerry's room. He was sitting on the floor with his hands over his ears.

He was crying. I sat down beside him. "Jerry, Jerry, daddy's beating mama up real bad! What are we going to *do?* Jerry! What are we going to do?"

"We're going to hide Albert and Leo right now!" Jerry stood up. "Come on!"

We ran into their room. They were asleep. We had a place where we could lay them down and daddy would never find them.

"You stay here with them, Emelia," Jerry said.

"No, I can't! I'm going with you," I said.

"Okay, but we need to check on them in a little while, okay? I promised mom I would look out for all of you."

We ran back to Jerry's room. It wasn't that far away from where we had hid Leo and Albert.

Daddy was still hitting mama. She was still screaming. We never heard mama scream like that before. "No, Jerry, *NO!* Please stop! *Please* stop!" she screamed. There were more sounds of glass breaking, banging up against the wall.

Jerry and I hid in the dark by mama's door. We knew that if we could still hear mama it meant she was still alive. Daddy was hurting her like never before. She was trying to say something, but it sounded like he was choking her. Jerry stood up. He couldn't stand it any more.

"No, don't, Jerry!" I cried. "If he sees you he will do the same to you! I can't take care of Leo and Albert by myself—and it will make it worse for mama. Every time daddy sees you he gets madder at mama."

"You're right, Emelia," he relented, "he does get madder at mom every time he sees me."

There was a big bang and daddy yelled. *Good for you, mama,* I thought. Then the gun went off! I grabbed Jerry for dear life. I was so scared. I couldn't hear mama anymore. The gun went off again! *Oh! mama, what did daddy do!*

"I can't hear mama anymore, Jerry!" I said. But he was so stunned he didn't seem to hear me. "Jerry!" I shouted, "I can't hear mama anymore!" Jerry woke up from his shock and came to me. I was crying so loud that he had to put his hand over my mouth so daddy wouldn't hear me.

We just sat there and cried together. We didn't know what to do. There was no more screaming, no more glass breaking, no more shots fired, no noise at all. Not one sound.

Jerry went and checked on Leo and Albert. They were still asleep. I was so glad they didn't hear everything that had happened during the night.

"Do you think mama is still alive, Jerry?" I wept as I asked.

"I don't know," said Jerry.

Everything was so quiet.

"Wait! I hear something—*shhhh,*" Jerry said.

We peeked and saw daddy come out of the door at the far end of the bedroom. It was a long bedroom with a door at either end. He was limping and seemed to be in a lot of pain. *I wonder why?* I thought. Jerry and I sat there waiting for mama to come out, but she never did.

"We have to go in there," Jerry said.

"I'm too scared, Jerry," I whispered. "I think we'll find mama dead, Jerry."

"Come on, she might still be alive," he said.

My breath was taken away when we walked into the room. Mama and daddy each had a full size bed. They each had a vanity with a big mirror and each a dresser where mama kept all her statues.

"Jerry, *look!* Everything's broken!"

The mirrors were all smashed, the mattresses were all torn apart and cut up, and mama's statues were stuck in the holes upside down. Broken glass lay scattered all over the floor. Everywhere you walked the glass would crunch.

"I can't find her!" Jerry said.

We looked under the beds, in the closet, under the covers on the floor.

"*Mama, where are you!*" I screamed.

"Mom, it's okay, dad is gone! Where are you?" Jerry called.

But mama was nowhere to be found. There was blood all over the place.

"Where can she be, Jerry?" I asked. My heart was beating wildly.

"I don't know, but at least she's not here," Jerry said, forever level-headed and sensible. "If she was, she'd be dead, wouldn't she?"

"Do you think daddy killed her and hid her somewhere?" I asked.

He shook his head. "We were here all night, he has a sore foot and had a hard time walking. I don't think he could have carried mom anywhere. She must have left on her own."

I was glad when Jerry said that. Mama *must* still be alive—but *where* was she?

"We better go check on Leo and Albert to make sure they didn't wake up and get scared," said Jerry.

Leo was just waking up when we got there, and Albert woke up right after we started talking to Leo.

"*Now* what, Jerry? What do we do now?"

"We go and feed Leo and Albert," Jerry replied sensibly.

Jerry and I stayed home from school to take care of Leo and Albert. Mama never came home that day. Neither did daddy.

The next morning I walked into the kitchen and daddy was taking a beer out of the refrigerator. I didn't even know he had come home.

"Where's Jerry?" daddy asked.

"He's getting Leo and Albert dressed," I said.

"What are you looking for?" he asked.

"I was going to make some toast for us to eat." My heart was pounding so fast.

There was a knock at the door just as Jerry walked into the room with Leo and Albert.

"Jerry," daddy said, "answer the door."

It was the babysitter that sometimes took care of us when mama and daddy went out with his friends. It wasn't often that mama went out and she could never go out alone. Daddy would never permit it.

"What do you want?" daddy sneered at the sitter.

"Irene called me late last night," she said. "She asked me to take care of the kids. I told her I would come first thing in the morning, and here I am."

"My kids don't need a sitter! They're Dions and they can fend for themselves. Where's Irene? Where did she call you from? Do you know where she is?"

The babysitter stared at him, confused.

"I want to know right *now!*" he yelled. "Tell me where she is!"

"I don't know where she is, Jerry, she didn't tell me. I asked her but she said she would rather I didn't know."

"If you hear from her again, you better let me know, you understand?" daddy yelled again.

"Yes, Jerry, I… I'll let you know."

She was getting upset and wanted to leave. I think she would have said anything just to get away from him.

Daddy was so angry after she left. He started kicking the kitchen table. We escaped being beaten only because we got out of there as fast as we could when we saw he was getting mad at the sitter. We knew that if we were still present he would be kicking us instead. In the end daddy went storming out the door.

"Did you hear that, Emelia?" Jerry said with surprise. "Dad called us his kids! That's the first time I've ever heard him call us his!"

I nodded. "It sounded kind of funny, didn't it, Jerry?"

"I wish mom could have heard that," Jerry said.

"Where can mama be, Jerry?" I asked.

"I don't know," he replied, "but one thing's for sure—she's still alive!"

This was the third day and we still hadn't heard anything about mama.

"I want you two to put your coats on and go outside and take a walk," daddy said. "I want you, Jerry, to walk up one side of the street and you, Emelia, to walk on the other side. All the way up Main Street, then all the way down Main Street. I want you to keep doing it until I tell you to stop. I think that if your mother is around, she'll try and make contact with you. I want to know if anyone talks to you no matter what it is they say—you remember it so you can tell me! I want to know where your mother is and you two are going to help me find her. Have I made myself clear to the both of you?" Daddy fixed his eyes on us. His expression was severe.

"Yes, dad," Jerry said.

"What about you!" he said to me.

"Yes, daddy," I said in a small voice.

"Okay, then. Leave and make sure you don't hide anything from me. You know what will happen if you do!"

It was nice to get outside again. We hadn't been out for three days now. Jerry went to the left on the other side of the street and I went to the right on my side, because Jerry didn't want me to cross over in the traffic.

We walked up and down the street five times. The street was long. *Oh mama, where are you?* I kept thinking to myself. *I miss you so much, mama. I just want to put my arms around you and tell you I love you.* I started crying because I wanted my mama back.

Then I saw a familiar figure. *I know that lady*, I thought to myself. She was walking towards me. I stopped crying. My mind was focused on her coming near me.

But she walked right by me! I kept walking in the direction past the Princess Theater. When I got around the corner, a voice spoke to me: "Don't turn around. Keep walking the way you are, not too fast! If someone walks by me, I'm going to stop talking until they pass me. I don't want you to say anything—just listen."

It was the voice of the lady that I saw walking towards me—who walked right by.

"Your mother is safe," said the voice. "I have her with me. If you look to your left you will see a small boarding house. Walk real slow. There's a door towards the back of the building on the left—do you see it? Just make a loud cough if the answer is yes."

I looked—and I coughed.

"Okay then, you can see it. Now listen, I want you to tell your brother Jerry—but only him. Do not tell your father, do you understand?"

I coughed in reply.

"Okay. Your mother wants to see you and Jerry tonight after your two younger brothers and your father are asleep. Make very sure that your father is asleep. If he wakes up, you are *not* to come. You are not to tell him I spoke to you. If he finds your mother, he will hurt her even more than she is already hurt. You know that, right?"

I coughed again.

"Okay. Make sure that your father doesn't hear you when you tell Jerry. Now for the hardest part. You have to convince your father that you don't know anything when you get home. And you have to stay calm to do that. Let him ask you the questions and your answer is that nobody talked to you. You don't know *anything*. Do you understand everything I just told you?"

Again, I coughed.

"Okay. You and Jerry come to the back door tonight. No matter what the time is, it will be okay. I'll look for you. Now wait about a minute, then turn around and head the other way—and good luck!"

When I turned around she was gone. I was so excited I could hardly stand it. I was going to see mama! Oh, I couldn't wait to tell Jerry! But I *had* to stay calm. Then I saw Jerry approach me.

"Jerry, what are you doing on my side of the street?" I asked.

"Dad has been yelling for you. He sent me to find you. Did you find out anything?"

Just as I was about to say something, I was face to face with daddy.

"I've been yelling for you!" daddy said through gritted teeth. "Where *were* you?"

"I… I guess I wasn't walking so fast anymore… my legs got tired, daddy." I was so nervous I stumbled over my words.

"*I'll* give you tired legs!" he shouted. "Get yourself home right now!"

He didn't have to say it twice. I ran all the way home. *How am I going to tell Jerry?* I asked myself. Daddy will almost certainly be watching us to see if we talk about anything.

"Did you find anything out?" daddy asked.

Jerry and I both shook our heads.

"Did anyone talk to you?" daddy asked.

Again Jerry and I said no.

"I thought I saw you talking to a woman, Emelia?" daddy said, watching me closely.

My heart leapt into my throat. *Be still now*, I said to myself, *he's trying to trick me.* I knew that he couldn't see her or me from where he was.

"No, daddy, I didn't talk to no woman. I didn't talk to anyone." *Stay calm*, I thought. My voice was shaky. Could he tell? *Please don't ask me anymore questions*, I thought to myself.

"What about you, Jerry? Did anyone talk to you?"

"No, dad," he said truthfully, "not one person."

Daddy paused, giving us a long, calculating look. "Well," he said, "I'm going to tell you what happened to your mother. She ran away with another man, see? She didn't want you kids anymore. She told me she didn't care about any of you." He sneered, looking for our reaction. "So how do you like that? Even your own mother can't stand you—ha–ha–ha!" How he laughed! "Go get Albert and Leo to bed, then you two do the same," he said. He wasn't laughing anymore.

I couldn't say anything to Jerry in front of Leo and Albert because if I mentioned mama, they would get all excited; so I had to wait until they were in bed. When they were in bed I tiptoed into Jerry's room.

"Jerry, Jerry! Wake up!"

"What… what's going on?" he blinked.

"I have to tell you something," I whispered.

"Can't this wait till morning?" he said.

"No, it can't. It's about mama."

Jerry jumped up out of bed."

"What about mom?"

"*Shhhhh*," I said. "I talked to a lady today."

"Then dad was right when he said that to you?"

"No, he wasn't. I really didn't talk to her. She talked to *me* and I had to cough if the answer was yes."

"What did she say?" Jerry asked, his eyes wide.

"Mama wants to see us tonight, but we have to make sure daddy is sleeping—and Leo and Albert, too. She showed me where to go to find mama. It's not far from here."

"Well, you don't have to worry about dad," he grinned. "He had a lot to drink tonight. He's passed out. Let's check on the boys."

"Okay—good. They're sound asleep."

"Let's go," said Jerry. "Just put your coat on. You don't have to get dressed."

And so we crept out into the night. I found the door the woman had mentioned.

"Are you sure that this is the place, Emelia?"

"Yes—I'm sure. It's dark, but the door is here. I saw it earlier today. The lady showed me. Here it is, Jerry."

We knocked on the door. The lady that had spoken to me opened it.

"Come in, kids." The lady made us wait as we entered. Her forehead was creased with concern. "I want to tell you something first. You have to be careful when you see your mother. She's still hurting pretty bad, so try not to squeeze her, okay?"

"Okay," we both said, and she led us into a room where we saw mama half lying on a sofa.

I gasped. "Oh mama! Look at you! Your face is all black and blue! I can hardly see your eyes. Your arms are all cut up, mama—and your legs too!" The tears gushed into my eyes. "We know what daddy did, mama! We saw all the broken glass on the floor. Can I give you a hug, mama?"

"Come here!" mama said. "Don't squeeze me, okay? I have three broken ribs and they're sore."

The lady had mama's ribs taped up. "I couldn't take her to the hospital," she said, "your father would have found her."

"Thank you for taking care of mom," Jerry said.

"Listen kids," mama said. "I have to tell you something: I'm going away. I have to—or your father will kill me this time. I can't take any more of his beatings. I'm going to stay here for a few days, then I'm leaving Berlin. I'm not sure where I'm going yet. I have to wait until I can at least walk and get around. You can't tell your father where I am, but I'm sure you won't." She smiled at Jerry. "Jerry, I guess I'm counting on you to be the big brother that you always had to be. I know I don't have to ask you to watch out for them. I already know that you will. I've always been able to count on you, Jerry. You're the joy of my heart. You all are." Then she smiled at me, her green eyes glistening with tears. "I know your father won't hurt any of you—he wants me first. But do try and stay out of his way as much as you can."

"Can I come with you, mama?" I asked. I was hardly aware of the tear that ran down my cheek.

"No, Emelia, I can't take any of you with me."

"You're going to leave us, mama?" My voice broke and I couldn't swallow the lump in my throat. "Oh mama, don't leave us! *Please,* mama! Let us go with you. Don't leave us with daddy!"

Mama smiled through her tears. In spite of her bruises, she had a wonderful smile. She stretched out her arms and I crept closer. I knew she hurt inside, but I was hurting too.

"Mama, it hurts inside! My heart is hurting, mama—please make it stop!" And I began to cry. I couldn't stop my sobs and the hot tears streaked down my face. Mama held me the best she could with the pain that was in her broken body.

"Emelia, listen to me. Some day I will have all of you kids back with me. Do you hear me? I will have you all back. I don't know how long it will take, but it *will* happen. I promise you. Do you believe me?"

"Y...yes, mama. I believe you, but... but it still hurts." I wept and I reached out to touch her brown hair that was cut just below her ears. Normally so neat and with a curl to it, her hair was disheveled from her ordeal.

"I know, honey, I know, it hurts me too." She turned to Jerry. "Jerry," she whispered, "take Emelia home. I won't be seeing any of you again until we're all together for good. Remember, I love all of you. Don't ever forget that."

When Jerry pulled me away from mama, it was like someone reached through my chest, grabbed my heart, and tore it out of me.

10

Jerry and I hadn't been to school for almost two weeks. The truant officer was after daddy to do something about it. Daddy wouldn't let the sitter come to the house to take care of Albert and Leo so we could go to school.

Daddy drank most of the time and started beating us again. Sometimes he would get both of us, not just one—but we did manage to keep him from hurting Leo and Albert.

"Jerry!" daddy yelled from downstairs. "Get yourself down here *now!* The fire is going out in the furnace! Tend to it!"

Jerry ran downstairs as fast as he could, but he had to go around daddy to get to the furnace. As soon as Jerry got close to him, daddy reached out and took Jerry by the back of the neck and rammed his body up against the wall, over and over again. I ran downstairs and got in his way so daddy would let Jerry go. Daddy kicked me and I ran. He chased me back upstairs and I ended up getting the belt. But I didn't care—Jerry had got away! But it didn't make the belt feel any better. He seemed to hit even harder than before.

I didn't have mama anymore to put cold washcloths on my back and bottom.

I miss you mama. If only I could see you just one more time. Then I thought, *Yes! I'll go see mama just once more!*

Jerry was back, daddy was lying down, and Albert was napping. Jerry went in to watch Leo play with his blocks.

"I'll be right back, Jerry," I said.

"Where are you going, Emelia?" he asked.

"I'll be right back," I said as I ran out the door.

Mama, I'm coming! I can't wait to see you! I ran just as fast as I could. I got to the door of the boarding house and the lady opened it.

"Emelia! What are you *doing* here?" she asked.

"I want to see mama."

"You can't," she said, her eyebrows drawing together in a worried frown.

"I'll only stay for a minute! Please let me see mama."

"You don't understand, Emelia. She's gone. She left four days ago. Some people picked her up and took her with them. It was someone that she knew from the restaurant. They were moving out of Berlin. They said they would take good care of her. Don't worry. I'm sure she will be just fine."

Her words made my mind go numb and I just stared at her.

"Emelia, are you listening to me?" she asked.

I was still hearing her say, "She's gone."

I found my voice. "Mama's gone? When is she coming back? When will I see her again?"

"Don't you remember when your mother told you she had to leave? She told you that someday she would have you all back together again. She promised you, remember?"

"Yes," I said, my voice almost a whisper. "I remember."

I took my time walking back home. The tears in my eyes felt hot. When I got there, I didn't see daddy anywhere.

"Jerry, why are you sitting on the floor?" I asked. "What happened to your lip?"

He looked up at me. His eyes were wet with tears barely held back.

"Emelia, they're gone," he said.

"Who is gone?"

"Albert and Leo are gone!"

"Where are they?" My heart missed a beat.

"A couple of women came here while you were out and dad gave Albert and Leo to them."

"When are they coming back?" I felt dazed.

"They're not."

"How do you know they're not coming back? Of course they're coming back, Jerry!"

"*No!*" he shook his head. "They're *not*. One of the ladies told dad it was hard to put the two of them together so they would have to split them up and put them in different homes. And…and dad said, 'I don't care, split them up—just get them out of here!' I spoke up and told dad I would take care of them and he gave me a fat lip. When the ladies went he belted me."

"Are you okay now, Jerry?"

"I'll be okay, Emelia. I'm used to it."

"What's going to happen to us now, Jerry?" I asked. It was like the world had fallen away from beneath my feet. *This isn't real,* I thought. "I'm scared, Jerry."

"I am too." He raised his eyes to me in a forlorn look.

"Oh Jerry, mama's not there anymore! She's gone. The lady said she left four days ago!"

His eyes widened. "You weren't supposed to go back there! You heard what mom said."

"I know," I said, beginning to cry. "I just wanted to see her one more time… but it didn't matter anyway. She's already gone away. Do you think that mama has gone to *memere's* and *pepere's* house?"

"No!" daddy said as he stepped into the room. "She didn't go to *pepere's* house."

I jumped and my heart leapt into my throat. I hadn't heard him come in.

"Where were you!" he yelled. "Out looking for your mother again? I *told* you she ran off with some bum. She doesn't care about any of you! She left you! She's no good. Even her own father sent her back to me when she ran away the last time. You were there, remember? Nobody cares about her! No one wants her!"

"That's not true!" I cried. "*I* care about her. *I* want her."

By the look on Jerry's face I realized that for once I wasn't thinking those things—I had actually said them out loud!

Daddy jerked me by the arm and dragged me down the stairs, into the car and drove off.

I can't believe it! I thought. *I yelled at him and I'm still alive.* I was crying so hard but only on the inside because I didn't want daddy to see me on the outside.

Daddy never said a word to me. He just drove. I was so scared, I could feel myself shivering—as you do when you get out of the water and the cold air hits your body and you can't make yourself stop no matter how hard you try.

Where was he taking me? Maybe if I closed my eyes and opened them again it would be morning and I'd find out that all this was just a bad dream. If that was the case, I thought I would rather have the witch come after me and tie me up on the windowsill again.

I opened my eyes. Daddy had stopped the car. He reached over and grabbed me. I don't think my feet ever hit the ground until I was standing in mother superior's office.

"Is this the child you spoke to me about, Mr. Dion?" mother superior asked.

"Yes, it is," daddy said.

"I thought you weren't bringing her until next week?" she said.

"I don't have any more use for her, so take her now." He turned towards the door and said, as he walked out, "And make sure you let me know if she or you hear from her mother."

No hug, no kiss, no nothing! Not even a goodbye from him. I never got to kiss and hug Leo and Albert when they were taken away, either. Mama was gone, and I didn't know what was going to happen to Jerry—and now my daddy was gone too.

I could still hear his words burning in my heart: "*I have no more use for her.*"

Mother superior looked stern and forbidding, and my heart raced. Her voice was impersonal and formal. "We don't have names here," she announced. "We have numbers. Let's see—your number will be 64."

She read it off to me while she sat behind her great big desk. "Everything you will be using will have that number sewn on it—your uniform, undergarments, and so on. Your knee socks will have a 64 on them, and you are responsible for washing them out every night before bed so you can have them for the next day. We don't have a supply of those. Someone will show you how. We go to church every morning at five, and right afterwards we go to the dining room for breakfast. You will be assigned to a nun. Each nun has ten girls in the group she is responsible for. You stay with your own group of girls—that way your nun can keep an eye on all of you. Don't make her look for you. At nighttime make sure you go to the bathroom *before* getting into bed. If for any reason you need to go during the night, you are to put your slippers on and do *not* turn any lights on—not for *any* reason." She pulled herself up straight, her eyes still fixed on me. "Do you have any questions?"

My heart had slowed down a little and I took a deep breath.

"Is… is this a convent?" I asked.

"Yes, it is," she said.

Then I felt my whole body cry out with excitement!

"Is my sister here?" I asked. "Her name is Cecile."

"What is her number?" she asked me.

"I… I don't know."

"Has she been here long?"

"Yes." I nodded.

"Well, I can't help you then. You have to know her number. We have a lot of girls here."

My excitement drained away. I felt so alone. How could everything go so wrong all the time?

"Come with me," mother superior said.

I followed her. I walked by one of the classrooms and the door was open. I saw the nun in charge walk over to one of the girls and hit her right across the knuckles with a ruler.

"You'll see more of *that* if you're not on your best behavior!" mother superior warned me. "The same will happen to you."

I was confused. "Mother superior, what did that girl do?"

"Oh, probably nothing," she said as we walked on. "Sometimes we do that to someone that doesn't deserve it in order to make the others think twice about it before acting up. We can control them better that way."

All I could think of was that daddy must have given these nuns some of his lessons.

"Here we are," she said as we reached another room with a nun seated at a desk. "Come in here with me. Sister Pauline, this is number 64—to be placed."

"Thank you, mother," said sister Pauline, whose unsmiling face looked very severe. "Have a seat!" she said to me as mother superior left. I sat down. "Just one minute," she added. "I have something to take care of first."

Sister Pauline got up from her chair and I saw how tall and thin she was. She walked to what looked like a closet door, opened it and said, "You can go back to your room now!" A little girl came out of the closet, her face swollen and red from crying. "Next time I have to speak to you, it will be a *lot* longer than two hours that you'll spend in there!"

Two hours! I thought, *that's a long time to spend in a closet!* It felt like I'd never left home. Now I knew for sure daddy had been showing these nuns a few things.

"Now, who did mother superior say you were?" sister Pauline asked.

"My name is Emelia," I said.

"I don't want to know your name!" she spat out. "Our girls don't have names here. They have *numbers!* I'm sure mother superior told you that!"

"I'm sorry, sister Pauline. My number is 64." I was fidgeting in my seat. I still had a sore bottom from the last beating daddy gave me with his army belt.

"I can see that you're going to be a handful," said sister. "*Stop your fidgeting!* Can't you sit still? *Come here!*"

She pulled up the back of my shirt. "I *knew* it! I can tell by looking at these blisters that you've been a very naughty girl!" The tone of her voice hardened. "Don't think for one minute that you'll get away with anything around here!" Then she yelled: "You'll be good or else! I wish I had the room for you in *my* group. I would calm you right down in a hurry!" She was thoughtful for a moment, then spoke with satisfaction: "It just so happens we *do* have a sister that will straighten you out—*and* she has room to take you. She walks around with her ruler in her hands all the time. She *never* has any trouble with her girls. Even the other sisters stay out of her way. She gets the job done and that's all we care about. She has the best–behaved girls in this convent. Yes—she'll be *perfect* for you! We have about ten minutes before her class is done."

My heart was like lead and I felt nervous, lost and frightened. I quickly wiped away a tear that wanted to spill out onto my cheek. I scratched an itch on my head.

"*What* did I see you do!" sister yelled at me.

"I… I didn't do anything, sister," I said in a shaky voice.

"Did I see you scratch your head? Come here! Let me see your fingers," she commanded. She took hold of my fingers, examining them. "You see that shiny spot right there? That's oil. Not just plain oil but holy oil," she said. "Don't you know it's a sin to scratch your head! You're getting all that holy oil on your fingers, then touching things with it. It's a sin!"

I never read that in my catechism book, but she was a nun—she should know. Boy! I thought to myself, the priests and the nuns must have to scratch their heads a lot in order to get enough oil to fill the bottle in the church.

Pow! That ruler of hers came out of nowhere just like daddy's belt used to. She hit my knuckles just as hard as she could. There was blood on two of my knuckles where the steel part of the ruler hit. I always thought I'd like to be in the convent to be with my sister, but now I knew I'd hate it there!

Oh Cecile, where are you? I wondered. *I always thought you had it much better than the rest of us—that you didn't have to get daddy's beating every other day. I can see now that it probably wasn't much better for you being here.*

"Lets go," sister Pauline said. I followed her with tears in my eyes. I held my head down so nobody would see them.

"You wait here," she said to me. I didn't dare move. I'd only been there for one hour and, so far, I didn't have a name anymore, just a number, I had sinned against God by scratching my head because I had an itch, I had gotten my knuckles cracked by a ruler, and I was told I was a very naughty girl. What next, I thought.

"All right, 64! Come in here," sister Pauline said, taking me into an office. "This is the nun I told you about. She'll be looking over you. You are one of her ten, but I'll be watching you from a distance. I know how naughty you are!"

"Sister Pauline!" the other nun said severely as she stood up.

"Yes?" said sister Pauline, taken aback.

"You are *not* to punish any of my girls! I do that myself! I can see you've already done that with 64. I'll take care of punishing her my own way, agreed?"

"Oh… yes, sister, I agree," said sister Pauline as she left the room.

"Come over here," the nun said to me. I didn't move—my feet were frozen to the floor. She stood up and I saw she was short and a little chunky, unlike sister Pauline who was tall and thin. She walked over towards me, tapping the palm of her hand with the big ruler in her other hand. Sister Pauline's ruler wasn't as big as this one, I thought. She looked over by the door and saw sister Pauline standing in the hallway.

"Will you please shut that door, sister Pauline?" she said severely.

"Oh my, yes… I will! Thank you, sister."

"You're welcome!"

Sister Pauline closed the door.

"Now, do you see this ruler in my hand?" the nun said to me.

I couldn't say anything. I was so scared I just nodded my head ever so slightly.

"Well... it's not for you," she said. Her voice had unexpectedly softened.

Eh? I didn't think I'd heard her right. If that ruler wasn't for me, then what was? I didn't think I wanted to find out.

Sister went back to her desk, laid the ruler down, then came back to where I was. She took my hand and led me back to her desk. She sat me in a chair next to hers.

"Let me see your hand," she said as she opened her desk drawer and took out a tube of something. She squeezed some of it onto my hurting knuckles. "We'll clean them good later. Does that feel better, now?" she asked kindly.

"Y...yes, ma'm," I said, confused.

She reached for her ruler and I jumped out of my seat!

"It's okay, my dear," she soothed. "I'm not going to use it on you. I only have it so the other nuns *think* I do. That way they leave my girls alone, see?"

I blinked, stunned with surprise.

"Come here," she said gently. "Now, what is your name?"

"Number 64," I said.

"No, I want your name."

"Emelia," I said.

She turned me around and pulled up my shirt. *Here we go again*, I thought nervously.

"Oh, you poor child," she said softly as she pulled me towards her and hugged me. "You'll never be beaten again—not while I'm around."

I couldn't believe what I was hearing! This nun sounded just like mama!

"Now, you can't tell anyone how I treat my girls, okay?" she continued in a gentle voice. "If they find out, the girls will be placed with other nuns. I only use the ruler to scare the other nuns into thinking I punish my girls the same way they do. I wish I could do more for the girls here; but the way I see it, they always give me the smallest and weakest ones and at least I'm able to protect them from the other sisters' abuse. Do I have your word that you won't tell anyone? Not even any of the girls that you might become friendly with? I ask this because I don't want the other girls to feel worse than they already do."

"I won't tell anyone, sister," I promised, blinking away my tears.

"Sergeant," she said.

"Sergeant?"

"Yes, that's what you call me. The reason is because the other nuns *think* I'm the meanest of all of them. I walk around with my ruler all the time." She gave a little laugh. "They wanted to call me captain, but mother superior didn't want them to. I was glad, so I ended up with the name Sergeant. If it makes them stay away from my girls, then it's okay with me."

"You're so nice!" I smiled. "I'm so glad you're my nun."

"Now you be careful, just the same! The other nuns will be keeping an eye on you because you're new here. After sister Pauline tells them all about your marks on your back, they'll automatically think the same way she did—that you're a very naughty girl. That's the first thing she had to tell me when she brought you to me. Try not to wander off too far from me. If you do, one of them might find a reason to punish you."

"Sergeant?" I said, a new hope springing up inside me.

"Yes?"

"How will I find my sister if I don't look for her?"

"Your sister is here?"

"Yes—I think she's still here."

"How long has she been here? Did she come at the same time as you?"

I shook my head. "She's been here for a long time, but I don't know how long. Do you know all of the kids' names, Sergeant?"

"No," she smiled. "I only know my ten girls' names. What is your sister's name?"

"Cecile."

"Cecile?" she frowned. "No, I never heard that name before. Do you know her number?"

"No, I didn't know about the numbers until I got here today."

"I'm sorry, Emelia, I don't think there is much that I can do; but I *will* try and find out whatever I can, if anything. How old is she?"

"She's two years older than me and I'm almost nine."

Does she look like you?"

I shook my head again. "No, she looks like my daddy, and I look like mama. Cecile has dark hair, not light like mine."

There was a knock at the door. Sergeant got up to answer it. "Come in girls," she said. "This is a new girl that's joining us, so I want all of you to make her feel welcome. Her name is Emelia, but all you need to know is that she is 64."

Later Sergeant took my hand. "Come Emelia," she said. "We're going to show you where you're going to sleep. We need to make up your bed and we have to get you a uniform and undergarments. Also, pajamas, slippers, and all the other things that you will need. You can only have one pair of knee socks but I'm going to try and find you two pairs. That way one pair will have a whole day to dry instead of just overnight. I'll take your things with me so I can sew your number on each item. I will start with your pj's so when you put them on tonight, they'll belong to you. I'll do the rest of your clothes this evening. I'll have everything ready for you when you get up in the morning."

She turned her attention to the other girls.

"Now, girls, we're going out where the other girls are, so be careful how you act."

I couldn't believe how everyone changed when they left Sergeant's office. I'll have to watch real good so I can learn to act the same way.

That night I closed my eyes and prayed, "God, please watch over my mama, Jerry, Leo, Albert and Cecile too. Let them know how much I love them. Keep them safe and God, please help mama get us all back together again. Thank you God for giving me such a nice nun to watch over me, amen."

11

Twenty-eight days passed and I still didn't know if Cecile was also at the convent. My birthday came and went. Daddy never came to see me.

I didn't hear anything about Jerry. And for that matter, I hadn't heard anything about Leo or Albert either.

I wondered if mama knew where I was? How could she? Daddy was the only one that knew I was there. I felt so alone. I cried myself to sleep almost every night. I had a friend that slept in the bed next to mine. I didn't know her name or her number. We didn't speak—we only saw each other at bedtime when no one was allowed to talk. Some nights she must have heard me crying. She reached out and held my hand and we swung our arms back and forth until we fell asleep.

The convent food wasn't very good. The first morning I went for breakfast it was *awful*. It was the same thing every morning—clumped-up oatmeal with no sugar or milk to put over it, and a dried-up piece of toast with no butter. You took one bite and the toast fell apart in your hands. I couldn't eat my oatmeal—it made me gag when I tried to put it in my mouth.

"Eat your oatmeal!" sister Pauline ordered.

I didn't know where Sergeant was, but I hoped feverishly that she would show up. "I can't, it will make me sick, sister," I said, and pleaded: "*Please* don't make me eat it."

"You're *going to* eat it!" she commanded. "I don't care if it takes all day!"

Two hours went by and I still couldn't eat it. I tried, but I knew it would make me sick if I put one more bit in my mouth. Sister Pauline lost patience.

"Open your mouth!" she ordered. She stuffed one spoonful after another down my throat.

Mercifully, Sergeant showed up. "Where have you been? I've been looking all over for you, 64!"

Sister Pauline was stuffing in the last spoonful. "She didn't want to eat her oatmeal! I told her she wasn't leaving until she ate every bit of it." She put down the spoon on the empty plate. "There, that didn't hurt, did it? You're all done now!"

I stood, and immediately I threw up all over sister Pauline's black dress. Boy! Was she upset! And I didn't even do it on purpose. I couldn't help noticing the smile on Sergeant's face as she hurried me out the door and brought me to the nurse. She gave me a warm drink, a pink liquid tasting of mint that made me feel a lot better. Sergeant wanted me to lie down for a while, anyway. I think it was her way of keeping sister Pauline away from me. I was sure glad about that! I didn't want to see her anyway. *I think she's out to get me now*, I thought: *it's only a matter of time!* It was clear Sister Pauline didn't like me at all, but then I don't think she liked anybody.

It's a good thing we could wash our own socks. Every morning at breakfast we had oatmeal. I cleaned my plate every day. This kept sister Pauline from picking on me. She thought I ate it because of what she did to me; but what she didn't know was that I still couldn't eat that oatmeal. It still made me sick and I still didn't eat it. I stuffed it down my knee socks every morning when she wasn't looking! By the end of the day my feet looked like prunes from being wet all day. It was so uncomfortable—but it was better than eating the stuff! Every night I cleaned out the oatmeal in my socks and washed them real good and hung them to dry. Sergeant was able to find me two pairs of socks, and that made it easier to keep up with wearing my breakfast all day!

I didn't like going to bed. It gave me too much time to think about all the people I loved so much and never could get to see anymore. How I wished I could find out where everybody was! It seemed like forever since I'd seen them. I just *knew* that mama was trying to get us all back together again. After all, she had *promised* and she never broke a promise to me—not ever.

"Oh, please God, make all the pain go away!" I prayed. "Help me to sleep and not think about how much I miss everybody."

There was my friend's hand again—she must have heard me crying again. *Thank you for my friend, God.* We never spoke but I knew she cared enough to hold my hand to try and make me feel better and not so alone. She had people who came to see her on visiting day and I wondered if that was why she felt so bad for me—because no one ever came to see *me*.

I had nearly dropped off to sleep, still holding my friend's hand, when a noise beside me startled me. Now it was under my bed! What was it? I strained my ears and heard some talking. Whoever was there was going to get into trouble if the nun heard her—she and my friend might even get the ruler!

"It's okay, *I'll* hold her hand," one of the voices said, "she's my sister."

Who said that? I *knew* that voice!

"Cecile! Is that *you*?" I could hardly contain myself.

"*Shhhhhh*. Yes Emelia, it's me." She crept closer, taking my hand, and whispered: "I only found out a week ago you were here—only because I heard some nun saying my name and that's something you don't hear around here. Numbers, yes, names, no. Then that same nun said your name so I listened to hear what they were saying. I couldn't make it all out but I had the feeling they were looking for me." She squeezed my hand. "I would have come sooner but I have a very mean nun and she watches me like a hawk! I'm always getting her ruler across my knuckles—or my back; and sometimes she makes me kneel down for long periods of time."

"What's her name?" I whispered back, still barely able to believe it was Cecile next to me in the dark.

"Sister Pauline," she said. "Some of the girls call her Geronamo, and the name suits her fine, believe me!"

"Oh! I know all about sister Pauline!" I said. "I have Sergeant."

"*That's* the nun who said your name!" she squeezed my hand harder. "She's the *worst* nun in the place, you poor kid!"

I raised myself on one elbow to try and see her better. "Were you under my *bed*, Cecile?"

"Yes!" she said. "That was the only way I could get to you. I had to crawl under every bed in this row to get here." She giggled. "Let me tell you, I don't think they dust under the beds around here. I kept sneezing the whole time I was crawling. I was afraid that the nun would hear me."

"I missed you so much, Cecile!"

"*Shhhhh*, I think I can hear sister Pauline." Cecile was silent for a moment, then decided the danger was over. "I'm sorry mom went and stuck you in here, Emelia. You don't deserve this."

"But Cecile, she didn't!"

There were sounds of footsteps approaching.

"Sister is coming!" Cecile whispered hurriedly. "I have to go."

"Wait!" I said. "What's your number?"

"It's 121. I got to go! I'll talk to you somehow. I love you." Then she crawled under the beds out of sight.

I could hear sister Pauline talking. She was asking one of the nuns if they'd seen number 121.

I couldn't believe it! Big sister *was* in the convent! And I saw her! I couldn't wait to tell Sergeant. She would know what to do now that I had her number. 121! Oh boy! I was so excited. It had been so long since I'd seen Cecile, I didn't think I could sleep. *Please morning, hurry up and come!*

"My, my, aren't we all wound up this morning!" said Sergeant. "What's gotten into you?"

"Sergeant! I saw my sister!" I exclaimed. "She came and saw me last night!"

"Oh no!" she said with dismay. "It was your sister, then, that sister Pauline was beating last night!"

"What!" I said. "Is my sister okay, Sergeant?" My joy had turned to anxiety.

"I don't know how bad it was, but I'll find out," she said kindly. "So just calm down." She dropped her voice. "Now, Emelia, you don't want to let anyone know she's your sister, see? Especially if sister Pauline has her. What's her number? Did she tell you?"

"Yes, I asked her. It's 121."

"Good job!" she smiled. "That will make it easier for me to check up on her."

"Sergeant," I said, returning her smile, "Cecile thinks you're the worst nun in the convent! She might not trust you. What will we do?"

Her smile broadened. "You just leave that to me! I'll think of something."

Another thought struck me. "Sergeant," I said, "when Cecile was leaving me last night, she said she loved me—and I didn't have a chance to answer her back. If you get to talk to her, will you tell her that I love her, too?"

"Surely I will," she said thoughtfully, her brows drawing together. "You know something that might work?"

"What might work, Sergeant," I asked.

"Was there anything else your sister told you that no one else heard last night?"

"Well, she said that sister Pauline watches her like a hawk. Oh, and she said that some of the girls call sister Pauline by a nickname they gave her—Geronamo!"

"Very good, Emelia!" She gave me a sly wink. "Now you go about your business—and act like nothing has happened. As soon as I find out something, I'll come and find you and let you know."

Oh, Cecile, I thought, *I do hope you're okay. It's my fault this has happened to you. If you hadn't come to see me, sister Pauline wouldn't have done anything to you. Please hurry, Sergeant, find her!*

"Sister Pauline?" Sergeant said.

"Yes, sister? What can I do for you?"

"I hear one of your girls was seen in my dorm last night. I believe it was 121. Am I right in saying that?"

"Yes, sister, you are," sister Pauline replied with satisfaction. "but I took care of it last night when she came back to her bed. She was severely punished by me and I don't think she will ever do that again, believe me."

"Did she say why she had done that?"

"No, she didn't—but I thought she might be trying to run away again. I've been keeping a close eye on her ever since she tried the last time."

"Indeed!" Sergeant nodded. "I would like very much to see this girl 121. I know that she is under you—but I wouldn't mind asking her a couple of questions. I don't want her giving my girls any ideas about running away. I'm sure you have everything under control, but I'd like to see her—if *you* don't mind, of course?"

"Consider it done!" Sister Pauline gave a grim smile. "In fact, it would do her some good. I hear she's scared to death of you."

"Indeed! Where can I find 121?"

"Right there in my closet," she said, pointing. "She's been there since last night!"

"I see." Sergeant narrowed her eyes. "If I am going to get the full effect of frightening her, do you mind if I see her alone?"

Sister Pauline nodded. "I could use a break. I'll be back in twenty minutes. Is that long enough?"

"That will do nicely."

Sergeant opened the door of the closet.

"121—out you come!"

There was no reply so Sergeant turned on the light. Cecile was seated on a stool, her hands tied behind her back and her feet tied together. She had tried in vain to rub off the piece of tape that sealed her mouth.

"121?" Sergeant queried.

Cecile looked up in alarm and started to shake all over. *Oh no!* she thought as her heart raced, recognizing Sergeant, the worst nun in the convent.

Sergeant took the tape off Cecile's mouth and untied her. "Follow me," she said.

They went to the nurse's office. Sergeant knew the nurse wouldn't be there at that time. She wanted to talk to Cecile in a safe place. She knew sister Pauline would try to come right back so she could hear what was being said. Sergeant locked the door behind them.

Cecile was beside herself. She didn't know what to think. What was Sergeant going to do to her?

"First of all, Cecile," Sergeant said kindly, "I don't want you to be afraid of me. Just tell me—why did you go to my dorm last night?"

"Um—for no reason," she began nervously, wide–eyed, her brain racing for a suitable excuse. "I...I was just out walking around. Then I heard sister Pauline's voice and I tried to hide. That's all."

"Is that what you told sister Pauline?"

"Y...yes."

"Good! Sergeant smiled. "I don't want you telling anyone it was your sister you went to see. It will make it rough on Emelia—and you—if people find out you are sisters. The only way that you two are going to be able to see each other is on Saturdays when we wash the girls' hair. I know I will be able to change shifts with another nun—for her time slot; I know she will, because she already agreed to do so some time ago. She has her own reasons and I don't pry. That way you two girls will at least be able to see each other for a couple of hours a week, for the time being—until I can find other ways for you two to get together."

Cecile's eyes were as big as saucers. She couldn't believe what she was hearing from the meanest nun in the convent! *It's a trick!* she told herself. *I bet it is! This is a set up! I just know it!*

"I don't know what you're talking about, sister," Cecile replied with her heart in her mouth. "I was out for a walk, and sister Pauline caught me, and…and…that's all there is to it."

Sergeant gave a knowing smile. "Well, I guess I'll have to convince you. Lets see, now…The girls in your group have a nickname for sister Pauline, right? It's Geronamo! And how about this? When you left Emelia last night you told her that you loved her, but she didn't get a chance to answer you back; so she wanted me to tell you that she loves you too."

Great big tears welled up in Cecile's eyes. Sergeant put her arms around her and hugged her.

"It's okay, Cecile, I'm your friend. I'm not the enemy—only the other nuns think I am. But you can't give away my secret, you hear? You can't tell anyone—not even your best friend."

Cecile smiled through her tears. "Don't worry—I don't have any best friends. I won't tell anyone your secret, anyway." Her smile widened. "At least now I don't have to worry about Emelia having you for a nun!" She wiped a tear from her cheek, then moved a strand of her dark hair that had fallen across one eye as she looked up at the nun. Her face became serious and it gave her a pinched look. "Did you really mean what you said about fixing it so Emelia and I can see each other on Saturdays?"

"I sure did!" Sergeant nodded. "I'll go right now and fix it up with sister Jane. You will be seeing her in two days—but no more sneaking around, okay?"

"Okay," she smiled again.

"Right! Come on now, I have to get you back to sister Pauline's office There's not much I can do when it comes to the other nuns—you know that, don't you?"

"Oh, yes, Sergeant, I know—it's all right, I'm used to it."

"Very well," she nodded again. "Let sister Pauline know how stern I was with you, and that you're sorry for what happened and that you will try and do better."

She led Cecile back to sister Pauline's office.

"Sister Pauline, I brought 121 back to you. I took her to the nurse's office, but no one was there. In fact, the door was locked."

Cecile spoke in a small voice. "I'm sorry, sister Pauline, for all the trouble I caused you. I'll try my best to do better—I promise."

Sister Pauline's eyes widened in surprise. "Well! I guess Sergeant must have shown you how naughty you've been! In that case, you can be excused—but no more trouble!" She turned to Sergeant. "*Thank* you, sister—that's the best I have ever seen 121 act! I don't know how you do it, but whatever it is, it works!"

"Just apply a little love," Sergeant said under her breath as she walked away from sister Pauline—advice she wouldn't dare express loud enough for her to hear.

"Emelia?" Sergeant called out when she returned.

"Oh, Sergeant! What did you find out?" Emelia had been anxiously waiting for the nun's return and readily responded to the sound of her voice. "I've been so worried! Did you see Cecile? Is she hurt real bad? Where is she? Did you talk to her? Did she believe you?"

"Slow down, Emelia!" Sergeant laughed. "One question at a time! Yes, I *did* see Cecile. She has a few bruises on her. But it was more of a mental punishment than anything else. She was put in that closet that you told me about when you first came here. I got to have a nice talk with her. She's a very nice girl and she certainly cares about you, dear. And yes, she believed me—but only when I told her you wanted me to tell her that you loved her too. She told sister Pauline that she was sorry that she caused her trouble and she would try and do better. Sister Pauline let her off from her punishment, so I guess everything's back to normal. Oh yes, and I asked Cecile to keep my secret and she said she would—and I believe her."

"Oh, Sergeant! Thank you for finding Cecile and doing everything that you did! You're the best!"

Sergeant smiled, then looked serious again. "There's one more thing. Would you like to hear it?"

"Yes, I would."

"I already told Cecile that I was going to do this, and I did do it. I talked to sister Jane and it's all taken care of."

"What is it, Sergeant? Tell me, you're teasing me, aren't you?" My cheeks dimpled in a shy smile.

"I fixed it up with sister Jane to change the time for my girls—that means for you, too, Emelia—for Saturday mornings for all of you to get your hair washed."

"What does that mean?" I said.

"That means that you will be able to see your sister Cecile for two hours every Saturday morning." She smiled impishly. "How do you like that?"

"I like that a lot!" I exclaimed. "For two whole *hours*? Every Saturday? *Thank you*, Sergeant!"

This time there were happy tears in my eyes.

12

"It's Saturday!" I said.

"Emelia," Sergeant said, "I don't want you running right over to Cecile, okay? You want to take it a little slow. Let her come to you. She'll be able to judge it better since she has to watch out for sister Pauline."

"I don't understand, Sergeant," I said. "Why does she have to be so careful with sister Pauline?"

"Ever since Cecile tried to run away, sister Pauline has been watching her really close. We don't want her finding out that you two are sisters yet. And another thing, don't forget sister Pauline still hasn't gotten over you throwing up on her!"

"Cecile tried to run away?" I asked, surprised.

"Yes," Sergeant nodded. "I don't know all the facts. I only found out recently from your sister when I was talking to her."

When we entered the washroom I spotted her immediately.

"There she is, Sergeant!" I said.

She nodded. "Now, remember what I said—and refer to her as 121. I'll just sit over here."

I thought to myself: *Cecile, I'm over here, can you see me?* My stomach did a few flip-flops.

She spotted me! She began walking over towards me!

"121!" sister Pauline yelled across the room.

"Yes sister," Cecile said, stopping in her tracks.

"Come here!"

Cecile walked away from me. My heart fell to my feet. I ran over to Sergeant.

"Sister Pauline made Cecile go back to her," I said, crestfallen.

"Calm down, Emelia," Sergeant smiled. "Sister Pauline is doing her hair first. She'll be done in a few minutes."

"Then I won't get to see her for that long," I said, disappointed.

"Come here," Sergeant said. "I'll wash your hair first. That way you'll be done about the same time."

"Oh Sergeant, you think of everything!"

It wasn't that long before Cecile managed to walk over to me again.

"Come sit over here, Emelia," said Cecile. "I didn't think I would ever get to talk to you again! How come *you're* in the convent?"

"Mama's gone. She left daddy."

"*Mom* left *dad!*" exclaimed Cecile. "Where are Leo and Albert?"

"I don't know. Daddy sent them away just before he brought me here," I said. "Jerry told me that a couple of ladies came to the hotel and took them away."

"What about Jerry? Where's he?"

I shook my head. "I don't know that either. He was still home when daddy brought me here."

"Where did mom go?"

"She didn't tell me where she was going. She's been gone for a long time now. It seems like forever. Jerry and I stayed out of school to take care of Leo and Albert. Mama tried sending the sitter to take care of us but daddy wouldn't let her. He said we were Dions and we didn't need anybody to take care of us—that we could fend for ourselves." I was aware of her drinking in all the information I was giving. Her blue eyes, set in her dear face framed by the cleanly washed, long brown hair that was thicker than my blonde wispy hair, studied mine. I could barely believe she was real—that I could reach out and touch that face. The tears welled up in my eyes. "Oh, Cecile, I'm so glad I'm with you. I was so scared all the time. I still am, but now I have you—and Sergeant."

"I can't *believe* how nice Sergeant is!" Cecile said. "She's the one I was always afraid of the most! What a surprise to find out she's not like the rest of them here. I'm real happy that you have her, Emelia."

"Sergeant told me that you tried to run away once. What happened?"

She shrugged. "I was homesick, I guess. I wanted to see all of you—but I didn't get too far. Sister Pauline caught me."

"You used to be able to tiptoe so good, Cecile. How come you got caught?"

She gave a little laugh. "Sister Pauline can tiptoe better that I can, I guess. Besides, she has longer legs than me. She can take bigger steps."

"What did she do to you after she caught you?"

"She beat me with her ruler across my back, my fingers and my knuckles! I couldn't write anything for two days. I had athlete's feet at the time from not wearing my 'thongs' or 'flip–flops' when I took a shower and they were all scabby. When I ran away it opened up some of the sores. She held my feet over a bucket and poured alcohol over them. It hurt so bad I thought I was going to pass out. She'd also wake me up one hour before everyone else and make me kneel down; then she would walk around me and hit me with her ruler. It didn't matter to her where she hit me, as long as she was doing it. She seemed to get so much enjoyment out of it! She would do the same thing to me right after school and again at bedtime. Sometimes she had work to do in her office so she would take me with her and make me kneel for two to three hours at a time in front of her so she could keep looking at me. I had to hold my hands in a praying position. I would get so tired that I would clasp my hands together. She didn't like that so she would tape my fingers so they would stay straight; then she would tape my two hands together. It sure made it hard if I had an itch. I couldn't even scratch myself. But then if I did she would say it was a sin anyway."

"I know!" I exclaimed. "I scratched my head once and she told me it was a sin—because my head had holy oil on it and I wasn't supposed to touch it!"

Cecile nodded. "Yes—it's weird."

"Does she still do that to you?" I asked.

"Not so much now," said Cecile, "but she does try to keep me away from the other girls. She says I'm a bad influence."

"I'm sorry, Cecile, that you have such a mean nun. I wish you had Sergeant too. Then we could spend all kinds of time together."

Our talk was interrupted by sister Pauline suddenly yelling: "121! Let's go!"

"I have to go," Cecile whispered. "I'll see you next Saturday. I love you!"

"I love you, too," I whispered back.

These weekly meetings went on for some time. The only time I saw Cecile was on Saturdays when we got our hair washed. These were the times when we would tell each other what went on during the week, like who did what to whom, and what for. Cecile was still getting the ruler from sister Pauline. As long as I was around Sergeant I was okay, but when I had other classes the nuns would find my knuckles with their rulers, and sometimes slip and get my back as well.

"Emelia!" said Sergeant. I jumped. I must have been day dreaming again.

"Yes, Sergeant?"

"You have a visitor."

"I do?" I said, taken aback. "I haven't had a visitor since I've been here. Are you sure it's for me?"

"Yes, I am. She asked for you, Emelia."

"Oh! Is it mama!" My heart missed a beat.

"I don't know what your mother looks like, but I don't think this is her. This lady looks and sounds Italian."

Cecile was standing next to the lady who had her back to me. She must have said something to her. The lady turned around and I recognized her at once, the mother of Jerry's best friend Clint who did that naughty thing to me while I was hanging from the broken bridge. Clint was a jerk, but his mother had always been kind to us.

"Mrs. Dee!" I exclaimed. "I'm so happy to see you."

"Hi, Emelia," Mrs. Dee said. "I received permission from mother superior to come and get you girls for a couple of hours. I found out where Albert and Leo are."

"You did!" I exclaimed.

"Yes—and I thought you two girls would like to go and see your brothers for a little while."

"I sure would!" I said.

"Do you think they will remember me?" asked Cecile. "It's been a long time since I've seen them—a lot longer than you, Emelia."

"I'm sure they will," said Mrs. Dee. "Come, let's go. There's only one way to find out."

I couldn't believe it! I was going to see Leo and Albert! It had been almost a year since I had seen them."

It was so nice to see Mrs. Dee again. I missed going to her little grocery store. Mama's tip money used to buy all our snacks there. She used to sit me up on a bench and let me watch her make Italian sandwiches and they smelt so good! She would always cut extra pieces of meat and cheese and give them to me. She was ever so kind to do this for us. She must really care about us, I thought.

Albert and Leo were going to be so surprised to see us! I couldn't wait to see the look on their faces.

"Mrs. Dee," I said, "you found us so easy! When I came to the convent I couldn't find Cecile *anywhere*. I didn't know her number. How did you know it—and mine too?"

"I didn't," she smiled. "I had a picture of you and Cecile. I showed it to mother superior and she knew the both of you; but she didn't know that you two were sisters."

"Sister Pauline sent for me," said Cecile.

"That's one of the nuns that mother superior called to get you."

"And the other one was Sergeant," I said.

"That's a strange name, isn't it?" said Mrs. Dee. "Mother superior called her to get you, Emelia."

"I wonder if mother superior told sister Pauline that we were sisters?" said Cecile.

"Wouldn't she have said something to you when she told you that Mrs. Dee was here?" I asked, confused.

"No," said Cecile. "She sent one of the girls in my group to tell me to go outside. She said that someone was here to see me."

"Sergeant didn't say anything to me," I said. "And she would have if she had found out. She would have been worried about us. Maybe mother superior didn't tell sister Pauline."

"Did I cause you girls a problem?" Mrs. Dee asked from the front seat of the car.

"No, Mrs. Dee," Cecile assured her. "Nothing we can't handle."

I wasn't so sure, though.

"Here we are," said Mrs. Dee. "This is the house where Albert is."

"*Look*, Cecile!" I exclaimed. "There he is!"

"My goodness, hasn't he gotten big!" said Cecile.

Albert looked so nice, all dressed up in a little suit. There were no other kids around. He was so excited to see us.

"Cecile, he still knows you!" I said. "And you thought it had been too long."

"Albert, *look* at you!" Cecile said. "You're so big!"

He was jumping up and down. He wanted me to pick him up, so I did. The lady that Albert was staying with came over to me.

"Would you please put him down," she said primly. "I don't want his clothes wrinkled. I believe that a child should look nice all the time."

It broke my heart that I couldn't hold him for even a minute! But I did as she said and I put him down. He landed on his feet, but tipped over just enough to make him put his hands down and touch the porch floor. He stood right up without falling on his bottom.

"I *told* you not to get yourself dirty!" the lady said crossly.

"He didn't fall," I said. "He only touched the floor with one of his hands. It didn't even get dirty."

"Come with me!" She took Albert by the hand and fairly dragged him into the house, yelling behind her: "You girls will have to leave now!"

I could hear Albert crying inside the house. I felt so bad for him. I hated hearing him cry.

"Albert can't even play and get dirty!" I said in dismay.

"Cheer up, Emelia, everything will be okay," said Cecile.

"Let's go and see how Leo is," said Mrs. Dee.

"Have you heard anything about where Jerry is, Mrs. Dee?" asked Cecile when we were back in the car.

She shook her head. "No, I haven't," she said thoughtfully. "If I find out anything I'll let the both of you know." The car slowed down. "Here we are, girls."

"That looks like Leo right there!" I said. "There are so many kids around here, not like where Albert is staying. At least Leo has other kids to play with."

Leo ran up to us gleefully.

"Look at you! You're so dirty, Leo!" said Cecile, laughing.

"Did you come to bring me home now?" asked Leo. "I want to see mommy. Where's big brother?" He looked around. "I want to show him how big I am!"

"Mrs. Dee brought me and Emelia to see you for a few minutes, Leo," said Cecile. "But then we have to go back to the convent."

"Take me with you, please!" said Leo.

"We can't," said Cecile.

"Please, Cecile, *please* Emelia—take me with you! I don't want to stay here anymore."

He started to cry. He grabbed me by the leg and wrapped his arms and legs right around me.

"Please, Emelia, take me with you!" he cried.

The lady that Leo was staying with came and pulled him off me.

Why was there always so much pain? Why couldn't we all be together? Why did it have to hurt so much? I thought: *Please take me away from here, I can't stand it, my heart is hurting and I can't stop it!* All the bad feelings that I had when I was home at the hotel when daddy was there were back. *Please God, make the hurt go away,* I prayed.

Mrs. Dee took us back to the convent.

"I'm sorry that it turned out the way it did," she said.

"It's not your fault, Mrs. Dee," said Cecile

She smiled. "Is it okay with you girls if I come back and see you again sometime?"

"Oh yes, Mrs. Dee," Cecile assured her. "We would like that very much. You're the only one that has come to see us. My dad used to come to see me once in a while, but he hasn't been back since Emelia's been here."

But I didn't want to go back there again. I didn't want to ever see Albert and Leo again, not ever! I cried. It hurt too much!

"Well, well! What do we have here?" sister Pauline said. "I should have known that you two were sisters!"

Sister Pauline was waiting for us to return so she could show us how mean she could be.

"121, you come with me," she said. "Don't plan on seeing your sister anymore on Saturdays! I just put a stop to it!" Her mouth twisted into a cruel smile as she walked away with Cecile.

I ran to my room, lay on my bed and couldn't stop crying.

"Emelia, please don't cry," said Sergeant.

"Oh Sergeant! Sister Pauline won't let me see Cecile anymore!"

"*Shhhh,*" said Sergeant, "I know. I heard all about it when you were gone to see your brothers."

"I don't want to see them anymore either, Sergeant," I cried. "I don't want to hear them cry any more!"

"You poor dear child," she soothed with her soft, gentle, loving voice. "You are so young to have all this pain in your life." Sergeant held me in her arms close to her heart. "*Shhh* Emelia, everything will be all right. God will see to it. You just wait and see." She held me for a long time, then said, "I have something for you, Emelia."

"You do?" I lifted my face to hers.

"I was going to give it to you on your birthday, but I don't want to wait any longer." She got up. "You wait here. I'll be right back."

It wasn't long before she returned with a parcel under her arm.

"Here you go, open it!" she smiled.

I untied the string and a garment of soft, flowing material unfolded. I held it up, spellbound.

"A dress! For *me*?" I said.

"Yes, for you," Sergeant smiled. "All the girls have a dress of their own—even your sister does. You're the only girl in the convent that doesn't have one. You always have to wear your uniform."

"Daddy didn't take the time to pack any clothes for me like mama did for Cecile. He was too angry with me."

"Well, I thought you could wear your dress on Saturdays—like the other girls do." She smiled again. "Wouldn't you like that? It's not new, but I think it's pretty, just like you."

"It's beautiful, Sergeant!" I said, holding it up to the light. "It's the most beautiful dress I've ever seen. I love it, Sergeant. Thank you! It looks a lot like one of the dresses mama bought for herself once, but daddy cut it all up with a pair of scissors."

Sergeant looked shocked. "What in the world are you talking about?"

"It's a very long story, Sergeant, and not a very nice one; and I don't like thinking about it. Daddy isn't a very nice daddy at all. Sometimes he was very mean—worse than sister Pauline."

"That's okay, Emelia. Let's not talk about it right now. Would you like to talk about something else?"

"Yes, Sergeant. I don't like talking about daddy. My mama is gone because of him, and I miss her very much."

"Do you want to try your dress on?" asked Sergeant.

"Oh yes!" I said. "Can I? It's not my birthday yet, though."

"That's okay." She smiled. "Come here." She unbuttoned my uniform and helped me get into the dress. It hung beautifully and felt wonderful.

"It's a perfect fit," Sergeant said. "Look in the mirror and see how it looks on you."

It was the most wonderful present! It looked so pretty on me.

"I love it, Sergeant! I really do."

"Well, my dear, its all ready for you to wear next Saturday."

"Would it be okay with you if I save my dress?" I asked.

"Save it? Why?"

"For when I get to see mama again," I said. "I want to look pretty when she comes to take me with her for good—like she promised me. Is it okay, Sergeant?"

"Sure it is, my pet," she said.

13

Sister Pauline kept her word. Three weeks went by and I hadn't seen Cecile. My birthday was the following week and I had been hoping to spend it with Cecile—but it didn't look like it would happen. I had spent my ninth birthday alone, and it looked like my tenth would be alone too. At least I had Sergeant. That's more than Cecile had.

Speaking of Sergeant, I wondered where she was? She was never late for class. Before long mother superior came in.

"I have an announcement to make," she said. "Sergeant is ill today. That means you girls will be split up into different classes. Each nun will take one of you girls in her class."

The nuns came into the room and picked out a girl, each one leaving with the girl of her choice. My heart sank when I saw sister Pauline coming towards me. *Oh no,* I thought to myself. *Please don't pick me!* Those were my first thoughts, but then I hoped she *would* pick me—for then I might have a chance of seeing Cecile.

"64! You come with me!" said sister Pauline. I was scared—but happy!

"I always said I would get a chance to get my hands on you!" sister Pauline pronounced with satisfaction. A smile twisted her lips. "And now I have."

My heart missed a beat at that remark.

"Follow me!" she ordered. When we reached her classroom she indicated a seat. "There's an empty desk and chair right there. Sit in it! I don't want to hear one sound out of you during class. Do I make myself clear?"

"Yes, sister," I said meekly.

Cecile! I saw you when I came into the room, I was thinking. *I can still see you! You're just four seats in front of me. You have such pretty hair, unlike mine: yours is so dark and thick! I wish that we could talk to each other like we used to. I miss you, Cecile!* I was daydreaming again. I'd better pay attention, I thought, or sister Pauline would ask me a question and I wouldn't know the answer.

Sister Pauline talked and talked, then almost at the end of class she asked us to get a book out of the desk. I did, but with one problem. When I opened the top of the desk, it didn't stay up like mine always did in Sergeant's class. It fell down and made a loud bang. All the girls turned around and looked at me and started to laugh. Sister Pauline was furious and came at me with her ruler. She continued to slash at me with the ruler that struck me repeatedly on what seemed like every part of my body. The girls weren't laughing anymore. While she was bombarding me with hits her ruler landed so hard on my right wrist that it damaged the bone. (I couldn't use my right hand for two weeks or more after that. That meant I couldn't do my homework. One of my punishments afterwards was to go to her class every day after school to do my homework. There was no way she was going to let me get away with not doing it, seeing she was the one that had caused the damage in the first place. She was responsible for me to get it done. I was right–handed and my hand was all taped up. She made me do all my assignments with my left hand on the blackboard and every time I wrote something that she couldn't read, she would give me a crack with the ruler instead of speaking. I still have the marks on my legs that the steel part of her ruler took chunks of meat out of.)

"You stay right there!" sister Pauline said icily after that first hard crack on my knuckles. She was pointing her ruler at Cecile. "And don't you dare move!"

She grabbed me by my hair and banged my head against the top of the desk and held it down with her hand.

"You are *not* to move from that spot!" she said through clenched teeth, still pressing down my head. "There will be no supper for you! You're here for the night! I'm going to let you go, now—but I don't want to even see your face! You keep it right there!"

She removed her hand and I didn't dare move, I was so scared. My head hurt awful where it had hit the desk.

◆   ◆   ◆

Everyone is gone now. It's dark in here. Oh mama, please come soon! I don't think I can take much more of this place. I know Cecile can't, either.

I tried to sleep but I couldn't. I needed to pee but I didn't dare move from that spot. I just *knew* she was watching me from somewhere. I think she had eyes in the back of her head. I grew cold and began to shiver. Could she see me? If she did, she would think I was moving—but I wasn't. It was just my body that was shaking, and I tried to make it stop.

I thought I heard my name—just a whisper! Yes—there it was again!

"*Emelia, are you okay?*" the whisper said.

It was Cecile!

"Oh, I'm so glad to hear you, Cecile!" I whispered back, trying not to move.

She sat down on the floor to talk to me.

"I needed to check on you," Cecile whispered. "I was so worried about you. I tried to get Sergeant but I couldn't find..."

"*WHAT* ARE YOU DOING HERE!"

Sister Pauline's strident voice made my heart stop.

I heard Cecile's nervous reply: "I...I came to check on my sister."

I was really shaking now, but it wasn't because I was cold anymore. *Why did you have to show up, sister Pauline?* I thought. *I got to talk to my sister after you kept her away from me—and now you spoiled it all! Why did you have to catch her! Go away, sister Pauline!* I wished I could say all those things out loud. My heart was beating again, faster than ever!

Sister Pauline spoke to Cecile and her voice grated in my ears: "You're going to take your sister's place, 121—but not with the luxury of sitting down. Kneel down! *Now!*"

Then she said in a voice dripping with false sweetness: "Sixty–four, you can go to your room now—your sister was nice enough to take your place!"

I went to my room crying all the way. *Cecile, you should have stayed in bed! Then you never would have gotten caught. Oh, why is sister Pauline so mean?*

It was 2:00 a.m. Maybe I could get a little sleep before I had to be up at 5:00. *For what it's worth, Cecile, thank you for coming to see me and taking my place. I know that wasn't the intention you had—but thanks anyway.* These thoughts ran through my head as I fell asleep.

◆   ◆   ◆

"You had a rough day yesterday, didn't you?" asked Sergeant while she bandaged my wrist.

"It was an awful day!" I said. "Are you feeling better now, Sergeant?"

"Yes, I am. I'll try not to get sick again—ever." She smiled. "If I do, I won't tell anyone. I don't want you ever to go through anything like that again."

"It's not your fault if you're sick, Sergeant," I said. "Do you think you can find out how Cecile is for me?"

"I already did," she said, gently touching my forehead where a bruise showed. "I knew you would want to know as soon as I found out what had happened. Cecile wanted me to tell you that everything was okay and not to worry."

"You *talked* to Cecile?"

"Yes, I did—and she's fine." She smiled again. "Do you feel better now?"

"Much better. Just my wrist is sore."

"It will take time to heal," she said kindly. "Oh, I almost forgot—this will make you feel better—you have mail!"

"I have mail!" The surprise sent a flow of excitement through my veins. "Who is it from?"

"Well, I don't know. I didn't wait for the mail nun to open it, either. I saw it lying there. It had your name on it, so I brought it to you."

I tore the envelope open. "It's a birthday card!"

"Who is it from? Hurry, look inside!"

"It's… it's…" I couldn't believe it! "It's from *mama!* I got a card from my mama! Oh Sergeant! Mama knows where I am!"

"What does it say?" Sergeant asked.

"It says, 'Don't give up on me. I love you very much. I will keep my promise. Love, Mama.' Oh, and there's a P.S. too! It says, 'Please tell Cecile that I love her too!'" I looked up at Sergeant with imploring eyes. "Will you tell Cecile for me, Sergeant?"

"Of course I will," she replied warmly. "I'm not sure when I will be able to, but I'll do my best."

"I know you will, Sergeant!"

Mother superior was angry with the mail nun when she was told I had received mail that wasn't opened first. She was supposed to let mother superior know if I got any mail—that way mother superior could let daddy know who it was from and where it came from. But there was *no way* that I was going to tell her! I knew if I did, she would tell daddy and he would find mom and kill her.

◆   ◆   ◆

"You have a priest here to see you, sixty–four," said mother superior.

"A priest?"

"Yes. He's a cousin of your father and would like to take you and your sister out for dinner to celebrate your birthday."

Why would he want to take us out? He didn't take us out on my last birthday.

"Come now, sixty–four," said mother superior, "don't keep him waiting." Her next words thrilled me: "Your sister is going with you," she said.

Cecile is coming, too! I couldn't wait to spend some time with her.

"Come along girls," the priest said when we entered the hall where he was waiting.

We went to a nice restaurant and ordered anything we wanted. I wasn't used to regular food anymore. I started to feel sick, but I didn't tell anyone. I didn't want to spoil it for Cecile. Then the waitress came out singing happy birthday to me—and brought out a little birthday cake. Everything was so nice, but I was feeling sicker than ever.

"Did you get any birthday cards from anyone, Emelia?" the priest asked.

There, I knew it! Daddy must have sent him to find out. Mother superior must have told daddy that I received some mail.

I shook my head.

"Oh yes, she did, father," Cecile piped up. "She got a card from mom."

"Can I see the card?" the priest asked. "I bet it's a real pretty one."

"I… I don't have it with me," I began, thinking on my feet. "It's back at the convent."

The priest nodded. "I sure would like to see it when we get back," he said. "You'll show it to me, won't you?"

"I'm sure she will, father," said Cecile.

Cecile, you have no idea what's going on right now, I thought.

"I would like to go to the girls' room," I said.

I was hoping Cecile would come with me so I could tell her, but she never came. I got into the stall and took my card out of my inside pocket of my uniform. I took it out of the envelope and put both pieces back into my pocket. When I got back to the table, I reached up into my pocket and pulled out just the card.

"I'm sorry," I said, "I do have the card with me."

The priest grabbed it out of my hand. "Where's the envelope?" he said.

"I think I threw that away," I smiled innocently. "I was so excited about the card that the envelope must have gotten thrown away."

I knew what he was up to but Cecile had no idea. I forgot to tell her all the bad stuff that was going on at the hotel—about daddy wanting to kill mama, and that it wasn't mama that put her in the convent but mommie and daddy. *Oh Cecile! I have to talk to you, but how?*

"Well girls," the priest sighed, rising from his seat, "we have to get back now." He looked at me. "Can I keep this with me for a little while?"

"No!" I shook my head. "I'll keep it with me—but you can see it any time you want to."

I said it! The priest looked surprised, so I added: "It's just that I waited so long to hear from mama. Now I have, I don't want not to have my pretty card. I want to be able to read it over and over again."

"I understand," the priest gave a bland smile.

We got into the car before the priest did and Cecile whispered to me. "Why didn't you want to let the priest keep your card for a little while?"

"You don't understand, Cecile," I said.

"What don't I understand?"

"The reason that mama left daddy!"

But the priest got in and I couldn't speak. He drove us back to the convent.

"We're here, girls," he said.

As we got out I whispered urgently to Cecile. "Cecile, I *have* to talk to you! It's important."

The priest handed us back to sister Pauline. "They're all yours, sister Pauline," he said, and added under his breath, "I got some of what I wanted."

"What did he mean by that?" Cecile asked after he left.

"You go to your room, 121!" sister Pauline cut her off gruffly, then turned to me. "As for you, get to your room as well!"

She didn't have to tell me more than once. I ran to my room.

"Sergeant!" I said with relief. "I'm so glad you're here! The priest only wanted to get the address of the envelope so he could give it to daddy!" I took a deep breath. "I lied to him, Sergeant."

"Oh? And what did you say, dear?"

"I told him that the envelope might have been thrown away—but I had it the whole time in my pocket! I went to the bathroom and took the card out of the envelope because he wanted to see it. I'm so sorry, Sergeant. I didn't want to lie."

She thought for a moment and her face brightened. "Well, dear, you didn't *say* that it was thrown away, did you? You said that it *might* have been thrown away. 'Was' and 'might' have two different meanings, haven't they? 'Was' is for *sure,* and 'might' is *could be*—but not *sure.*" She smiled. "You just pray extra hard tonight and I'll do the same," said Sergeant. "Anyway, the fact is you did it to protect your mother—so don't worry about it, okay? There can't be anything wrong with that, now, can there? Like I said, say your prayers and ask for whatever forgiveness you need to have. God will know best."

I put my card back into the envelope and hid it under my pillow. During the day mama's card went everywhere I went. I was never without it. I was hoping to see Cecile Saturday but sister Pauline was still keeping her away from me. How was I ever going to tell her what happened? Maybe next Saturday I'd see her.

Another week went by and still no Cecile.

"Sergeant," I asked, "do you think I'll ever see her again?"

"Hang in there, Emelia. I'm sure you'll get to see her again."

Just then a girl walked by.

"Sergeant," I gasped. "That girl has my new dress on!"

"Are you *sure?*" asked Sergeant, surprised.

"Look at it! It's the one you bought me!"

"You're *right,* Emelia!" she exclaimed. "That's one of sister Pauline's girls! In fact, it's the only girl that she likes. Let's go and see sister Pauline about it at once!"

Sergeant approached sister Pauline in her formidable way. "Sister!" she said in a commanding voice. "One of your girls has sixty–four's dress on!"

Sister Pauline blinked. "I don't think so," she said.

"Yes sister, she does," I piped up. I don't know what made me say anything—Sergeant was doing fine. "Can we go and see the number on the dress?"

"That dress belongs to her!" sister Pauline stated emphatically.

"I think sixty–four had a good idea," said Sergeant. "Shall we go see what the number on the dress is?"

"Oh, very well then," she relented.

The girl was called over and I looked at the label behind the neck.

"It's number 64!" I said triumphantly. "I *knew* that was my dress."

"How did you get this dress?" Sergeant asked the girl.

The girl looked up at Sergeant, wide–eyed. "Sister Pauline gave it to me. Sister said I could keep it. But I'll go change and give it back to sixty–four."

"Thank you," I said, and so did Sergeant. Sister Pauline didn't say anything, but her nostrils flared—as though she had a bad smell under her nose.

"I'll get it all cleaned up for you to put away again—for when your mother comes to get you, like she promised," said Sergeant.

That sounded so good to hear.

"I hope it's soon," I said

But it wasn't mama who came the next day. My blood froze when I heard Sergeant's announcement.

"You have someone who wants to see you, Emelia," she said. "It's your father."

Daddy is here! I thought. *I know what he wants! And here he comes! I won't be able to hide my envelope! Oh no! Cecile's with him—and I haven't been able to tell her anything yet!*

"Look Emelia!" said Cecile. "Dad is here to see us! We haven't seen him in a long time."

"Emelia!" daddy said without bothering to say hello or kiss me. "I heard you got a card from your mother. I thought you might show it to me."

"I'll have to go and get it," I said. That way I'd have a chance to take it out of the envelope, I thought.

"Don't be silly, Emelia," Cecile said, "you know you're never without the card!" She reached up inside my pocket and pulled it out. "Oh, you found the envelope!" she exclaimed.

Daddy reached over and took the envelope out of Cecile's hand. "New Bedford, Mass," he said, reading. "So *that's* where she is! I know people that live there and I bet it's the same people that will tell me where she is." He sneered. "Thank you, Irene, for being stupid enough to send a card with the city and state on it!" He threw the card back at me and walked off.

I started to cry. Everything felt so hopeless, and it was my fault! Why hadn't I thrown away the envelope! I could have flushed it down the toilet that time the priest took us out.

"Emelia, what was that all about?" Cecile asked, dumbfounded.

I tried to stop myself crying. "It's... it's what I've been trying to *tell* you... but sister Pauline kept you away from me and I never got to tell you. I never thought about it until I got the card from mama and the priest showed up."

"What do you mean?"

"Don't you *see*? Daddy is out to kill mama!"

"What are you *talking* about, Emelia! Dad isn't going to kill mom!" She touched me on the cheek. "He probably just wants to get her back. That should make you *happy*. You'll be able to go back home again."

I shook my head, my eyes still wet with tears. "You don't *understand*, Cecile. Didn't you hear what he said? Do you think he would call mama stupid if he loved her? Daddy beat her so bad just before she left. Broken ribs and everything! He even tried to get me and Jerry to help him find her. He said that he was going to kill her, and that he would kill us afterwards. Mama hid for over a week. Then she left. But before she did, she had me and Jerry go and see her. She said that she would get us back, that it might take a long time but she promised that she would do it. Read my card! It says not to give up on her and that she will keep her promise. Cecile, you have *no idea* of all the bad things that were going on before mama left. The doctor wanted mama to have daddy put in the nuthouse because he was crazy—but she was afraid to. She thought that he would get out and kill us all, but she knew that if she went away that he wouldn't hurt any of us until he found her."

"I don't believe it," said Cecile. "Why did mom put me in here? She doesn't care about me!"

"Oh yes, she does! Mama didn't put you in here. Mommie and daddy did!"

"That's not true!"

"Yes, it *is* true! I heard mommie tell daddy that she wanted you in the convent so you could become a lady; and I know that daddy told you that it was mama that said that—but it *wasn't*. I heard the whole thing. I heard daddy tell mama that he wasn't about to lose mommie's money when she died, that he was going to do what she wanted him to so she wouldn't cut him out of her will. I also heard him tell mama that she couldn't talk to you about it—that he would handle it and if she interfered she would never see you again."

Cecile said nothing. She just looked at me with big eyes.

"After I heard what daddy told you," I went on, "I went and told mama what he said. She couldn't tell you—she was afraid to lose you, and I didn't want to lose you either; so I kept my mouth shut!"

Cecile looked confused. "But I called up mom! I begged her to come and get me and take me home. She said that she would have to ask dad and mommie if it would be okay—but she never got back to me."

"Did you hear what you just said?" I asked Cecile. "Why would mama have to check with mommie? Don't you see, she was trying to *tell* you something! She was trying to tell you that it was daddy and mommie that put you here, not her! She *couldn't* get back to you. If she did, mother superior would let daddy know that she made contact with you. A phone call or a letter, he would have found out! Look what happened when I got my card in the mail from mama! Sergeant gave me the card before anyone had a chance to open it. Mother superior found out and let the priest know. That's why he was so interested in getting the envelope—so he could tell daddy where it came from. He didn't get the information, so daddy came himself—because he knew that the card came from mama and he swore that he would find her. I only wish I could have told you all of this when I first came here! But it took me so long to find you that I forgot to tell you about it."

Cecile had turned white as a sheet. "Oh Emelia—I believe you! What have I done! Poor mom! Oh, what have I done!" She wrung her hands.

"If only there was a way that I could warn mama that daddy is on his way," I said.

"I don't think there is!" said Cecile. "I feel so bad inside, Emelia—I had no idea that it was dad the whole time. But now, when I think about it, it all fits together. Dad told me not to say anything to mom about it. He said he would try and get me out, but every time I saw him—and it wasn't that often—he would say he was still working on it. Dad always got his own way, no matter what it was. How could I be so dumb as to believe him the way I did!"

"Cecile, don't be so hard on yourself," I said. "You had no idea that I had the envelope and that I had put the card back into it. You had a surprised look on your face when you pulled it out of my pocket, remember?"

"I know—but I still feel bad. Oh mom, I am *so* sorry!" cried Cecile.

"When we go to bed tonight, we need to pray for mama like never before, okay?"

"Like never before—yes," Cecile agreed.

14

Daddy found his way to New Bedford, Mass. He went to find the people that he knew lived there. One of the persons was a brother to Mr. Tony who lived in our hotel in Berlin.

He was told where to find Mr. Tony's brother who was at a land-clearing site. Daddy took plenty of home brew with him, knowing that if he could get them to drink enough, one of them would tell him what they knew about mama. They might even know where he could find her.

It just so happened that daddy was introduced to Larry, the husband of Annette who worked with mama and who had become one of her very good friends. I guess Annette was the only close friend that mama had.

Larry and Annette had no idea that daddy was out to hurt mama. She never told anyone how mean he was—only her lawyer knew the truth about him. "The more people that know, the better chance he has to find me," was the way that mama looked at it.

Larry took daddy to the apartment where mama was staying. He knocked at the door. When mama answered it, daddy reached in and grabbed her by the neck in a choking grasp.

Larry, shocked, spun daddy right around and yelled: "Run Irene, run!" Mama ran off as fast as she could to Annette's house that was about six houses away, and stayed there.

Larry held daddy until he calmed down, then he let him go. Larry was a much bigger man than daddy was.

Daddy took off, trying to find mama, but had no idea what direction she went in. He could barely drive his car, he was so drunk. Mama stayed at Annette's house for a few hours. When she ventured out there was no sign of daddy.

"More than likely he's sleeping it off somewhere," said Larry.

Larry and Annette walked mama back to her apartment to make sure she was safe.

"Don't worry about Jerry," said Larry. "He'll never be able to find you. He had so much to drink he won't remember where you live."

Even so, mama was still terrified and spent the night looking out of her window, hoping and praying that he wouldn't come back.

The next day mama saw daddy riding up and down the street. He did this for almost the entire day—until a lady from another building who was getting very nervous about the car, called the police to notify them of what was going on.

The police showed up and stopped daddy. "What do you think you're doing?" they asked. "You're making a lot of people uncomfortable, riding up and down this street."

"I'm looking for my wife!" daddy said bluntly. "She lives here somewhere on the upper part of the street. I'm not leaving until I find her!"

His rude manner didn't win any sympathy. "Okay, buddy," the policeman said decisively, "you get back into your car right now and go back where you came from!"

"I'm *not* driving back to Berlin until I find my wife and take her back with me!" he insisted.

"I guess you're not hearing me too good," retuned the policeman. "You don't have a choice. If your wife wanted to go with you, she would have been out here by now. You're causing havoc on this street—and if you don't leave now, I'll arrest you."

"You can't arrest me!" he said and swore at the policeman. "I'm not doing anything wrong!"

The second officer called from his car: "Hey Mike! I just got another call from the station. They said this guy's bad news. Some woman said he tried to choke his wife yesterday."

"Okay, okay," daddy relented with bad grace. "I'm leaving!"

"Right—and I'm going to follow you to see to it that you find your way out," said the policeman.

"You don't have to," said daddy. "I'm going back to Berlin—but I'll be back!"

"I wouldn't do that if I were you," said the policeman. "If another person calls the station about you for any reason, even if you're parked on this street, we'll be back and you'll be arrested. Do I make myself clear? Furthermore, we'll have to check into this phone call about you choking your wife. That might detain you for a while—and I don't think you want that, do you?"

"No, I don't want that," said daddy, adjusting his tone. "It was only a misunderstanding on her part. You'll see."

So daddy drove off. "I bet it was you, Irene, that called the police!" he mumbled to himself. "That's okay—I'll be back and I *will* find you!"

Cecile and I had no idea this was going on. Daddy never told us he had found mama—probably because he lost her again. He couldn't remember what building she was in, for they all looked alike. He couldn't even remember if he had to climb stairs to get to her.

◆　　　◆　　　◆

"Emelia," said Sargent. "I just saw Cecile. She wanted me to tell you that she received a birthday card from your mother! She got it right on her birthday. She was *so* excited when she told me about it! Her birthday is only a month after yours, eh? Oh, and she said that just like your card, it had a P.S. that said, 'Tell Emelia that I love her too.' It must make your mother feel better, knowing you two girls are together."

"The only thing, Sergeant," I said, "is that we are *not* together. We can't even talk to each other anymore because of sister Pauline. I might as well be alone."

"You've got *me*," said Sergeant.

"Oh, I know—I'm sorry, Sergeant. I guess I'm just worried about mama. Now that daddy knows where to find her it's making me sick to my stomach—and it's all my fault."

"Why do you think that?" asked Sergeant.

"I should have thrown the envelope away! Then none of this would have happened."

"Emelia, put it in God's hands and try not to think about it," she said kindly. "Everything will be okay. It's getting late now—you better get to bed before we both get into trouble!"

"Goodnight, Sergeant," I said.

Sergeant said the same as she walked away. I fell asleep thinking about how it was getting more difficult remembering what mama looked like and I wished I had a picture of her.

I was hardly asleep when I woke up. I had forgotten to pee before I went to bed. I needed to go—real bad!

I ran down the hallway to the bathroom. *Oh no,* I thought, *I forgot to put my slippers on!* I couldn't go back. I decided I'd just make sure I didn't turn any lights on. I hoped nobody caught me, or I would be in big trouble!

I just made it. I didn't think I'd ever stop! I must have had a lot to drink that day.

I became aware of something tickling my feet. What in the world was it?

I turned the light on and I froze. *Eek! Bugs!* I thought, *just look at all the bugs!* I'd never seen so many except at the hotel—and they were some roaches! Daddy had to have some men come in once a year and do something to get rid of them, but they always came back.

But these weren't roaches, for I knew what *they* looked like. I remembered seeing these bugs in my science book. They were termites! They were the bugs that eat wood!

I turned the light off and ran as fast as I could back to my bed. No wonder they didn't want us to turn any lights on and make sure our slippers were on! Now I knew why. They had bugs! I didn't say anything to anyone. I was sure the nuns all knew, even Sergeant. *What do I do? Who do I tell?* I asked myself.

◆　　◆　　◆

"Your friend is here to see you again," said Sergeant.

"My friend?" I asked. "Who?"

"I believe you called her Mrs. Dee," she said.

"Oh boy! That means I'll see Cecile, too," I said.

"Go ahead," said Sergeant. "She's waiting for you."

"Hi, Mrs. Dee!" I beamed when I saw her in the hall. Cecile was already there. "Hi Cecile! Happy late birthday!"

"Thanks," Cecile smiled.

"Do you girls want to do anything special?" asked Mrs. Dee.

I remembered what happened the last time Mrs. Dee visited us. We went to see Albert and Leo. It was awful. I didn't want to see them sad ever again.

"No," I said. "Let's just sit and visit—is that okay?"

"Sure it is," said Mrs. Dee.

"Mrs. Dee, can I tell you something really important?" I asked.

"What is it?" She gave a concerned smile.

I turned to Cecile. "Cecile, you can't say anything, okay? I don't want to get in any trouble."

"Emelia, you know I'm not about to get you into any trouble!" Cecile assured me.

"I don't know who else to tell," I said.

"Tell me what it is," said Mrs. Dee kindly.

"Well—this place is full of bugs!"

"Bugs?" Mrs. Dee looked scandalized, her mouth open.

"Yes," I said. "They only come out at night time. They're termites."

"Termites! Are you sure?"

"Yes. I remember what they looked like from my schoolbook."

"We have to tell someone," said Mrs. Dee.

"But who?" I asked.

She shook her head. "I don't know. But I'll think of someone. Don't worry about it for now, okay? I'll try and do something about it tomorrow. Nothing is open on Sundays."

"How did you find the termites, Emelia?" asked Cecile.

"I went to the bathroom without my slippers and turned on the light."

"You went to the bathroom without your *slippers!*" Cecile's eyes widened. "I can't believe you did that! I'm surprised you didn't get caught when you turned the light on!"

I smiled. "It's a good thing you taught me how to tiptoe, Cecile. I got pretty good at it. Besides, I don't think my feet hit the floor, I was running so fast!"

Cecile and I laughed.

Of course, Mrs. Dee had no idea what was so funny. It was a nice visit—just what I needed after feeling so bad just a little while before.

Two days later there were a couple of men walking and prodding inside and outside the building. Then, three days after that, we were told that the convent would be closing down—they didn't know for how long or for what reason.

I had to leave my uniform and put my new dress on that Sergeant got for me. She gave me a pair of socks and under–panties because the ones I went there with were too small now.

"Is it because of the termites, Sergeant?" I asked.

"What are you talking about?" she said.

"Why are they closing down? Is it because they have termites here?"

"How did you know that?" she asked.

"Because I saw them one night when I got up to go to the bath-room," I said. "Oh Sergeant, is that the reason?"

"It was *you*, then?" Sergeant asked, her eyes widening. "For goodness sake, Emelia, don't tell anyone! No one knows how they found out. You told your friend Mrs. Dee? That's how it got out, am I right?"

"Yes, Sergeant," I nodded. "You're right. I'm sorry. What will happen to you now?"

"I don't know—but listen to me! Mother superior never came out and said the reason. She only told us that we would be closing down for a while—so you have no reason to think that you were the one responsible for this, do you understand?" Sergeant smiled. "I don't want you thinking that way, okay?"

"What's going to happen to Cecile and me? Where will we go? No one wants us." I started to cry. "How will mama find us?"

"Mother superior told me that your father will be picking you up in a little while. At least you'll be able to talk to your sister when you want to—and that's more than you've got right now. So cheer up—let me see that smile!" She kissed me on my forehead.

"I wanted to save my new dress for when I saw mama again," I said.

"I know," said Sergeant, "but look at it this way—no matter when you get to see your mother, it will still be new to her, right?"

"You're right, Sergeant." I gave her a hug. "I'll miss you so much."

"I'll miss you too, Emelia. I'll never forget you."

"I could never forget you either, Sergeant. You've been my only friend since I've been here." I was starting to cry again and I could see tears in Sergeant's eyes too. I didn't want daddy to see me like that. He would get angry so I had to stop talking. It was hurting too much to say anything else.

Sergeant reached down and hugged me just like mama did the last time I saw her—about one and a half years before.

Cecile was already outside. She always made it out there before me. She must be closer to the door, I thought.

We sat down and watched all the parents and grandparents come and pick up the girls.

Eventually everyone had gone except for Cecile and I.

"I wonder where dad is?" said Cecile.

"I don't know. I almost hope he doesn't come!"

"Why?" asked Cecile.

"I'm scared, Cecile. Do you have any idea where he will be taking us?"

"I don't know," she shrugged. "Maybe to the hotel."

"I wonder if he cleaned up mama's bedroom," I said. "There was broken glass all over the floor. Jerry and I were going to clean it up after mama left but daddy wouldn't let us. He said that mama would clean it as soon as he found her."

"That looks like dad's car now," said Cecile.

"It is!"

"Come on, Emelia," she said. "Let's go."

I turned around and Sergeant was in the window, waving. I waved back and whispered, "Bye Sergeant. I love you."

Daddy drew up next to us. "Cecile, go get in the car," he ordered. "You too, Emelia."

I got into the back and Cecile followed me.

"I was going to sit in the front but dad sounds ugly," Cecile whispered, "so I think I'll sit back here with you, Emelia."

Daddy drove off without saying a word, and neither did we. He stopped the car in front of mommie's and poppie's house.

"Stay here," daddy said as he got out of the car.

That was okay with me. I was glad that I didn't have to go in.

"Cecile," I said after he got out, "please don't tell daddy that you know it was mommie and him that put you in the convent, okay?"

She nodded. "Don't worry Emelia, I won't."

We could hear mommie yelling at daddy: "I don't want them kids here! I told you that already!"

"It will only be for a couple of days!" daddy yelled back. "Then I'll take them away. I'll take all of them away!"

I couldn't believe what I was hearing. Daddy wanted us to stay with mommie! *Oh please daddy, don't leave us here!* I was screaming inside.

"Cecile, I don't want to stay here!" I said.

"I don't either," Cecile said. "Don't worry, Emelia, you have me around. I won't let mommie hurt you, okay?"

We both knew there wasn't much that she could do for me when it came to mommie, but her words were a great comfort, just the same.

When daddy's brother, uncle Arthur, was alive, he and aunt Ad weren't getting along very well. Then uncle Arthur suffered a stroke. He couldn't think very clearly after that. Aunt Ad never had a chance to resolve the problem before his stroke—and then it was too late. While uncle Arthur was still in the hospital, mommie got her lawyer and had some papers drawn up, giving everything to mommie—the property, money, the house. Mommie had him sign the papers, then had him moved into her house. There wasn't anything aunt Ad could do about it. There was no money left over for a lawyer.

Mommie had aunt Ad and their five children evicted from their home. They had no place to go and no money. Mommie not only took everything away from them—she also disowned uncle Arthur's wife and five grandchildren. She didn't even let uncle Arthur's kids come and visit him.

Even when uncle Arthur died a few years later, the kids weren't allowed in the funeral home at the same time she was. Mommie had money—and money talks. I used to hear her say that all the time when she was talking to daddy.

Now she was trying to do the same thing to daddy's kids. She would just as soon disown us too.

The only grandchildren that mommie cared about were the ones that came from her daughters. Mommie thought the world of *them*—and the rest of us kids knew it. She didn't try to hide it from us. She would always tell us how good they were and how bad we were.

Never once did mommie, who was my own grandmother and Cecile's too, come to visit us in the convent, yet she only lived six miles away. As far as that goes, never once did any of the Dion family come to see us—and they all lived within six miles of us.

Relatives on mama's side lived one hundred miles away and most of them didn't even know what was going on, because mama's dad told her that she should take daddy back without realizing how dangerous daddy was. Pepere wouldn't listen—he didn't believe mama. She couldn't go to them for help, so she had to run to a different state to get away from daddy. *Oh Pepere, if only you could have helped mama, maybe all of us would have been together instead of being all split up.*

I think daddy was trying to make brownie points when he named me Emelia, after mommie, but it didn't work—did it, daddy? She didn't want us in her house either, just like our cousins.

Mommie was still yelling at daddy to take us away.

"Just give me a couple of days to get ready—that's all I need," he said.

"Okay, okay!" she relented. "A couple of days—that's all! And another thing, I don't want them other brats here. You can keep them right where they are! And Jerry can stay with your brother. He doesn't have to come here either!"

"Did you hear that, Cecile?" I gasped. "Jerry is with uncle Al and aunt L. I'm so glad! They're the nicest people I know."

"They don't have any kids of their own," said Cecile.

"I know," I said. "It's hard to believe that uncle Al and daddy are brothers."

"Uncle Al must take after poppie," said Cecile.

"Yeah, and daddy must take after mommie," I said.

Daddy marched back to the car. "All right, you two!" he said. "Get in the house before she changes her mind!"

15

"**I** will have supper ready in twenty minutes," said mommie. "Go wash your hands." She stood there looking at us as though we had just come in from outside after playing in the dirt.

Mommie still looked the same with her white bun on top of her head and her hands resting on her hips. The same frown creased her face.

I can remember when we went to visit *memere* in Sanbornville. She always had a big hug for us and was so happy to see us—but not mommie. I can't ever remember seeing a smile on her face when it had anything to do with us. I would have thought that after all this time of not seeing us that just a hello would have been nice. We sat down and ate our French toast that tasted very good.

"I would have had something different, but I was not expecting you two to be staying here," she said unfeelingly. "I told your father that I didn't want you here."

It hurt the first time she said it—when she didn't know we could hear her yelling at daddy; but it hurt even more now because she was saying it to our faces.

"You two can sit in the living room until it's bedtime, and I don't want to hear any noise out of either one of you!"

Did she think we were little kids? I was ten and a half and Cecile was twelve and a half. Why couldn't she treat us like her grandchildren, like blood relatives? Then again, she never did, so why should she change now?

It was 8:00 p.m. when mommie said it was bedtime.

"Come with me," said mommie. "You can wash up in there!" She pointed to the upstairs bathroom. "Then get into your pj's. I'll be back."

I didn't have any pj's like Cecile had. I washed up and just had my t–shirt and panties on.

"Why aren't you in your pj's like I told you!" mommie said crossly.

"I don't have any," I said.

"Very well," she sighed. "Come with me. The two of you will be sleeping in this bed." She took us into a beautiful bedroom, one that I had never seen before. I had never seen the upstairs of mommie's house.

Then fear hit me like never before. *I can't sleep in this bed!* I thought. I remembered that every time I slept in a bed for the first time, I'd pee in it. After that I never did it again. What was I going to do? I was going to have to tell mommie the truth. She would understand, I hoped.

"Mommie," I said. "I have a problem. I can't sleep in this bed—I'll pee in it."

"You'll *what!*" She stared at me in horror. "Did I hear you right? You'll *pee* in it?"

"Y… yes mommie, that's what I said. It's just that every time I sleep in a new bed I never slept in before, I pee in it the first time I sleep in it. I don't mean to—it just happens."

"How old are you now?" she asked sternly.

"Ten and a half."

"Ten and a half!" she glared. "Don't you think that's old enough to stop wetting the bed?"

"Yes, mommie, it is." I hung my head in shame.

"Then you *will* sleep in this bed like I told you—and you will *not* pee in it! Do you understand me?"

I looked up at her, imploringly. "Please, mommie, don't make me sleep in it. I know I will pee and I don't want to! Please mommie, please," I begged.

"Get into that bed and I don't want to hear anymore about it!"

I got into bed and mommie left the room.

"I didn't know you had a problem like that," said Cecile. "When is the last time that you wet the bed?"

"The first night that I was at the convent."

"Emelia, that was ages ago! What makes you think it will happen again? You're older now. You'll be okay."

I shook my head. "No Cecile, I won't be, okay? I will pee in this bed if I sleep in it. I know I will! I can't sleep in this bed—I'm scared!"

I got up and lay on the floor. It was cold but I didn't care—it was better than wetting the bed and having to face mommie in the morning.

I was just drifting off to sleep when a loud voice startled me awake. *"What are you doing on the floor!"*

I jumped up. My heart was pounding.

"Mommie..." I began. "Y...you don't understand. I will pee in that bed if you make me sleep in it. Please don't make me, please, mommie," I begged again.

"Stop your foolishness right now!" she yelled. "You get into that bed right now! And don't you dare get back out of it again!"

I tried to stay awake for as long as I could. When I woke up I had wet the bed—just like I knew I would.

"Emelia," Cecile gasped. "You really *did* wet the bed! You're going to be in big trouble with mommie!"

"I *know*," I cried. "I *tried* to tell her but she wouldn't listen to me. What am I going to do now?"

◆   ◆   ◆

"Emelia! What did you *do!*" yelled mommie. "I can't *believe* you wet the bed—at your age! Get out of my way!"

Mommie stripped the bed, threw the sheets into the machine to wash, dragged the mattress over by the window and took her pail of water and started scrubbing the mattress. She was so mad that all she did was mutter. It didn't make any sense except for when she said that I wouldn't have another chance to do that to her again.

"What did she mean by that?" asked Cecile.

"I… I don't know, but I'm scared, Cecile. What will daddy do to me when he finds out what I did?"

Mommie didn't speak to me all day except when she told me I couldn't have anything to eat or drink for the day.

I was so thirsty. Cecile went into the bathroom and when she washed her hands, she left the faucet with a tiny drip for me.

"You wash your hands out here where I can watch you!" said mommie when I used the bathroom. "I can hear that faucet so don't even think about sneaking water out of it!"

I was thankful to Cecile. There wasn't much of a drip because she didn't want to get caught by mommie, but it was enough for me to at least wet my tongue.

◆　　　◆　　　◆

It was time for bed again. I was glad in a way. *Maybe she'll let me have something to drink tomorrow,* I thought.

"Cecile, get into bed," ordered mommie. Then she turned to me. "Emelia, you come with me!"

Where was she taking me? Mommie unlocked a door and took me by the hand and dragged me up a flight of stairs. Where were we? I had never seen this place. Mommie had a third floor. It looked like an apartment. She took me over to a crib that was in front of a window, took all my clothes off and put me into this crib that had only a rubber sheet on it. There were no blankets, or a pillow, not even a regular sheet.

"What are you doing, mommie?"

She tied my ankles to the crib bars opposite one another and did the same with my arms. I was on my back and couldn't move my arms or legs.

"Mommie, *please* don't leave me here like this!" I pleaded. "You don't have to tie me up. I won't get up, I promise." I screamed: "Please mommie—don't do this to me!"

"There!" she said with satisfaction. "Now you can pee all you want! You can't get your clothes wet, and better still, you can't get the sheet wet—it's made of rubber! And if you don't keep your mouth shut I'll tape it shut for you!"

Oh mommie! Why are you like this? Why are you punishing me for something I told you would happen if you made me sleep in that bed? Why did you have to tie me up? Why mommie, why? You're just like daddy, I thought to myself. I could hear the door being locked. Mommie even felt that she had to lock me up there, besides everything else.

Please morning, come fast, I prayed. *Mama, mama, where are you? Take me away from here, please mama.*

My back was sticking to the rubber sheet and the rest of me was cold. Flashes of light seemed to flicker through the very dark room. I could hear thunder and it was getting closer. *Pass quickly,* I prayed. The thunder and lightning was right over my head, it was so loud! I wished I could get up and get away from the window. Then I could see a different light shining at the window. I heard sirens blowing just like when our farmhouse was burning down.

"Is there anyone else in the house?" I heard someone yell.

"No, it's empty," mommie's voice replied.

"I'm *here!* I'm tied to the crib, I'm upstairs! Can anyone hear me?" I screamed, but no one answered.

Then I heard a voice calling me from down the stairs. "Emelia, are you okay?" It was Cecile. "There was a fire across the street. The firemen have it out now. Don't let mommie hear you screaming—there's no telling what she'll do to you next."

"I thought that this house was on fire," I answered. "I heard mommie tell them that there was no one else in the house!"

"Why didn't you look out the window?" she asked. "Then you wouldn't have gotten so scared."

"I *can't*," I said. "Mommie tied me down in the crib and I can't get up."

There was silence. Then Cecile spoke again. "I wish I could come up there and see you, but mommie locked the door."

"I know," I said. "I heard it when it locked."

"After everyone goes back to bed I'll sit by the door down here so you won't feel so alone, okay, Emelia?"

"Thank you, Cecile," I called out to her.

Daddy came about two hours later.

"What are you doing sleeping here on the floor, Cecile?" he asked her.

"I was keeping Emelia company, so she wouldn't be scared," said Cecile.

"Why would she be scared?" asked daddy. "Where is she?"

"Upstairs," said Cecile.

Daddy tried to open the door but it was locked.

"Who locked the door?" he said. "Was it Emelia? That's what it is, eh? She doesn't want to get into trouble so she has you here protecting her, right?"

"*No*, dad, mommie locked the door! She's punishing Emelia for wetting the bed, and Emelia begged her not to make her sleep in that bed—but mommie made her anyway and now she's tied up in a crib upstairs."

Daddy became outraged. I was shaking all over. *Now* I've had it, I thought—but at least the reason for my being locked up sounded better coming out of Cecile instead of mommie.

Mommie woke up from all the noise.

"Where's the key to unlock this door!" daddy yelled at mommie.

She reached in her pocket and gave daddy the key. "Emelia pissed in my bed," said mommie. She was very angry, too.

Daddy came upstairs and untied me from the crib. Cecile gave me my t–shirt and under–panties while daddy and mommie were yelling at each other.

"*I* am the only one that has the right to punish these kids!" he yelled. "Not Irene, not you—nobody but me! I own them! They're mine! Don't you ever lay another hand on them again! If you have a problem with any of them, you tell *me*. I'll punish them *my* way! You got that!"

Daddy never said a word to me about it.

"Go to bed," he said, and I didn't have to be told twice—I was gone instantly.

"Where are you going to finish sleeping?" asked Cecile.

"I think on the toilet," I said. "That seems to be the only safe place around here."

"I'm sorry that mommie did that to you," said Cecile. "It must have been real scary for you."

"It was—I'm glad it's over. I don't want to think about it anymore, okay, Cecile?"

"Okay, then. Come on, let's get some sleep. It's almost time to get up."

Next morning I woke to daddy and mommie arguing.

"I want those girls out of here today!" said mommie.

"They will be," said daddy. "I plan on leaving tonight."

"Good!" said mommie.

"Did you hear that, Emelia?" asked Cecile. "Dad is taking us some-where tonight!"

"I heard," I said. "Where do you think he's taking us?"

"I don't know—but let's keep our ears open and we might find out," she said.

Dad had all kinds of things in the driveway. It looked like he was going on a camping trip.

"Burt picked daddy up a couple of hours ago, Emelia," Cecile said. "He said something about clothes. He's back—outside with Burt. Let's go see if we can hear them talking."

"I'm right behind you," I said.

"Look Cecile, they're taking a big brown trunk out of Burt's car. I wonder what's in it?"

"Let's get closer so we can hear," said Cecile.

Daddy had a map that he laid out on the hood of the car. He was mapping out his route.

"How long do you think it will take to drive there?" asked Burt.

"Mexico is pretty far," said daddy. "I don't know. I don't care, as long as it's far enough away so I'm not bothered by Irene's lawyer anymore."

"Irene will never find them there," laughed Burt.

"Mexico! Cecile, we can't go to Mexico! Mama won't be able to find us!" I said. "You heard daddy—he said that mama will never find us! What are we going to do?"

"Jerry!" mommie yelled out the front door.

"What!" daddy shouted back.

"Irene's lawyer is on the phone! He wants to talk to you!"

"Tell him to call later! That way I'll already be gone."

"You better come right now!" mommie shouted.

After a few swear words daddy went towards the house. I ran up beside him.

"Where do you think *you're* going?" asked daddy.

"I'm going in to use the bathroom," I said. I also wanted to hear him on the phone, but I didn't tell him that. In the bathroom I kept my ear close to the door and soon heard his voice.

"Yeah, speaking," said daddy. "What? Is that right? We'll see about that!" He slammed the phone down.

"What's Irene's problem now?" asked mommie.

"That bitch decided she didn't want any part of me—or the kids," said daddy. "She's been fighting me all this time for them. Now she doesn't want them any more because they're part of *me!*" He yelled: "That bitch!"

Mama doesn't want us anymore! I thought. *You said that we would all be together again, mama, you promised! I miss you mama, I love you mama. Why did you change your mind?* All these questions rushed through my mind.

Daddy went out and slammed the door behind him. I thought it would break. I ran out. I had to find Cecile! I had to tell her. "Cecile," I whispered to her when I found her, "mama doesn't want us anymore!"

"Burt!" daddy yelled, "you see that trunk right there? You take it to the dump! I bought those clothes and she's not getting it! Get rid of it! *I* paid for it, not her!" He turned to Cecile. "Cecile, grab your sister and get in the car!"

Daddy was driving faster then he usually did. We pulled up outside a house. I'd seen that house before, I thought—that's where we went to see Albert. Daddy got out of the car and went inside. I don't think he was gone for two minutes when he came out carrying Albert. He opened the back door and just about threw Albert in—at Cecile. He slammed the door and drove off.

Albert was stunned. He sat there with a dumbfounded look on his face, almost as though he had just been woken from a nap, though it was too late in the day for that—it was already dark outside. Daddy made another stop.

"Emelia," said Cecile. "This looks like the place where Leo was when we came to see him."

"I know," I said. "I wish I knew what was on daddy's mind."

"He's probably in a hurry to leave for Mexico," said Cecile.

Daddy came out of the house dragging Leo by his arm. "Get in there with them," he said.

Leo was so surprised to see us—you could see the twinkle in his eyes! But before he had a chance to open his mouth I put a finger up to my lips. "*Shhhhh*," I said.

Leo smiled from ear to ear and gave me a great big hug. After a while I leaned over and whispered to Cecile: "Daddy never went to uncle Al's house to get Jerry."

"I'm sure Jerry's okay," said Cecile.

"We've been riding for a long time now," I said.

"I know—and I'm starved," said Cecile.

We never did have supper. I was hungry too, but more tired than hungry.

Leo and Albert switched sides. Albert crawled up in my lap and went to sleep. He looked so big, three years old now.

Leo sat beside Cecile and had his head on her lap. For only five, he knew when he could play and when he had to be quiet. He had to learn young, just like the rest of us. I'm so glad that neither of them had had the beatings we had, and I prayed they never would.

Leo learned a long time ago how to stay out of daddy's way. Cecile and I were going to have to teach Albert how to do the same thing. It was so nice sitting there, all together as before, except for Jerry not being there—and mama was missing too, of course.

Oh mama, did you mean what you said? It can't be true, it just can't be!

Daddy slowed down. He turned down a dark street. He stopped.

"Get out!" he ordered.

So that's what we did—we all got out of the car. Daddy pointed to a bunch of buildings and said, "Your mother lives in one of these apartments—go find her! Kids belong with their mother!"

Then daddy drove off, leaving us there.

Dumbfounded, we all sat down on the curb and for a while didn't say a word. I heard the big clock strike twice. It was 2:00 a.m. and daddy had just left us there on the side of a street!

"What are we going to do now?" asked Cecile. "Everyone is still sleeping. It's too dark out here—I can't see *anything*. There are only two streetlights that work. We don't know what house mom's in."

I could hardly hear what Cecile was saying. I was deep in my thoughts.

I'd waited so long for this to happen—and now to be so close to mama and yet so scared! What if she really didn't want us! What would happen to us then?

"Emelia," said Cecile. "Are you hearing me? What are we going to do?"

"We have to find mama," I said.

"I'm not looking for her at this time of the night. We can always wait until it gets light."

"You stay here with Leo and Albert," I said. "I'm going to find mama."

"Be careful!" she said as I walked away.

16

It was the end of August and it was a cool night in New Bedford. At least I think that's where we were. It had to be if mama were there. In all the times that I have been terrified—slapped by daddy, hollered at, hit with a ruler by the nuns in the convent, gotten the belt too many times to remember, seen Jerry and mama beaten, and now been tied up by my grandmother on the vacant third floor of her house in a crib during a thunder and lightning storm with a fire raging across the street where a tree was hit by lightning and tipped over to lean on the house that I was in where I could see the orange flames reflecting on the ceiling while I could only look up at them in terror—I have never ever been so frightened as I was right then. And it was not just that I was scared of the dark or of being alone in a strange place in the middle of the night. I was mainly scared because the thought haunted me that maybe my mama didn't love me and didn't want me anymore!

I had six buildings to choose from—that would be thirty–six apartments, three in the front and three in the back. Daddy had dropped us off right in the middle of them.

I walked up the street to the first building, stopped and looked it over; then walked down past Cecile to the last building and stood looking at it—and prayed.

"Dear God, please help me to find mama. *You* know where she is. Oh, and God—*please* let mama still love me!"

I started to walk back towards Cecile but something was pulling me to the house next to the one I was just at. I decided to start with that one. I went in and climbed the stairs to the third floor. Something bad had happened on the third floor at mommies, so maybe something good would happen on *this* third floor. I was hoping, anyway.

Knock, knock. Nothing. *Knock, knock.*

"Who is it?" a lady's voice asked.

"Emelia," I said.

At first I didn't recognize the voice, but I hoped that the lady would know where to find mama.

"Who?" she said.

Yes, that was it! That was the voice I was looking for!

"It's your daughter—Emelia!" I said, my heart beating wildly.

The door swung open and there she was! Even though she was pale and thinner, she was a beautiful sight to see. She reached out and put her arms around me and squeezed me so tight. It was the best feeling I ever had.

"Mama, don't cry!" I said. But I was crying, too.

"I can't help it—I'm so happy to see you," she said.

"Cecile is downstairs sitting on the curbing, mama—with Leo and Albert."

"She *is!* They *are!*" mama said, letting me go and staring at me in disbelief. She laughed through her tears. "Let's go get them!"

We were all in mama's apartment. Everyone was so tired. In fact, Leo and Albert never woke up when they were carried upstairs. Mama made a bed on the floor for Albert and Leo to sleep on. Cecile took the couch and mama took me into her bed. She only had a one–bedroom apartment.

Mama and I were both sitting up in bed when mama wrapped her arms around me for the second time. "I've missed you so much," she said. Then she whispered in my ear as she held me, "I love you."

"Oh mama! I was so afraid that you didn't love me anymore. Daddy told us that you didn't want us anymore."

She held me and looked me straight in the eye. "Emelia, listen to me," she said, "I have been fighting for you kids ever since I left Berlin. Your father wouldn't let me have you. He said that I would have to come back. I couldn't... I knew what he would do to you kids and me if I did go back."

"I know mama," I smiled. "It's okay."

"I stopped pushing my divorce because your father said that I would never see you kids again—that he would take you out of state if I continued with it. I couldn't take that chance. He had my hands tied."

"Mama," I said. "Daddy was going to take us out of state tonight. He was taking us to Mexico."

"Mexico!" mama exclaimed. "I almost lost you! I almost lost all of you!"

"It's okay, mama, you have us now." I hugged her again. "Your lawyer called daddy and he got real mad and he brought us all here."

She nodded. "That's because I decided I had to do something different. I didn't want to be without any of you any longer. Your father has never given me anything I've ever wanted and he knew how much I wanted you kids. I failed to get custody of you because his lawyer convinced the judge that I was unfit to be a mother—because I deserted all of you and ran away. My lawyer tried to tell the judge how cruel your father was, but he wouldn't listen. The fact was that I had left. I took a big chance and told my lawyer to tell your father that I didn't want anything that was a part of him. I just wanted him and his children out of my life. You see? It worked! Your father gave all of you to me because he thinks I don't want you any more and he didn't want me to have my own way—so he brought all of you here, except for Jerry. I wish I knew where he is. I had hoped that if he brought all of you to me that Jerry would be here too."

"I know where Jerry is!" I said. "He's with uncle Al and aunt L."

"He is? How do you know?"

"I heard mommie say something to daddy about Jerry being with daddy's brother—and uncle Al is the only one left; uncle Arthur died already."

"I'm so glad that Jerry is there," smiled mama. "Your uncle Al and aunt L. are good people. Jerry is in good hands—but I still miss him and I want him back."

"I was scared, mama! I didn't want to believe daddy when he told mommie that you didn't want us anymore!"

"Oh Emelia, I love all of you so very much! Thank God I have you back."

My arms slipped round her neck again. "I love you too, mama," I said.

Mama held me as I went to sleep. I never felt so safe as I did right then.

Albert and Leo had no idea where they were when they woke up the next morning, but didn't they get excited when they saw mama! School had already started but we couldn't go. We had no clothes other than the ones we had on. Albert and Leo didn't even have any shoes. Daddy was so angry when he went to pick them up that they were only half dressed when he rushed out the door with them.

Mama was working but didn't make much money. She started looking for another apartment for two reasons, the first one being that the one she had was way too small, and the second being that she didn't want daddy changing his mind and coming right back to take us away.

Annette's husband didn't want her working anymore, so she told mama she would take care of Albert.

So mama found an apartment on the lower end of Dean Street. Again, we were on the third floor, but it had a lot more room for all of us to move around in.

One of the neighbors, Doris, who had a lot of kids, noticed that we weren't going to school.

"Why aren't you kids going to school?" she asked.

"We don't have any clothes yet," said Cecile, "but mom said that we wouldn't have to wait too long and she will get enough money to buy us some."

"Daddy threw all of our clothes away," I piped up.

"He did?" she asked with raised eyebrows. "Maybe your mother can get some help somewhere. Has she tried yet?"

"We don't know," said Cecile. "We come from New Hampshire. I don't think mom knows where to go for help; besides, I don't think she would ever ask for it anyway."

Doris was a really nice lady who was very ill with T.B. She called A.D.C. (Aid to Dependent Children) to let them know we needed help.

When mama came home, Doris went to her to tell her what she had done.

"I hardly know you," said mama. "Why would you want to help me?"

Doris smiled. "I know how rough it can be when no one wants to help—especially if you're a person that won't ask for it. Sometimes we have to rely on ourselves so much that we forget that there *is* help out there. I hope you're not angry with me because I did this?"

"No, it was very thoughtful of you," mama said, returning her smile. "Thank you for your concern."

The next day a lady came to the apartment to talk to mama about putting her on A.D.C.—that way she would have the money to buy us some clothes and a few groceries.

The check came in two days later. It didn't take long because they were trying to get us into school as soon as possible. It wasn't a very big check but it was enough to get us started. Each month the check came and mama would buy all of us a couple more pieces of clothing and a few groceries.

On the third month mama came home to find the A.D.C. woman in our apartment.

"What are you doing here?" mama asked with a tight smile. "Who let you in?"

"The landlord let me in," she said.

"You couldn't wait until I got home?"

"We like to do surprise visits," she said flatly.

"Yes, but what are you doing in my bureau drawers?"

"Just checking to see if you bought yourself any new clothes."

"What?" Mama thought she must have misheard the woman.

"We want to make sure you're using the money we give you for your children—not for yourself." She spoke while she looked in

Cecile's drawers. Then she looked in my drawers. She had already looked into Leo's and Albert's before mama got there.

Mama was getting increasingly upset, her face turning redder.

The lady's high heels clicked into the kitchen where she started to open up the cupboard doors to see what we had for food.

"I think I've had just about enough of this," mama said icily. "As far as I'm concerned, you have no right to come into my home anytime you feel like it and open my drawers and touch my personal things—or my children's."

The lady raised her eyebrows. "Oh? A.D.C. sends you a check! *That* gives me the right!"

"You know what you can do with that check?" mama said. "You can keep it! Nobody has the right to treat people this way. I don't spend *any* of that money on myself! What little you people give is spent only on my children." Mama assumed a regal posture. Her anger, as always, made her both formidable and beautiful.

"Oh really!" the lady said in a haughty tone. She took her bag and her high heels clicked across the floor as she made her way to the front door. She turned and gave mama a frozen look. "Very well, then," she said icily, "don't expect any more help!" Then she was gone.

"Mama, what are we going to do now?" I asked.

"Don't worry, Emelia," said mama, still bristling with outrage. "Everything will be *just* fine!"

Mama had a friend whose name was Ben. He was always trying to help mama out but she always refused it. Ben was crazy about mama but she didn't want anything to do with another man in her life. She met Ben when she was still living with Ray and Lou, the couple that took her with them when they moved out of Berlin. Ben was Lou's brother–in–law. Ben's brother and Lou's sister were married and Ben became friends with Ray, Lou's husband. Ben worked with a company that kept him away for weeks at a time, but every time Ben was in the area he would make it a point to stop in and see Ray, hoping he would have a chance to see mama at the same time. Ben had been trying to get mama to at least go and have dinner with him for the better part of a year, but mama wouldn't be moved.

Things continued to be rough and were getting worse. Annette wanted to adopt Albert because she had become so attached to him. She and Larry couldn't have any children of their own. But mama said no. "My children stay together, and with me," she said. "I will never lose them again." Annette understood, but couldn't take care of him anymore. Mama put Albert in a day–care center that cost $9.00 a week. She was only making $29.00 a week. The rent alone was $10.00 a week. That left her with $10.00 a week for groceries, heat, lights, and anything else that we needed.

Mama persuaded a little grocery store to take her diamond for $100.00 worth of food. We tried to make it last as long as we could. Mama would make syrup with sugar and water, then add a touch of vanilla to it for a little color. We would take day–old bread and dip it in the syrup. That sometimes would be our supper. We had hot ketchup soup. Mama would give us a cup of hot water and we would shake some ketchup in it, and it would become soup. Many times we went to bed a little hungry, but we knew that mama was more hungry because she would give everything to us and take nothing for herself.

There were times when public service would come and turn off our power because the bill hadn't been paid. There wasn't enough money to go around. It would get so cold! Public service thought more about their money than us kids being so cold that we had to wear our coats to bed. When mama was able to have food that she could cook, she would run down to the cellar and turn the power back on, then run back upstairs and cook whatever she had to feed us; then she would run back downstairs to turn the power back off before she got caught—but not before we kids had a chance to warm up a little!

Mama heard from uncle Al. He wanted to adopt Jerry because they couldn't have any kids of their own. Again mama said no for the same reason she said no in Albert's case. Uncle Al understood and told mama that he would bring Jerry to her. Mama was so happy she was going to have her heart's joy back—not that any of us weren't her heart's joy, too!

I was so excited when I found out that Jerry was finally coming home! I couldn't wait to see him, but mama said it would be just a little while longer so Jerry could finish his semester at school.

There was a knock at the door. I opened it and there was a man, tall and striking, verging on thin, with a mop of brown hair that had a little wave in it. He smiled with eyes that were soft—and green, like mama's.

"Is your mama home?" the man asked with just a hint of a French accent.

"Yes, she is," I said. "I'll get her for you."

I called mama and she came to the door.

"Ben!" she exclaimed. "It's been a long time!"

Ben's face lit up. "I've been home one other time! I tried to find you but I couldn't. I had to leave right off for another job. This time I was going to find you no matter what!"

Mama invited him in.

"Ah! You must be Emelia?" Ben smiled.

I was so surprised that he knew my name.

"Yes, that's right," I said.

"Your mother has talked about you—often. I'm glad to get to meet you!" He put out his hand.

I smiled as I took his hand that closed on mine in a warm and firm grip. I couldn't help thinking what a nice man he was. I learnt later that he was a French Canadian.

Ben noticed how cold my hand was—and then how cold it was in the apartment. "What happened to the furnace?" he asked.

"Nothing," I said. "Mama didn't have enough money to pay the bill."

"Emelia!" mama said, horrified. "You shouldn't tell people that!"

"Why not, mama? It's true."

"Sometimes you don't tell everything you know," she said softly. "It can be a little embarrassing."

"It's okay, Irene," Ben said. He stood up and pulled out his wallet.

"Oh no, you don't!" said mama. "I'm not going to take your money, Ben, so you can just put that wallet away."

"Come on, Irene, let me help you!" urged Ben.

She shook her head. "I'm not going to take your money now any more than when you offered it to me before."

"Irene, you were by yourself before. You have your children with you now. You need to think about them. You can't keep living the way you are right now. Let me help, please. How about a loan? Would you take it if it was a loan?"

Mama broke down and started to cry. "Okay, only if it's a loan."

Ben handed the money to mama. I don't know how much there was but knowing mama the way I do, I know she meant what she said about paying back every cent of it.

Ben gave mama a hug to try to stop her from crying. "How about if I take you all out for a burger or a pizza or something?" he asked. "Irene, you always said no when I asked before. You said that you would never do anything that would hurt the chance of getting your kids back. What do you say now? The kids are here with you now!"

"*Can* we mama?" I asked. It sure sounded good to me!

"Okay," mama said. "Go and let Cecile know and I'll get Leo and Albert."

"All right!" I said. I was really happy, almost as happy as the day that Ray and Lou asked mama if they could adopt me. They had grown to care about me with the visits that I took to go and help them at their home, with cleaning and ironing. They even asked me if I would like to become their little girl before asking mama if they could adopt me. I didn't want to—I wanted to stay with my mama; but mama said no to them anyway, so I was really happy—just as I was at that moment when Ben invited us out.

Ben's smile stretched from ear to ear. I'll never forget it!

17

Mama's divorce finally went through. She got custody of all of us kids. Her lawyer was able to prove to the court that daddy was indeed crazy. The doctor that treated daddy at the V.A. hospital had died, but mama's lawyer was able to get a court order to open up his files and in it was a copy of the letter he had written to mama telling her how dangerous daddy was along with all the medical terms of his condition. The judge granted mama's divorce on the grounds of Extreme Cruelty to the Extremist.

"Emelia, get the door," said mama.

"I didn't hear anybody knock," I said as I walked to the door.

Knock, knock, it came again.

"Sorry mama, someone *is* knocking." I opened the door and froze with surprise.

"Jerry!"

"Hi *Sheote*," Jerry smiled.

Jerry used to call me that sometimes. He told me it was a slang French word that meant 'out–house.' I wouldn't let anyone else call me by that name—just him. It was a big brother thing.

"Who is at the door?" mama asked as she walked into the room. Then she saw him.

"Jerry!" she yelled.

She ran to him and wrapped her arms around him and began to cry. I didn't think mama would ever let Jerry go. He had gotten so tall, the same size as mama.

Albert was running around the house saying, "Eo! Eo! Derry is home!" He couldn't pronounce Leo and Jerry's name right. They didn't appreciate it much but the rest of us thought it was funny.

"Jerry!" Leo said. "Look how big I got! But you got bigger?"

"That's okay, Leo," said Jerry. "Someday you'll be bigger than me."

"I will!" said Leo. "I can't wait!"

"I'm so happy to see all of you with me again," said mama through her tears. "You're my heart's joy. All of you."

Every other weekend when Ben was in town he would stop in to see us. I think he liked mama a lot. We started calling him uncle Ben, which pleased him. It was nice to see mama smile again.

Things were still pretty tight money–wise. Ben kept trying to give mama more money but she wouldn't take it; in fact, every time he came to see her, she gave him a little back from what she borrowed from him six months before.

Christmas was the next day and there was no tree or presents for us. Jerry, being fourteen, Cecile, thirteen and I now eleven, we under-stood—but Leo was six and Albert only four, and they didn't under-stand. They kept hoping that Santa would find us, the reason being, they said, that we had all moved from different places and Santa would have a hard time figuring it out. But Jerry, Cecile and I knew that Santa hadn't been able to find us for a very long time. Albert and Leo went to bed hoping there would be a surprise waiting for them the next morning, but there wouldn't be.

"Cecile," I said, "I can hear mama crying."

"I know," said Cecile. "It must be because mom couldn't do any-thing for us for Christmas."

"We've got to go tell her that it's okay and not to cry," I said.

"Wait—Mom just called Jerry into her room," said Cecile. "Let's go see what it's all about."

Mama was speaking to Jerry.

"Jerry, take this ten dollar bill," she said. "I want you to take your sisters and brothers to the little store around the corner. I'm sure they're open—they're never closed. I want you to let them each spend two dollars, and there is two dollars for you there too."

"But mom," said Jerry, "this is all the money you have. You don't have to do this. We understand, mom."

"Please, Jerry," cried mama. "Do this for me—it's not much and God only knows that you kids deserve more, but I don't have any more to give."

"That's what I'm saying, mom. We know that you don't have the money. It's all right."

"Please Jerry!" cried mama, "I need to do this."

"Okay, mom," said Jerry, taking the money but looking concerned. "I'll do it."

Cecile and I stayed hidden by the bedroom door. We heard everything that was said. Cecile had a hard time holding back the tears. I tried to hold them back but I couldn't.

"Come on, you two," said Jerry. "Let's get Leo and Albert and do what mom wants."

"It's not a very merry Christmas, is it?" said Cecile.

"Let's try and make the best of it for mom's sake," Jerry said.

"Is there enough money to buy mama a present?" I asked. "It might make her feel better."

Jerry frowned. "Not unless we pool our money together." Then he smiled. "I'm willing if you two are."

"*I'm* willing," said Cecile.

"I am too!" I said.

"Lets go see what we can find, then!" said Jerry.

When we got to the store, Albert and Leo found themselves each a truck that was two dollars and twenty–nine cents each.

"Can we buy these trucks?" asked Leo.

"It cost more than the money you have to spend," said Jerry. Leo and Albert looked crestfallen.

"They can have some of my money," I said.

"That's not a bad idea," said Cecile. "Let's all put the extra in so they can get the trucks."

"Okay with me," said Jerry. "Let's see if we can find a present for mom now."

"*Look*, Jerry! It's a statue of the Blessed Mary!" I said.

"Wow!" exclaimed Jerry.

"Mom already has one of those," said Cecile.

"Not anymore," Jerry shook his head. "Mom doesn't have any of her stuff that she had before. Dad has it all."

"*Yeah*," I said. "And all of mama's statues got broken!

"How much is it?" asked Cecile.

"Two dollars and fifty–nine cents," said Jerry.

"Can we get it, Jerry?" I asked. "Please, it would make mama so happy."

"We sure can," said Jerry. "Hey!" he exclaimed, "what do you say about putting up a tree with decorations?"

"That would be great!" said Cecile. "But where are we going to get a tree?"

"Will a branch do?" asked Jerry. "I saw one on the ground on the way over here."

"Yeah!" I said. "We can make it work, can't we Cecile?"

"I don't see why not," said Cecile, "but how will we decorate it?"

"Jerry, can we buy a bag of popcorn?" I asked. "We can string it and put it around the tree."

"Okay," said Jerry.

It cost twenty–nine cents. We bought a bigger bag so we would have enough.

"I have some colored paper at home," said Cecile. "We can draw some pictures on it, then cut them out."

"That's a good idea!" said Jerry. "Then we can put little holes in the top of each one and hang them on the tree with thread."

"Can we buy this angel?" asked Leo.

"That would look good on the top of the tree," said Cecile. "It's only fifteen cents."

"Lets get it!" said Jerry. "We have two dollars and thirty nine cents left. Cecile," he said, "you and Emelia pick out seventy–five cents worth of penny candy and I'll do the same. That is, if that's what you would like to spend your money on."

"That sounds good to me," said Cecile.

"Me too," I said. "How about Leo and Albert? Is there any money left over so they can have some candy too?"

"Fourteen cents," said Jerry. "I'll pick them up each seven pieces and hide it in their trucks."

"Won't they be surprised!" I said.

Leo and Albert wanted to carry their trucks home. "Can we have them now?" asked Leo.

"No," said Jerry, "you have to wait until we get home and get the tree ready to surprise mom. You guys can help us. Would you like that?"

"Oh yes, that's great!" said Leo. "Did you hear that, Albert? We can help with the tree!"

"I have a small piece of Christmas paper," said the store lady. "Would you like me to wrap up your little statue?"

"That would be really nice of you to do that," said Jerry.

"I can't wait till mama opens her present!" I said. I thought to myself: *I don't want her to cry anymore. This will make her happy again. I just know it will.*

Jerry paid the lady and we left the store.

"That branch should be right around this corner," said Jerry. Then he paused.

"What's the matter?" asked Cecile.

"It's gone!" said Jerry. "The branch is gone."

"What are we going to do for a tree now?" asked Cecile.

"I don't know," said Jerry. "Let's look around. Maybe we can find another one."

"Look Jerry!" I said. "That man is throwing out something. It looks like a little tree."

Jerry ran up to the man without hesitation. "Hello mister," he said. "Are you throwing that away?"

"Yes—I am." The man looked up and smiled. "It's just a dried up dead plant; the leaves have all fallen off and the plastic dish has a crack in it."

"Would it be okay with you if we were to take it home with us?" asked Jerry.

"Why in the world would you kids want this dead plant?" the man asked.

"So we can make it alive again—with color and popcorn and an angel," Jerry said enthusiastically. "So it can be our Christmas tree."

"It's all yours," the man smiled.

"Thanks, mister," said Jerry. "This is much better than the branch I saw on the way to the store." He turned to us. "Come on everybody! We have a lot of work to do."

We hurried home and set to work.

"You guys have to be real quiet, okay?" asked Jerry. "We don't want mom coming out here to see what's going on."

We all worked so hard. Cecile started drawing pictures on her colored paper and cutting them out while Leo helped her. Jerry took some of Cecile's paper and covered the plant dish so you couldn't see the crack. Albert helped me string the popcorn. He would hand the pieces to me, and every once in a while I would put one in his mouth and his eyes would light up. I would say *Shhhhhh* so he wouldn't tell anyone. After a while, Leo caught on, so he came over and wanted to help and he did. We had our own little private party until Jerry saw us.

"If there's not enough popcorn, I'll know why!" said Jerry. Then he smiled.

We had it all finished! It was the most beautiful Christmas tree I ever saw!

"You guys sit here and be still," said Jerry. "I'm going to go get mom."

We all sat there just as quiet as could be with smiles on our faces, full of anxiety, waiting for mama to come into the room.

"There she is!" I whispered.

"Oh no, mommy is crying again," said Leo.

"It's okay, Leo," said Cecile. "Those are happy tears."

"That's the most wonderful tree I have *ever* seen!" said mama. "You kids did a good job decorating it!"

"Sit down here, mama," I said. "You can see what Albert and Leo got for their presents."

They each opened their bag and—what a look on their faces when they found their candy in the trucks that Jerry had put there! Mama and the rest of us laughed, they were so funny.

"What did you other kids buy with your money?" asked mama. "You couldn't have had much left over after buying those trucks for Leo and Albert!"

"We all got penny candy," said Jerry, "and we have something for you too, mom!"

"You do?" she said, puzzled.

Jerry handed her the little three–inch package that was so beautifully wrapped. As mama reached for it you could see the tears filling her eyes.

"This is beautiful!" cried mama. "This is the *best* present anyone has ever gotten for me!" And she began to hug each of us in turn. "This will be one Christmas that I'll never forget. It's the best one I ever had and it's because of you kids! I wish I could have gotten all of you each your own special gift."

"Mama," I said. "You *did* give us a special gift, don't you know?"

"No, Emelia, I guess I don't know what you're talking about. What special gift did I give you?"

"Oh mama, you kept your *promise* to me! You said that you would have us all back with you again someday—and you *did it*, mama! You did it! We are all here with you again. This is the best present in the world that you could have given me. Don't you see?" My eyes glistened with tears as I smiled. "This is all I ever wanted!"

Mama cried happy tears. I guess we all did.

"That goes for me too, mom," said Jerry.

"Don't leave me out," said Cecile. "Me too."

Leo and Albert were too busy playing with their new trucks on the floor to notice what we were talking about.

Mama started singing Christmas carols and we all joined in. *She has the voice of an angel,* I thought to myself, *one that I haven't heard for a very long time.* It was so nice to hear it again. I had forgotten how beautiful it was.

What a wonderful day it turned out to be!

18

"Irene," said Ben. "I would like to apply for a job."

"A job?" asked mama. "What are you talking about?"

"I would like to apply for the position of being the father of your five children."

"What!" said mama, not believing what she was hearing.

"Will you marry me, Irene?" asked Ben.

"I… can't," she said, still dazed from the shock of the proposal.

"Why not?" asked Ben. "Don't you love me?"

"Well—as a matter of fact, I do," smiled mama.

"Then marry me," Ben said seriously.

"Oh, but I can't, Ben." Mama's smiling eyes were touched with sadness.

"Give me one good reason why you can't marry me," persisted Ben.

"I still owe you money."

"Is that all," laughed Ben. "You don't have to give me any more money, Irene—we'll be married!"

"I won't marry you until I pay you back every cent I borrowed from you," mama said firmly.

"Do I take that as a yes, then?" asked Ben. "After you pay me back, of course?"

"Yes," smiled mama. "But only after I pay you back."

"You better hurry then, because I want to marry you as soon as I can!" Ben laughed as he went out the door.

"Do you mean it, mama?" I asked. "Are you really going to marry him?"

"Is it okay with you if I do?" asked mama.

"It sure is!" I said. "Mama, do I call him dad after you're married?"

"If you want to," she smiled. "It would be up to you. I'm sure Ben would like that very much—and so would I. Now, how about going out and checking the mail?"

"Okay mama," I said. "Be right back."

It was starting to get colder outside now. I hoped it wouldn't get too cold. Cecile and I didn't have a warm coat yet. Mama had been giving all her extra money to Ben to pay him off except for a little she put in our coat fund. Mama said that it wouldn't be much longer. She had enough to buy one of us a coat now, but Cecile and I agreed that we wanted to get them at the same time—that way mama wouldn't have to choose between us. It made it easier for her that way.

Jerry got a part–time job so he was able to buy some of the things that he needed. It helped mama out not to have to worry about him, anyway. She had enough to worry about.

The kids at school had been making fun of Cecile and I. It was a cold second week of October and we were still wearing nylon wind-breakers. And it looked like we were in for an extra cold winter, for it had been awfully windy.

Within a few days Jerry came home with a bundle of what looked like clothing. He showed it to mama.

"What's this, Jerry?" asked mama.

"I've been saving to buy Cecile and Emelia a Christmas present this year, and I thought I would give it to them early—seeing that they could really use it right now."

"You bought them coats?" said mama.

"Yes, I did," said Jerry. "I thought it would help you out a little, mom. I know you've been working hard to make ends meet, and I knew the girls needed coats real bad—so here they are."

"Jerry!" said mama. "I don't know what to say! You must have paid a lot for these—they're beautiful! Wait till the girls see them!"

"Do you think they will like them?" asked Jerry.

"Oh, I *know* they will," said mama. "Quick! Hide them. I can hear the girls coming."

"Hi mama," I said right after Cecile had already said it—she always beat me through the door.

"Did you girls have a nice day at school?" smiled mama.

"Yes, I did," I said.

"It was okay," said Cecile.

"I bet I can make your day even better," said Jerry.

"And just how do you propose to do that?" asked Cecile.

"Try looking on top of your beds," said Jerry. "It's a surprise for you—an early Christmas present from me."

Jerry was so proud—and with good reason.

"It's beautiful, Jerry!" I said, holding up my coat. "Can I try it on?"

"Of course you can," smiled Jerry.

"Look, Emelia!" said Cecile. "There's a hat inside the pocket! This is really nice, Jerry—thank you!"

"I love it!" I said. "Thank you, Jerry. Can I wear it to school tomorrow? Or do I have to wait until Christmas?"

"You can wear it any time you want to," laughed Jerry as he left the room, only to come right back holding something in his hands. "I think you might like to have this too," he said. "One for each of you."

"Oh my! Look at that," said mama. "A muff!"

"What's a muff?" I asked as I turned and looked at Cecile. She had her hands in it, one at each end. "It's a big mitten—wow! I like that!"

"Wait till the kids at school see us in these," said Cecile. "They won't be teasing us anymore!"

Cecile was right. Everyone was asking me where I had gotten my pretty fur coat. It was beige fur with little black pine needle designs on it. The hat and muff were made out of the same material. My big brother bought it for me, I would say. He's the greatest big brother anyone could ever have.

Certainly, he *was* the greatest brother—except, maybe, three months before when he came home after playing basketball and took his sneakers off and put his smelly feet in my face! Mama only had so many chairs in the living room and some of us had to lie on the floor to watch television. Jerry would always end up in the chair closest to me and stick his stinky feet in my face. I would complain to mama; she would tell him to stop, but Jerry thought it was funny so kept doing it! One day mama told me that all I had to do was bite Jerry's toe the next time he did that to me.

"Put his smelly toe in my mouth!" I said in disgust. "I can't do that!"

"Trust me, Emelia," laughed mama, "it's the only way you'll break him of doing that to you!"

It was TV time again. It seemed like I'd never make it in time to get a chair. I lay on the floor next to where Leo was sitting, figuring it would be safe there; but when Jerry came into the room Leo spoke up.

"You can have my chair, Jerry," he said. Leo idealized his big brother.

"Oh no, here we go again!" I thought.

Sure enough, Jerry took off his sneakers and his feet began to come towards me—and did they stink! *I can't stand this anymore*, I thought. *Well, here goes.* I closed my eyes once I had his big toe in the right position, held my breath, and bit down hard.

"*Emelia!*" yelled Jerry, springing up and jumping around on the floor. "You bit me! Mom! She bit me!"

"I told you, Jerry," said mama calmly. "Didn't I tell you that one of these days she would get you? Well, she did."

"Yeah," I said, "and I'll do it again if you ever do that to me again!" I sincerely hoped he wouldn't, remembering how nasty it was for me. Yuk! But Jerry never attempted to do it again. Mama was right—it worked.

Two and a half weeks went by since Ben came to visit, but mama said he would be around the coming weekend. He didn't know it yet, but mama at last had all the money to pay him off. She was able to take the money that she was saving for our coats and add it to her savings to have enough. *Won't he be happy!* I thought.

"Mama," I called out when I saw Ben's car pull up in front, "Uncle Ben's here!"

"Hi, Irene," said Ben as he gave her a hug. "How has everything been going?"

"We've been doing just fine," said mama.

"What's this?" he asked, as he read the envelope mama thrust into his hands. He looked inside and found the money. 'Paid in full,' he read on a slip of paper. "How about that!" said Ben. A smile lit up his face. "Now we can get married, right?"

"Well...," began mama.

"Well nothing!" said Ben. "We had a deal. You can't back out of it now!"

"Yes, Ben," mama flashed her beautiful smile. "I would like very much to marry you."

"Yeah?" he beamed. "How about tomorrow?"

"Now you're kind of pushing it, aren't you?" said mama. "We have to get a license and blood test, and I need time to get a dress, and..."

"Okay, okay, I get the picture!" said Ben. "I'm working local this week. We can get all that stuff done this week, all right?"

"Okay," said mama. "We can get married next weekend. Is that soon enough for you?" She smiled demurely.

"Sounds good to me!" said Ben. "I just don't want to wait too long." He winked at us. "I don't want you changing your mind."

"I won't," said mama.

"Now, I want you to do something for me," said Ben. "I want to buy your wedding dress. Will you let me?"

Ben was so sincere!

"Okay, Ben, you can buy my dress if that's what you want."

"It *is* what I want," he said. "It's my wedding gift to you." He gave a bland smile. "I can't believe it! After all these years I'm finally getting married!"

"And with a ready–made family," said mama. "Are you sure you want to do this? You're not only getting me but my five children as well."

"I know," he laughed—he always laughed with such feeling! "I love your kids and I might even have a little love left over for you!"

So mama and Ben were married at the end of October 1962. It was a wonderful ceremony. Mama looked so beautiful in her new dress that Ben bought for her. He took us all to the family pub to celebrate afterwards. We ordered pizza and soda. It was so good.

"I'll have a beer," said Ben.

Did I hear him right? I think he just ordered a beer!

Then a little while later he ordered another beer. *Oh no!* I thought in alarm. *Ben drinks just like daddy!*

Mama got up and went to the ladies room. I was right behind her.

"Emelia, what's the matter, dear?" mama asked.

"Uncle Ben drinks beer!" I warned her.

"I thought you were going to call him 'dad' after we were married?" said mama.

"Didn't you hear me mama?" I asked. "My step dad *drinks*—just like daddy does!"

"Calm down, Emelia," smiled mama. "He doesn't drink *that* much—nothing like your father. There's nothing to worry about, okay?"

"Okay, mama," I said, and hoped the sick feeling in my stomach would go away.

Leo went up to step dad. "What do we call you now?" he asked.

"You can keep calling me uncle Ben if you want to," he said.

"Can we call you daddy?" asked Leo.

"If you want to," step dad said, a smile spreading across his face. "I would like that very much."

"I want to," said Leo.

"Okay then," said step dad. "Yes, you can call me daddy."

"Me too," said Albert. "Can I call you daddy too?"

His smile widened. "You can *all* call me dad if you want to! I just don't want any of you to think that you have to." You could see that he was happy to be called dad and I think mama was even happier.

Things went well for about a year. Then step dad got laid off from his job. He tried to start his own land–clearing business but winter was coming, so he knew it would have to wait. He managed to get a job at a dairy farm. It didn't pay much but jobs were hard to come by. He wasn't there very long before he broke his leg in three places. He had a rope on a bull and the bull started running; he hung onto the rope and the bull pulled him across the ice—but as soon as step dad hit bare tar, his leg snapped. That put him out of work for some time. He started getting depressed and being out of work gave him more time to drink.

"Irene," said Ben, "get me another beer."

Mama was trying to get him to stop before he got drunk. "I think you've had enough to drink, Ben," said mama.

"I said, *get me another beer!*" yelled Ben.

"If you want another beer, you'll have to get it yourself," said mama.

Step dad couldn't move around very well with the cast on his leg. He became so angry that he picked up his crutch that was leaning up against the couch where he was sitting and swung it towards mama. It missed her and hit some milk bottles, breaking two of them. I jumped up off my chair, ran over to step dad, grabbed the crutch out of his hands and held it in a raised position, ready to hit him with it.

"Don't you dare hit my mother!" I screamed. "Ever since I can remember I watched my father beat her. No one will ever beat her again! Not you," I yelled. "Not anyone! No one is going to make my mama run away again! I couldn't stand it if mama left again. She has been through enough!" I cried. "We've all been through enough!"

"Emelia!" screamed mama, "Put that down!"

I paid no attention to mama.

"Why do you have to drink like daddy does?" I asked. "Everything was going good until you broke your leg. I won't let you hurt mama, not now, not ever!"

"Emelia! Did you hear me?" mama yelled as she took the crutch out of my hands. "You're not ever to disrespect your step father!"

"It's okay, Irene," said Ben, the shock of my response apparently having sobered him. "Emelia's right. I should never treat you that way. You've gone through enough—and so have your kids. I've been drinking too much. It's getting the best of me. No more alcohol for me—I quit."

"You *quit?*" Mama looked at him in total shock.

"Yes," said Ben. "I want you to take whatever's left and dump it."

"Are you really going to quit?" I asked.

"Yes," said step dad. "I didn't mean to scare you, Emelia. I'm sorry. Your mother has told me some of the things that took place with your father, and there's a lot of things that she doesn't want to talk about. I can only imagine how bad it must have been for her and you kids too. There is no way that I want to be compared to anyone like that." He managed a weak smile at me. "I'm glad that you had the courage to stand up for your mother." He took mama's hand. "Irene, I'm sorry. I give you my word that this will never happen again."

Mama was so happy and so was I. We both gave step dad a hug.

"Emelia," said mama. "I want you to know one thing. I will never leave you kids again. No matter what. Do you believe me?"

"Yes mama, I believe you."

I was getting tired. I think all that excitement got to me. I decided to go to bed early.

Next morning Cecile and I left for school together. We were in the same class now. Cecile stayed back a couple of times so I caught up with her. It wasn't because Cecile wasn't smart or anything—she just didn't like school.

Cecile looked so pretty in the slip–on sweater that mama gave her. Mama gave her three of them because Cecile's blouses were getting too small in the front—they were popping open at the buttons. It suited me fine, for it meant her blouses came to me!

The nun at the school we were attending told Cecile she didn't want her wearing the sweaters.

"It's too distracting for the boys," the nun explained.

"But this is all I have to wear," said Cecile. "My mother can't afford to buy new clothes right now—so she gave me some of hers."

"I don't care!" the nun said flatly. "You're *not* to wear them again."

"I'll tell my mother," Cecile said, "but she won't be happy."

Mama wasn't happy. "What!" she exploded. "There's nothing wrong with those sweaters! I don't know why the nun would tell you that they look cheap! If anything, they make you look like a young lady. And I don't have the extra money to buy you any blouses at this time."

"I know, mom," said Cecile. "I told her that."

"If that nun says anything to you again, you can tell her from me that if she is buying, then she can pick out whatever clothes she wants you to wear; but if not, she will have to put up with what we have for the time being. You will *not* miss school because the nun doesn't like your chest!"

"Mom!" said Cecile.

"I'm sorry," said mama, "that wasn't called for. But just tell her that you have to wear them for now, and that I will do my best to buy you a couple of blouses with my next paycheck."

We had been sitting in class for over an hour and the nun hadn't said a word about Cecile's sweater. "Now open your books to page seventy five and read the whole chapter," the nun said.

The next thing I knew the nun was standing in front of Cecile's desk which was right next to mine.

"I thought I told you not to wear those sweaters anymore," the nun said in a peremptory voice. "Did you think I wouldn't notice when you walked into my classroom?"

"I'm sure you did," said Cecile.

"*What* did you say!" asked the nun.

"My mother told me to tell you that..."

Slap!

I couldn't believe it! The nun slapped Cecile right across the face before she could even complete her sentence!

"Don't you talk back to me!" screamed the nun.

Cecile got up from her chair, picked up her things and left the room.

The nun then stood in front of me and slapped my face as well. She hit me so hard that I fell off my chair! Why did she hit *me*? I never even opened my mouth! And I usually got straight A's on my report card! I had never given this nun any trouble at all.

"Why did you slap me?" I asked.

She pointed to the door that Cecile had walked out of. "Because that is your sister!"

I stood up and walked over to her and slapped her face just as hard as I could. Then I pointed to the same door she had indicated. "That's because she *is* my sister!" Then I walked out of the same door.

"Cecile!" I hollered, "wait up!"

"What are you doing here?" asked Cecile.

"I just walked out of class," I said.

"You *did*? I can't believe it!"

"I was worried about when mom found out, but now you did it too," said Cecile. "Maybe mom won't get so mad."

"I'm not so sure about that," I said. "I'll be in *much* bigger trouble than you."

"I don't see why?" said Cecile.

"You didn't slap her back. I did."

"You *what!*" Cecile gasped. "You *slapped* her? Why? Is it because she slapped me?"

"No, it's because she slapped me for no other reason than that you're my sister."

Cecile's eyes widened and we walked on in silence. At length we reached home.

"Well, here we are," said Cecile.

"That was a long walk, wasn't it?" I asked.

"Yeah, it was," she said. "Let's go face the music."

"At least we don't have to worry about it right now," I said. "Mama won't be home for another hour."

"Wrong!" said Cecile. "Don't you remember? Mom was getting out of work early today. Something to do with inventory."

Oh no! I thought. I took a big gulp and went through the door right behind big sister!

We explained to mama what took place and she never said a word. Cecile thinks it's because we were both involved. I think it's because mama was in shock!

Mama enrolled us into a public school.

"No more nuns for you two," said mama. "You both have had your share of abuse from them. I should have done this sooner. You start at your new school on Monday."

Cecile didn't go to public school very long before she turned sixteen and quit. Mama tried to talk her out of it but it was no use. Cecile hated school. I'm sure it had a lot to do with the way we were treated at the convent.

Cecile became determined to get married to a young fellow she had been seeing for some time by then. With a lot of no's, arguments and talking, mama finally gave in and said yes.

Her marriage didn't last for even a year. She and her husband didn't get along at all once they were married. She came back to live with us, but it wasn't the same in my eyes. She had changed so much—she had become too grown up for me. I had a hard time understanding her. I guess marriage changes one. At least she didn't have any children to have to worry about.

19

Step dad never picked up another beer or any kind of alcohol. He was true to his word—he said he would never drink again and he kept his promise. I have to say that, unlike daddy, he is, and proved to be, a man of his word.

Daddy had been coming around every once in a while, trying to get on the good side of us. He was brainwashing Cecile again. He even managed to convince her that mama and I lied to her about mommie and him putting her in the convent. He told her all sorts of things that weren't true. She was totally confused.

Cecile eventually went to live with daddy up in Berlin. He didn't have the hotel any more. He sold it to his sister and she changed the name to Fournier's Rooms.

I hadn't seen Cecile for some time. It hurt to think that she believed everything daddy told her, in spite of everything we'd been through together. I didn't blame her, for she wasn't around when daddy got really bad the last year before mama left him; and before that she knew how to tiptoe around him. Daddy always knew how to manipulate people, except for the ones he was abusing—but we knew better.

Hopefully, I'd see her again, and soon.

Jerry was still working part–time in the pizza place. He tried to join the service but they couldn't find any record of him. After a while they found out that his last name wasn't Dion—it was mama's maiden name, for that had been the name under which he had been registered.

Mama was furious when Jerry told her about it.

"I can't believe it!" said mama. "Your father was the one who took care of the birth certificate in the hospital. He told me not to worry about it—that he had taken care of it. He took care of it all right! No wonder he kept saying all those years that he wasn't your father! He knew what he had done! He *is* your father!"

"Calm down, mom," said Jerry. "I know he's my father. *Look* at me! I look just like him."

Mama was so upset, but Jerry was a little more than upset.

The service contacted daddy to take care of it, and he did.

Daddy went to see Jerry at the pizza place. It was closing time. Jerry saw daddy outside and came out. Daddy was laughing.

"I played a joke on your mother! I was going to change it, but I forgot!"

"I don't think it's funny," said Jerry.

He stopped laughing. "You better watch your tone with me," he warned.

"I still don't think it's funny," said Jerry. "I've gone eighteen years using the name Dion, and it was never legally mine to use."

"Don't talk to me that way!" daddy snarled and poked Jerry in the soft part of his shoulder. "Have you forgotten who you're talking to?"

"Don't poke me," said Jerry, his hackles rising.

"I'll poke you if I want to!" And he poked Jerry again.

"I'm going to tell you one more time," said Jerry, gritting his teeth. "Do *not* poke me!"

Daddy poked Jerry again, not once but twice. "There!" he said, "what are you going to do about it?"

Jerry balled up his fist and punched daddy—and down he went.

"*That's* what I'm going to do about it!" yelled Jerry. "I finally got big enough, dad! Don't you ever lay a hand on me again, not ever—or I'll knock you down again!" Then he walked back into the pizza place.

Daddy wasn't laughing anymore. He knew Jerry meant what he said. Jerry always told mama ever since he was little that some day he would be big enough—and that day had finally come.

Mama and step dad bought a house in Sanbornville, N.H.

I didn't want to move back to N.H. since I liked living in Mass. I was going steady with Freddy, a really nice boy. He liked my sister a lot, but she wasn't interested, so he started hanging out with me. I didn't care—he was someone to go to the movies with. Every time Freddy came to pick me up, mama would say, "Don't do anything wrong!" I had no idea exactly what she meant, but it didn't matter anyway because now we were moving away.

The house they bought was kind of nice. Much bigger than living in a third floor apartment.

I missed Freddy. He'd come to see me a few times, but it was just too far for him to travel. So we decided not to go steady anymore. School was okay. I missed my friends at the school I left behind but I resigned myself to it. I'd just have to get over it and, indeed, I was used to moving around by then.

I met a boy in school—a really nice boy, I thought. I was in class with him two months before he asked me out. I ended up going steady with him—Kenny—for over a year. The only problem I'd have with him was that he kept asking me for sex! I said no, repeatedly. Besides, I didn't know the first thing about it. I thought I did, once. When I was a little girl I believed that all a boy had to do was pee on a girl! My brother, Leo, was sleepwalking one night and came into my room. He climbed onto the foot of my bed and let it go all over me! I walked around for over a year thinking I was pregnant! I finally realized that I should have had the baby by then, so that threw that theory out of the window.

Mama was still telling me not to do anything wrong, and as soon as I figured out what it was, I thought, I would take care not to do it. If only mama had sat down and talked to me about these things! But she probably thought I already knew. The nuns certainly didn't tell me anything about sex. I was afraid to ask mama about it because then she would think that I was doing it and I wasn't!

Kenny started telling me things like, "I might get killed—I'm going into car racing and you wouldn't want me hurt, would you?" He'd say, "You might not ever see me again. I was in boot camp once, you know, and I was discharged because I was ill. They told me that I would never have any kids of my own because of my illness." He went on and on—and on!

I didn't want to be responsible for Kenny getting hurt or even killed, so I finally gave in to him. I said yes.

Kenny drove out to a field near where he lived in Milton, N.H. We got out of the car and walked hand in hand across the field until we came upon an old farm barn that stood there all by itself. I didn't know what to expect. Butterflies raced around in my stomach. The next thing I knew my back was up against the building. Kenny was kissing me like never before. I felt warm all over. He really loved me, I thought. It was so unlike the way daddy treated mama. Kenny's kisses were becoming more passionate. They made my whole body tingle and I found myself getting excited! I could feel his hand sliding up my leg under my dress. He reached my panties…

Old memories flooded my mind! I remembered that moment, years earlier, when I lived in Berlin, when Jerry's friend Clint had put his hands in my panties. It was different this time… Kenny was pulling my panties down! I didn't think I liked this… It didn't feel right.

I could feel something hard pressing up against me!

I pushed Kenny away from me and I saw what he had in his hand!

I gasped—and I knew!

This is it!… this is what mama always told me not to do…

I kept trying to push him from me…but Kenny was stronger than I was…

Again he pushed me up against the wall.

"I've waited too long for this!" he panted. "There's no way you're backing out of this now!" His spoke coldly as he pushed up against me once more. His arm was pressed up against my collarbone. I couldn't move.

My tears were burning my eyes.

His sweaty brow rested on my forehead. His hot heavy breath was in my face! Then I felt the horrible, searing penetration. I screamed for him to stop! It hurt so bad! But he wouldn't stop—he kept pounding into me with unbearable pain! Within seconds he groaned with pleasure and his hold on me relaxed.

Released, I ran from him, feeling my panties around my legs. I had to stop to pull them up.

Kenny caught up with me.

"Now that wasn't so bad, was it?" he laughed.

"Take me home!" I demanded.

The fifteen–minute ride home was unbearable. I couldn't speak, but neither did he. As I got out of the car I threw his class ring at him.

"I never want to see you again!" I yelled. "I hate what you did to me!"

Kenny squealed rubber as he drove off.

I felt so dirty!

Mama wasn't home. The house was quiet. I ran into the bathroom...

I had blood on my thighs! I was scared! I didn't understand.

My panties were stained. I scrubbed and scrubbed to get the blood out.

I went into the shower and stayed there until the hot water tank emptied... and still I felt dirty, so used.

I loved you, Kenny—at least, I thought I did. How could you do this to me! I cried and cried. *I guess this is my fault too...I never should have said yes—but why didn't you stop! Why didn't you stop when I asked you...?*

I had no idea what I had gotten myself into.

Two weeks later my period didn't come.

No! I thought with horror. *I can't be pregnant! Kenny said he couldn't have any children.*

I waited another two weeks, then I realized that he must have lied!

I knew I was in dreadful trouble! I was never late...never!

What am I going to do? I couldn't tell mama the way it really happened. She would think I was making up an excuse for myself! Mama didn't raise me that way...

I decided the right thing to do was to tell Kenny. I hadn't seen him since the day it had happened.

"Are you sure it's mine?" was Kenny's first response to the news.

"I can't believe you're asking me that!" I said, horrified. "*Of course* it's yours! No one has ever done to me what you did!"

"I guess we'll have to get married then," he said casually.

"I'm only fifteen!" I said. "Mama isn't going to let me get married!"

"You'll be sixteen next week," said Kenny. "Your sister got married at sixteen, remember?"

"Cecile was almost seventeen when she got married, and it didn't last long!" I said. "She's divorced already."

"You better tell your mother," said Kenny. "Let me know if she'll let you get married." He walked out the door as he spoke and left me standing there by myself. I had to face my plight alone.

◆   ◆   ◆

I sat in the dark for a long time trying to decide what to say to mama. John, a friend of Jerry's, came to the house and was waiting for Jerry who was taking a shower. He came into the room where I was sitting.

"Is it okay to turn the light on?" he asked.

"Please don't," I said in a choked voice.

"What's the matter?" he asked

"Nothing," I said.

"I know better then that," he said

"There's nothing wrong," I said.

"You're pregnant, aren't you?" he asked

I couldn't say a word. How did he know? I broke down and cried. I didn't know what else to do. Mama liked Jerry's friend a lot and she couldn't stand Kenny and was so glad that I had broken off with him.

"I have an idea," said Jerry's friend. "What do you say about you and I going to your mother and telling her that I'm the father of the baby, and you and I will get married?"

I looked at him aghast. "I can't do that! You're not the father: Kenny's the only one that did this to me. Why in the world would you want to do that?"

He shrugged. "I care about you—and I know that you're going through a lot of pain right now. I really would marry you—and no one has to know the baby isn't mine."

"No! I can't do that to you or anyone else," I said. "Besides, I already told Kenny about it."

"Do you want me to go and tell your mother for you?" he asked. "She likes me—she might take it a little easier."

"No," I said, shaking my head. "I have to do this myself. I just don't know how. Mama won't be home until late tonight. I'll tell her tomorrow."

He nodded. "Good luck, Emelia," he said as he walked to meet Jerry at the door. "If you change your mind, the offer is still good."

I couldn't believe anyone would go that far to help me out—and to think I never even liked Jerry's friend! But now I realized that he was a caring person—he must be. I felt guilty for thinking bad of him.

Most of the next day went by before I had the courage to tell mama. She didn't take it very well at all.

I couldn't stand seeing mama cry. I hadn't seen her cry like that since she was with daddy. The only difference was that I was the one that caused it this time.

I left the room and step dad caught up with me.

"Emelia," said step dad. "What were you thinking of? I can't believe you hurt your mother like that."

I loved step dad so much, and when I heard him say those words, "You hurt your mother"—my heart was torn in half!

"I didn't mean to hurt mama," I cried as I lay on my bed. The last thing I ever wanted to do was to hurt mama!

As I lay there I started thinking ... Maybe daddy was right to treat me the way he did. Somehow he must have known that I wasn't a good little girl. Maybe mommie hated and punished me because I deserved it! And sister Pauline, she was mean to me. Maybe she had every right to be… She was a holy person, a nun. She must have seen in me a bad person that would sin against God…

Oh! mama…What did you ever do that was so wrong to deserve a daughter like me! Only one thing in my life did you tell me not to do, and now I've done it! I've let you down mama! I'm useless!… I want to die!

I went to my step dad's toolbox and pulled out an exacta knife. It had a nice pointed blade on it. I went back to my room and without giving it a second thought I picked up the knife with my right hand and stabbed it into my left wrist!

The pain was so overwhelming that I passed out.

I don't know how much time had passed when I finally opened my eyes. The pain in my wrist reminded me of what I had done. I sat up on the floor. I took a look at it. There was blood, but not enough to make a difference—I was still alive! It had stopped bleeding of it's own accord. My sense of failure and desolation was unbearable.

I was a disappointment to so many people. Now I could add myself to the list. I couldn't even kill myself! And my wrist hurt too much to try it again. I still have the scar on my wrist to remind me of how close I had come to death by my own hand.

What was left for me to do? I would go on with my plan, to do what I thought was the right thing—get married and make the best of it. I thought if it was supposed to be any different, then God would have let me die. No one ever questioned the bandage that I wore.

A few days went by before mama came to me and begged me not to get married.

"You can stay here," said mama. "Have the baby. I'll help you, but please don't marry Kenny—it won't last."

"Mama, I can't put that burden on you!" I said. "You always said that we were responsible for our own actions. I have to see if I can make this work."

"Kenny is a lot like your father," said mama. "Don't you see that?"

"No, mama," I said. "Kenny isn't as bad as daddy—you'll see. I can change him for the better."

"You can't change people like that," said mama. "Why put yourself through it? You don't have to."

"I have to try," I said. "I know I can do it."

So I ended up quitting school. I didn't like doing that. I was in my second year of high school. But I couldn't stand the other students making fun of me all the time.

I turned sixteen the first week of May and Kenny and I got married the first week of July.

20

K enny turned out worse then I could ever imagine.

"I'm not giving up," I told myself. "I have to show mama that she was wrong about him."

Kenny wouldn't let me see a doctor until I was six months along. I had never been to the doctors to find out if I was pregnant—I just *knew* that I was.

I had a hard time finding a doctor that would take me. I was too far along and never had pre-natal care, but I finally did find one. I figured my due date to be the end of January and, after examining me, the doctor agreed.

I had a shoe shop job in Farmington, N.H. Every time I had a chance to work half an hour overtime, I did. The only thing was, I would miss my ride and have to walk home 5.6 miles to Milton, N.H., where I lived. I never made it home until after dark. It was tough being pregnant, but someone had to work—Kenny didn't. I never realized he was an alcoholic until after I married him.

I can't wait to get my paycheck today, I thought. I had worked four nights over the previous week!

There's the boss now... he's handing out the paychecks—but now his hand is empty?

"Where's my check?" I asked.

"I don't have it," he said. "The office must have forgotten it for some reason." He smiled and said, "Let's you and me go and see." So I followed him to the office lady's desk.

"Could I please have Emelia's check?" the boss asked.

The office lady looked up, surprised. "Her husband picked it up about an hour ago. He said his wife was out sick today and sent him to pick up her check."

My heart sank to my feet. Questions raced through my mind: How was I going to pay the bills? And buy groceries? There was no food in the apartment! Kenny will have it all spent by the time I got home—I just knew it! All these thoughts ran through my head.

"She's right *here!*" said the boss.

"Sorry," said the lady. "Her husband had a note. I have it right here."

The boss frowned. "You're *not* to give him another one of her checks again," he said. "I don't care if he has ten notes!" He tuned to me. "I'm sorry, Emelia. There's not much I can do about it."

"I know," I said dejectedly.

I didn't work over that night. When the boss realized how pregnant I was, and someone told him that I had been walking home, he stopped my overtime.

"It's too dangerous for you to be walking on that road after dark—let alone you being pregnant," he said.

I really could have used that overtime, but I guess it didn't matter anyway. Kenny always managed to find a way to crush me.

I didn't see Kenny for two weeks after that happened. The shop stopped me from working. I was seven months along. I took up baby-sitting six kids so I could continue to pay the bills. One night Kenny came home and decided that I should have the baby in December—that way he could claim benefits for the whole year.

"You don't even work!" I screamed as he belted me over and over again. "You can't claim the baby anyway!"

"No, but you can!" he yelled as he punched me in the belly.

"The baby isn't due for another month!" I cried. "Please, Kenny! Stop!"

After he was done hitting me, he threw me in the old–fashioned bathtub we had—the high kind that stood on pedestals. Then he walked away.

I lay there for some time, hurting all over.

I finally climbed out and washed the blood off my face. I lay down for a couple of hours—until the kids began to arrive for me to baby–sit them.

I started having an awful pain in my belly. I called all the mothers to come and pick up their kids. They were glad to, because it was storming outside and they were happy to have a reason to leave work and come home.

The weather got worse, as did the pain in my stomach!

Kenny showed up. He went out and borrowed his father's truck. We traveled about three miles from the apartment and Kenny got stuck. We managed to push the truck off the road a little more.

"You'll just have to walk back home," Kenny growled. "Find another ride to the hospital. I'm going to stay here with the truck."

I started walking. It was so cold. I was getting numb all over. At least it numbed the stomach pain a little.

I remembered how mama went into labor for Albert. Daddy had gone to the club earlier that day—it was only down the street from the hotel. Mama knew that she couldn't take the car to the hospital so she walked to the garage that daddy rented—just round the block. Mama picked up the car and drove to the sitter's house and brought her back to the hotel to take care of us kids. Then mama brought the car back to the rented garage and walked over a mile to the hospital! Daddy could only have one vehicle parked on Main Street and usually it was his truck.

Mama had lost so much blood that after Albert was born, they had to give her a blood transfusion; and to make it all worse, they gave her the wrong type of blood! It almost killed her. After that mama could never give blood or have another blood transfusion.

I'm here! I thought, relieved. But I was so cold I couldn't feel my fingers or my toes. *Oh good! The neighbor's home.*

"Emelia, *look* at you!" my neighbor exclaimed when he opened the door. "Why are you out in weather like this?"

"I think I'm in labor," I said. "Kenny is stuck off the road. He sent me back to find a ride to the hospital."

"Come on!" he said. "I'll take you." He had a few choice words about Kenny. I didn't pay much attention to them. I was warming up from the car heater and noticed how my pain had increased.

We drove past the spot where Kenny had been stuck. He was no longer there. It was all snowed in. He must have gotten out shortly after I started walking. *Why didn't you come for me Kenny?* I asked myself.

I stayed in labor for two days and on the morning of the third day, about 3:00 a.m. they decided to x–ray me and found out that the baby's head had turned. They went in with forceps and turned the baby's head. And so my little boy was born at 3:51 a.m. on the 30th of December, 1966.

That should make Kenny happy, I thought. He had managed to get his own way, after all. Kenneth was born before January, so now he could be claimed. My beatings weren't for nothing.

Kenny came to see Kenneth a few hours after he was born. After that I didn't see him until the day he came to pick me up. That was five days later.

Kenneth was so tiny, but other than a stomach problem with a special diet to keep, he was healthy. I had only carried him for eight months.

I had to hire a baby–sitter, even though Kenny didn't work. He was drunk 85% of the time. I couldn't trust him to watch the baby. When Kenneth was born, I had to have stitches. It didn't matter to Kenny what shape I was in. When he wanted sex he got it any time he felt like it. It was agony.

I was pregnant for the second time. Kenneth was only four months old. I was still sixteen, but at least I would turn seventeen before I had the second baby. I was due in January again. I knew what that meant! With all the beatings Kenny gave me, I could plan on one in December for sure.

One day there was a roar of engines outside. *What on earth was that racket?* I asked myself. I looked out the window to see six motorcycles parking out front.

Knock, knock.

"Come in," said Kenny. "Make yourself at home! I'll go get what I need. I'll be right with you!"

One of them looked like he was a good 300 lbs or more. Why were these guys here? I could smell the booze as they walked by me.

"Okay, whose first?" asked Kenny as he was putting his dyes and paints on the kitchen table.

It's too bad Kenny had a drinking problem. He could have made a good living with the talent he had. He could draw and paint better then anything I had ever seen.

Now I could see what was going on. Kenny was going to paint a design on their helmets. It also looked like he would be doing some tattoos as well.

Kenny showed me how to put tattoos on about a year ago—when he had me put some on his arms. I didn't like the idea at all and did it against my will. You had to wrap six needles together with thread that had to be placed exactly in the right spot. I never did any tattoos to anyone else, only him. Now he was telling me that I had to help him because these guys didn't have much time and he had to paint all six of the helmets.

Kenny drew the pictures on their arms and I had to apply the ink. I was so glad only two of the guys were getting tattoos—it took a long time to do.

Listening to those guys talking I found out that they were one of hundreds of groups that belonged to the hell's angels. They were on their way for the big gathering that took place once a year. They had a symbol that they were having Kenny paint on their helmets. He had two more to do when I was done with the last tattoo.

"Nice skirt you got there, Kenny!" one of them said, leering at me.

"Not bad," said Kenny.

"I wouldn't mind having a piece of that," the guy said.

"Take a piece," said Kenny. "The bedroom's over there—if you want it." And he pointed to our bedroom.

The guy grabbed me by the arm and began to drag me towards the room

I couldn't believe it! "Kenny!" I screamed. "You can't do this! I'm your *wife!*"

"Wow!" the guy exclaimed. "She's a wild one, Kenny! I like that! Your old lady on the pill?"

"I've already taken care of that," Kenny grinned. "She's pregnant."

"She's knocked up?" the guy said, looking disappointed. "Hell, I've got nothing against babies." Then he let me go.

Oh, thank you GOD for letting me be pregnant! is all I could think as the guy walked away from me.

I tried to leave the room but Kenny yelled to me to come back and touch up one of the tattoos.

"Hey, Kenny—your wife isn't very social, is she?" said another of the guys. "I think you should give her a drink! I've got some whiskey. Here, give her some of that!"

Kenny took the flask from the guy and poured some of it into a glass and brought it to where I was standing. Kenny knew I didn't drink. I never drank in my life. I hated just being around it. Everything bad in my life had to do with alcohol. I told Kenny about some of the things that daddy did; he didn't believe me, so I never told him anything else. I was only trying to show him how alcohol can ruin your life, and now he was bringing me some to drink.

"Drink this," said Kenny.

"I don't want to," I said.

"I told you to drink this!" he yelled.

"No!" I shook my head.

The guys were laughing at Kenny. "What's the matter, Kenny? Can't you make your old lady obey you?"

"*Drink this!*" he yelled again.

"No," I insisted.

Then I saw the familiar fist come at me. Down I went. I got back up.

"Now, drink this!" he yelled again.

"No," I said again, the tears in my eyes.

I couldn't see his fist as clear as I did the first time. He had hit my left eye. Down I went again. I stood up again.

The guys were laughing even louder and it made Kenny angrier.

"*Now I know you'll take a drink!*" screamed Kenny. "*Won't you!*"

I didn't dare say a word. He had hit me in the same eye. I just stood there and looked at him with my good eye.

"*Take it!*" he yelled.

I wouldn't, so he punched me for the third time in the same eye—and down I went again.

"We're taking off, Kenny," said the leader of the guys. "It's late. We have a long way to go yet."

I stayed down on the floor, rolled up into a ball. I knew if I stood up again I would pass out.

"Nice job on the helmets, Kenny," said the guy. "I'll let our brother hellions know about you. I'm sure they'll be looking you up." He handed some money to Kenny.

Kenny walked over towards me. He didn't have anyone around to perform to, now, so maybe he'd leave me alone, I thought. He did, but not before he kicked me on my backside. He always made sure he didn't hit my belly. He was careful to ensure I was far enough along so he wouldn't lose his tax exemption

Next morning he told me to make my excuses to his mother who lived in the apartment two stories above us.

He had nothing to worry about. I had a catalogue of all kinds of different reasons for my bruises. I heard them all when mama was telling her parents after daddy gave her a beating.

"You better tell them that you ran into a doorknob," said Kenny.

Well, that's a new one, I thought.

I'd seen fighting matches on television when the guy gets his face bashed in, but never saw one as bad as my left eye. I had no eye that you could see—not even an eyelid for it was buried: the swelling was so bad that it was difficult to even see my eyebrow. The bone just below my eye was clearly broken.

I had to tell Kenny's parents that lie, but I found it hard to believe that *they* would believe it.

"What happened to your eye?" asked mama when she came to visit. "And don't give me any of your excuses, either," she said. "I've heard them all." It was true. All my readymade excuses sounded only too familiar; in fact, some of them were word for word the same as mama's had been.

"I ran into a doorknob," I lied.

Mama's eyes widened with surprise. "Well—I have to give you credit! That's one *I* never used." She looked anxious. "Don't you think you should see a doctor? Your face looks crooked."

I'm glad mama didn't see it two weeks before when it happened, I thought. She would be pitching a fit for sure.

"No mama," I said. "I'll be okay."

Mama shook her head, sadly. "I know you won't admit it was Kenny that did this to you. You don't have to. I know it was him." Then she placed both hands on my cheeks, gently, her eyes looking straight into mine. "Emelia, listen, you don't have to live this way. Leave him. You and Kenneth can come and live with me. You have him to think about and also the baby that's coming."

"I can't, mama," I said through my tears.

"You don't have to prove anything to me," she said. "I know that's what you're doing. Emelia, listen to me! I'm here for you. My mother couldn't do anything for me because my father wouldn't let her. Please, let me help *you*."

Mama had to leave. We said our goodbyes. It was nice seeing her again. Our visits were few and far between. I promised her if I needed help I would call her, but she knew I was determined to get through this alone.

I changed jobs in order to make more money. The shoe shop was only paying $1.40 an hour. The only disadvantage with my new job was that I had to work a second shift.

I felt really ill one night at work and one of my co–workers offered to take me home at supper break—that was at 8:30 p.m. I didn't want to because of the money; but I left anyway, only to find Kenny in bed with a close friend of mine that I took in because she had no place to go. I was too sick to even get mad, but I did kick them both out. Kenny never gave me a hard time about it because he didn't want anyone to know about his evil temper. In three more weeks I had to go on maternity leave. They wouldn't let me work past seven months. I would have no income.

Kenny begged to come back. He even went and got himself a job! I knew I couldn't make it on my own but I didn't tell him that. I took him back. He was doing well—for him. He actually went to work two days in a row! It was nice for a change.

A week later, when Kenny came home from work, he told me about a house he found in Barrington, N.H. It was way out in the country three miles from the nearest neighbor. With Kenny working now, and with the prospect of me going back to work after the baby came, I thought this might be our chance to have something for ourselves. Maybe it was finally going to work out! I was so excited!

The owners were willing to take the rent money and put it towards the purchase of the house. It was great! It was a big house with plenty of room and a huge back yard.

I took my paycheck and paid the first month's rent. I had very little left over to buy food.

The baby was still small for being nine month's old. He was doing well on his formula but that's all the doctor would let him have.

"It won't be much longer," said the doctor. "He will be on baby food before you know it. But for the meantime you keep giving him only what I tell you to. Your baby is small because he is premature. You can rest assured that he will be just like the rest of the boys when he is a little bit older."

So I did everything just the way I was told. I wanted Kenneth to grow up healthy.

I broke out in a rash. The nurse at work told me it was from the wax I was using on the job and it would go away. Two days later I found out that it was chicken pox.

They wouldn't let me work out my three weeks. People were at risk of picking up the pox and bringing it home to their kids. So I was done that day.

That left me with a two–day paycheck—something I hadn't foreseen. I knew it would be another week before Kenny got his first check, so I took what I had and bought whatever I could for food, knowing I would run out but it would be close. I really scrimped on meals.

Thursday morning there was only two slices of bread left and one of those was a crust and I knew Kenny hated crust—but this time it would have to do. I boiled the last egg and sliced it on the bread. That took care of the last of the mayonnaise. Kenny never liked his eggs mashed, only sliced. I wanted him to at least have a sandwich to eat since he was the only one working now. The baby's formula was almost gone. I tried giving him extra water in order to make his milk last longer.

Kenny came home drunk Thursday night. I tried staying out of his way. He had begun to beat me again.

I don't know where Kenny got his beer. He didn't have any money to buy it.

"Get me something to eat," said Kenny.

"There isn't anything left," I said.

He became angry. He opened all the cupboard doors, looked in the refrigerator, and then swung at me. He got me on the side of the head.

"Why isn't there any food!" he demanded.

"You *know* why, Kenny!" I said. "Why are you *doing* this to me! I gave you all that was left for your dinner today! You know that!"

"I think *you* ate everything after I left for work!" he said.

"That's not true! I haven't had anything to eat since last night, when I had a piece of crust with a little mayonnaise on it. I saved the rest of it for your sandwich today. That's *all* I've had since yesterday!"

Kenny sat down but as soon as his bottom hit the chair he was back up again. He looked at me through narrowed eyes. "Isn't it about time you had that kid?"

"No," I said, my heart beating faster. "I still have over two months."

Actually, the baby was due in five weeks. I was still wearing regular clothes. We didn't have any food half the time so I'd only gained nine pounds. Kenny slapped me across the face, then punched me in my side.

"I don't want to wait until the last minute!" he shouted. "Kenneth came out late in the month. I want to make sure this one comes out earlier!"

I wondered how long I could fool him into believing how far along I was. *Oh mama, you were right,* I thought. *I'm never going to be able to change him. Women were made just for men to beat,* I thought as I washed the blood from my face once again.

Friday morning, just before Kenny left for work, I begged him to go right to the store to get the things I needed to make the formula for Kenneth. I only had two ounces of his milk left and I would be giving it to him within the hour. I forced him to have water during the night so I could save his milk, and there wasn't nearly enough. He could drink eight ounces as a rule. It was going to be a long day for Kenneth.

"If you want to have something to eat," I said, "bring home whatever you want and I'll fix it for you." I wanted to stay on the good side of Kenny for the sake of the baby.

"Hamburger and bread?" he asked.

"That sounds good to me," I said. And *did* it! I was so hungry. "But please, Kenny, the formula is the most important thing."

"Okay, okay," said Kenny. "I won't forget it."

Kenneth woke up at 6:45—a little late for him, but I was glad: it was that much less time to wait for his father to get home. I got him up and gave him a bath, trying to prolong his feeding time. "There you go, buddy," I said. "That tasted good, eh? Still hungry aren't you?"

I tried giving Kenneth some more water but he wouldn't take it. I searched the cupboards one more time. I found a jar of peanut butter that had tipped over and you couldn't see it. It had about three inches left in it. I also found a package of Kool–Aid. I only had enough sugar to make half of the packet. It was cherry flavored.

"You like that, don't you buddy?" I smiled.

I didn't dare drink any of it. I wanted to make sure it would last all day and especially since Kenny had to go to the bank and the store after work. That would make him a little later. Well, 9:00 p.m. came and still no Kenny. Kenneth was crying from being hungry. I knew how he felt. It had been two days since I'd put anything in my mouth.

Then I remembered—peanut butter! It smelt so good. I took a teaspoon of it to kill some of the hunger pains I was having. I put a teaspoon of it in a dish. I added a little water to it so I could take out the peanut chunks. I put some on my finger and gave it to Kenneth. He ate the whole teaspoon of it.

"My goodness!" I said. "That's the first smile I've seen today. Now let's see if you'll drink some water. Good boy!" I whispered as he fell asleep in my arms. I laid him in bed with me so I could keep an eye on him. I didn't know if the peanut butter would come back up. I wanted to make sure he was all right.

Next morning Kenny still wasn't home. I did pretty much the same thing as I did the day before. I could feel myself getting sicker. It had been three days since I had anything to eat, apart from the teaspoon of peanut butter. I didn't want to take any more of it. I saved it for Kenneth. You couldn't even tell I was pregnant: I was so skinny with a tiny little potbelly.

I *had* to do something. I couldn't wait for Kenny any longer. It had snowed during the night and it was still coming down. I tried calling mama but there was no answer.

I kept feeding the baby peanut butter. He seemed to be doing okay with it. At least he wasn't crying any more, but I didn't have much left. I had just finished giving him the rest of the Kool–Aid. *Where are you, Kenny?* I kept asking myself—as if I didn't know. I called mama again, hoping I could get her to bring me some formula for Kenneth. Again there was no answer.

Midnight came and I was feeling so faint.

Work! I thought. *Mama must be at work!* She and step dad worked from 3:30 p.m. to 1:00 a.m. I knew it was Saturday, but sometimes they put overtime in. I had to try. I called and asked for mama and sure enough she and step dad were there, but not allowed to come to the phone. They said that they would give her a message. I knew there was an all night store where they worked because it was the same place where I had been working. They didn't have any formula but I would take anything at this point. "Would you please ask her if she would bring me a quart of milk? I have nothing to feed my baby and he's very hungry. Please make sure you tell her."

"Will do," the voice said on the other end of the line.

"*Shshsh*, just a little while longer, buddy," I said. "Memere will be here soon with some milk for you."

Mama and step dad showed up a little after 2:00 a.m. on Sunday.

"Emelia, you look terrible!" said mama. "You're supposed to gain weight when you're pregnant, not lose it! When is the last time you ate anything?"

I didn't answer her. I knew how angry she would be if she knew the truth.

"Where's the milk?" I asked.

"That little store next to Davidson closes at midnight now," she replied. "Besides, since when does Kenneth drink regular milk?"

I sighed. "Mama, I need to give him some milk!"

"I have can milk, Karo syrup and everything else you need to make up his formula at the house," said mama. "I want you and the baby to come home with me and I won't take no for an answer!"

I had no intention to refuse. I was weak and I knew that the baby I was carrying needed nourishment as well as myself—and I had to think of Kenneth also. I was all done trying to prove to mama that she was wrong about Kenny. She had been right the whole time.

I started to get some things together.

"Take just what you need for now," said mama. "We'll come back to get the rest of your things."

Life will have it's little ironies, for this is the time Kenny chose to barge in, drunk on his feet!

"What's your mother doing here?" he demanded. "Did you call her?"

"Yes, I did," I said with a sense of hopelessness.

"You bitch!" he screamed as he punched me in the belly.

His fist was coming at me again, just as it had so many times before, just like daddy's fist came at mama so many times when I was growing up. I used to think, would it ever stop? And now I was looking at a fist just like mama did, asking the same question—would it ever stop? But Kenny's fist never hit me this time. When his arm went up to hit me, mama grabbed it, swung him around and belted him. He went flying across the room. Step dad got up to go after Kenny.

"You stay out of it, Ben!" said mama. "He's all mine!" She towered over him and glared. "Don't you lay another hand on her!" she said.

"You get out of my house!" yelled Kenny. "Or I'll call the cops!"

"You go right ahead," said mama. "Do you want me to dial for you? Because if you don't call them, I will!"

Kenny called the police and they came.

"Why don't you take your daughter and grandson home with you?" said the officer. "I'll keep him here," he said, nodding his head towards Kenny. "*He* won't bother you."

"Thank you," said mama.

Step dad carried Kenneth out and mama helped me with a few of the baby's things. I grabbed some of my own. I wasn't sure when we would be back to get the rest. I was in pain where Kenny punched me in the belly. I'm pretty sure it wasn't labor. I didn't know what it was.

This should have been a happy time. Christmas was in two days. I didn't feel happy, but I did—and still do—thank God for my step dad and my mama.

21

"**I** promised I would be there to help her, mama," I said.

"I don't think you're in any shape to go out," said mama.

Mama was right, I thought. The pains hadn't gone away from Kenny punching me in the belly two days ago.

"It's Christmas, mama," I said right after dinner was done. "I'll call you to come get me, okay?"

"Do I have your word on that?" asked mama.

"Yes," I said.

Step dad drove me and Kenneth to Kenny's parents' house. As step dad drove away, I noticed a car that had been parked up the street pull out and come to where I was standing holding Kenneth. It was Kenny.

"My parents don't know you went to stay with your mother," said Kenny. "I don't want them finding out yet. Don't tell them. Just act like there's nothing wrong—you got that?"

I didn't answer him.

"I won't bother you," he said. "If I do, then you can tell them. Deal?"

"Okay," I conceded. I didn't feel like arguing.

There wasn't much left to do to help getting the dinner ready. It smelt so good. I wished those pains would stop so I could enjoy the wonderful Christmas dinner, I thought as I walked from the counter to the table.

At that moment I had a sharp pain. My water broke!

"Looks like we'll have another December baby," said Kenny with a smile from ear to ear. He was unconcerned that the baby wasn't due for another month.

I didn't feel much like eating after that, though I did eat a small amount before I went and sat on the living room chair with a towel under me. My father–in–law gave me a watch so I could time my pains.

It was already fixed up ahead of time that my mother–in–law would take care of Kenneth while I was in the hospital having this baby.

I called mama to tell her I wouldn't be back right away, for I had gone into labor.

Kenney chose to leave. He told everyone he had something to do.

"That's okay, Kenny," said my father–in–law. "I'll take her to the hospital when the time comes."

I sat in the chair all night. When the pains were closer together Kenny's dad took me to the hospital—at 8:00 a.m. They asked me why I was there.

"I'm going to have a baby," I said.

The nurse laughed. "You're pregnant? Let's see." My belly was even smaller now that my water had broken.

"My goodness!" she said. "I guess you *are* in labor!"

My little girl was delivered at 11:01 a.m. on the 26th of December, 1967.

"It's a girl," said the doctor. Everything was quiet.

"I can't hear her crying," I said.

Everyone was rushing around. No one was saying anything.

"I can't hear her!" I yelled.

Finally a faint, tiny little cry filled the quiet room. They wouldn't let me hold her. She was put into an incubator and taken away.

I got to see her a few hours later in the nursery. She was so tiny—even smaller than Kenneth was. Kenny always said that if we had a girl he wanted to name her Tina. She looked more like a Lisa to me, so that's what I named her.

Kenny never came to the hospital to see her when she was born. I don't even think he knew if I had another boy or a girl. The only thing Kenny cared about was that I had the baby early enough for him to claim benefits for the year. My father–in–law was the one who came and got me when it was time for me to leave. The doctor said that Lisa had to stay there for at least a couple of weeks longer—then he'd see if she could go home.

I didn't see Kenny again until I was moving into my own apartment two days after I got out of the hospital. I had all my silverware laid out on the counter. I was admiring the beautiful knives that mama gave me. Step dad kept them nice and sharp for her.

I was so happy to have my own place again. The apartment was on the second floor above a grocery store that the landlord also owned. In fact, he and his wife lived in the apartment next to mine. Mama paid a month's rent for me on the understanding that I would give her back a little each week when I returned to work in three more weeks.

The landlady said I could charge my groceries until I started getting my paychecks again. Then I could give her a little extra each week until I had it paid off.

Everything seemed to be going great, except that the apartment only had one bedroom. That meant that the two kids and I would have to share. That's okay, I thought. They were so little, they wouldn't take up much space. Later on, maybe, I'd find a bigger place—but for now this would do just fine.

"I see you got your own place now," said Kenny.

I jumped! He scared me. I had no idea he was there.

"I'll go down and get my things out of the car," he said.

"Don't bother!" I said. "You're not moving in with us! I don't want you around me or my kids—I'm filing for a divorce."

"You're not divorcing me!" said Kenny.

"Yes I am," I said. "I'm not going through any more of your abuse. I don't have to! You're not going to keep doing to me what daddy did to mama. My kids are not going to grow up in fear like I did!"

Kenny walked towards me. I could smell the booze on him. He grabbed me by my neck with both hands, squeezing my throat and choking me. He wouldn't stop! I couldn't breathe. I was seeing black spots in front of me. I remember seeing daddy's hands around mama's neck many times, but this was the first time I was on the receiving end of hands that acted just like daddy's did.

Kenny, stop! my mind was screaming—but there were no words coming out of my mouth.

I reached behind me. My hand landed on one of the knives. I brought it towards me, handle first. As I turned my hand the blade of the knife slid along Kenny's side. It startled him and he let me go.

I put one hand on his chin and the other on his chest and ran forward, pushing him backwards. I kept running until I reached the refrigerator where I pushed Kenny's head up against it as hard as I could. Down he went!

I grabbed Kenneth who had earlier been kicking Kenny in the leg, only to be kicked back. I knew Kenneth was hurt but that didn't stop him from trying again to protect me.

I went through what I called my secret door. People thought it was a connecting door to the landlord's apartment, so they never fooled with it; but it was a door that led to an unfinished hallway that separated the two apartments. The landlady told me about it because of my trouble with Kenny.

"Don't tell anyone else about it, okay?" she had said. "Someday it might come in handy for you."

I'm glad she told me and she was right—it *did* come in handy. I went out there and sat on the floor. Kenneth knew how to be quiet, just like I did when I was little.

You've gotten so much bigger, I thought as I looked down on Kenneth who had curled up in my lap and was falling asleep. Just three days before he had turned a year old. I was so relieved that Lisa was still in the hospital. At least I didn't have to worry about her right then, even though my arms ached to hold her.

I must have knocked Kenny out. I wondered for how long I'd be stuck in that hallway. It had a hard cold floor, but at least we were safe from Kenny.

I started thinking about Cecile. Her baby should be coming soon. She'd moved back near where I was staying. I guessed she must have seen a side of daddy that I already knew about. I was glad she was back. It was nice having her around. I felt bad for her—she cared a lot about the baby's father, but he denied his child. I told her that she was better off without him. His loss, her gain.

A while back Cecile got me to take a trip to Berlin on a bus to see the autumn foliage. We were going to stay the night at a motel and come back the next day on another bus. Mama told me to go—it would do me some good to get away. So she took care of Kenneth and off Cecile and I went.

It was a beautiful ride—so much color and so bright!

I didn't know that daddy would be waiting at the bus stop, though Cecile did.

"Hello, girls," said daddy.

"Hi, dad," said Cecile.

"I wasn't able to get you girls a room," said daddy. "Everything was booked solid. There's been a lot of people coming up to see the foliage. Mommie said that you two could spend the night there."

I didn't want to, but I didn't say anything. Daddy took us out for supper. All he talked about was that Cecile and I had quit school.

"You're not going to get anywhere's in life without your diplomas," he said. "School is the most important thing that anyone could do."

"I know," said Cecile.

"Did you hear me, Emelia?" asked daddy.

"Yes," I said meekly. "I heard you."

It was getting late and we had to get up early in the morning in order to catch our bus. I noticed when Cecile was getting out of the car that her belly was much bigger than mine—except that hers was the right size.

I was happy to see that it was time for bed when we got to mommie's house. I didn't want to visit with her. I still had nightmares because of her.

"You girls take this room," said mommie.

"Thanks, mommie," said Cecile.

"I'm tired," said Cecile as she pulled the covers down on the bed.

"*Eh!*" I gasped. It felt like my breath had been knocked out of me.

"What's wrong?" asked Cecile.

"This is the same bed I wet in!" I said. "The first night we stayed here when we got out of the convent, remember?"

"Emelia," laughed Cecile, "that was seven years ago! You don't *still* wet the bed, do you?"

"No!" I said. "But I've had a couple of close calls this past month. Doctor said I'm carrying this baby very low—it's putting pressure on my bladder. I don't want to sleep in this bed! With my luck I'll probably pee in it again!"

"Oh, *come on* Emelia, you'll be fine!" Cecile smiled, patting the bed next to her. "Get into bed and get some sleep!"

"I guess it is kind of silly," I said, and climbed in. "Goodnight, Cecile."

"Goodnight," she yawned.

I was woken from my sleep by Cecile shaking me.

"Emelia! Get up," she said. "It's late. We have to hurry if we're going to make it to the bus stop on time. It's going to take a little time to walk there."

I began to sit up when I froze. "Cecile!" I gasped.

"What?"

"I wet the bed!"

"You didn't!"

"I did!" Dismay swept over me. "Just a little—but look, it's noticeable! What am I going to do?"

"Quick! Help me make the bed," said Cecile, jumping to the floor.

"What!" I said. "You can't make up the bed—it's wet!"

"Oh yes, I can," she said. "Don't you think mommie punished you enough for two bed wettings?"

"Enough for at least three!" I said as I hurried to help Cecile make the bed.

"In that case," said Cecile, "maybe we can come back sometime and pay mommie another visit."

"Cecile! That's terrible!"

I never heard Cecile laugh so loud before. Then I realized I was laughing with her.

Was that a cough? It was Kenny! According to my watch, I'd been sitting in the hallway for thirty–five minutes.

I could hear him walking around the apartment, looking for me, no doubt. Kenneth was waking up. *Shhhh*, I said. I wanted Kenneth to remember where we were.

Kenny was running down the stairs. I came out of my hiding place, put Kenneth in his playpen, then ran down the stairs to lock the door. The landlady told me it was okay to lock that door because it only led up to my apartment. Then I ran back upstairs and locked that door, too.

I had a sore throat for a few days. You could see the fingerprints on my neck. They turned black and blue.

It was nice having Lisa home now. The first day she was home Kenneth couldn't figure out where the crying was coming from, so he tipped the bassinet over. I ran to find him sitting on the floor beside her. She was lying on her pillow smiling away at Kenneth. All I could think of was, *here we go! I'm in for a good time with these two clowns.* They had already started their acrobatics.

Things were looking up. I found a house for rent down the road from mama's house. It had two bedrooms, one floor, but it had no cellar. I didn't care—it was a little house all by itself and I was close to mama.

Lisa was four months old when Kenny showed up at the house.

"I need some money," said Kenny. The booze smell could knock you over.

"I don't have any," I said.

"If I can't have any money, then I'll take you," he said and began to tear away at my pants.

"Stop it!" I yelled. "Get out of here!"

"Not until I get what I came for," he said.

My blouse was ripped and my pants were half off when Leo came to the door.

"Leo!" I screamed. "Go tell mama to call the police!"

Leo went running. Kenny stopped. I managed to pull my pants back up.

Kenny grabbed Lisa out of her swing and ran out the door with her. I was right behind him. He jumped into the truck and told his friend to drive off. As the door was about to close, I grabbed on to the handle. The truck was going down the hill dragging me alongside of it, ripping my pants down to the meat of my legs—but I wouldn't let go! No—one was going to take my child from me! I could hear the sirens of the police car. *Hurry! Please hurry!* I thought. The pain was unbearable.

Kenny's friend stopped the truck. I fell to the ground. Kenny took our four—month—old daughter and threw her at me. Thank God I caught her!

Kenny's friend ran off to leave Kenny to face the music, but not until he had driven out of sight.

I pressed charges against him. The day I appeared in court, Kenney's mother begged me to drop the charges. After a while I finally did, but not before I was told that Kenny would never bother me again.

My divorce went through. It took me a long time to save the money, but it was over with at last.

Kenny was ordered to pay forty dollars a week for child support. To the judge's surprise, I asked him to drop the amount to twenty dollars a week.

"Why?" he asked.

"There's no way that Kenny is going to pay forty dollars a week," I said. "I would rather think that I might have a chance of getting the twenty."

"For *two* children?" he asked. "That's not much money. You're entitled to double that amount."

"I know," I said. "But a little is better than nothing at all."

The judge nodded. "If you ever want to get it changed, all you have to do is apply for it through the court."

"Thank you," I smiled.

I had some extra expenses come up and Kenny was now three hundred behind. I called probate court and they had him arrested. I felt I had to do it this way because even at twenty a week Kenny never paid anything.

His bail was set at two hundred. Someone bailed him out and they sent the money to me.

Right after I cashed the check I found out that it was Kenny's grandmother that put up the bail money. That broke my heart. She was a very dear person to me. She had to live on her social security. *I can't take this money away from her*, I thought.

I went to visit her.

"Memere B, I can't take this money from you," I said.

"You need it for the kids," she said.

"The kids are not your responsibility," I said. "It's up to Kenny to support his kids, not you."

"How did you find out it was me that paid Kenny's bail?" she asked.

"It doesn't matter how I found out," I said. "I don't want you to let people use you this way. They think nothing of taking advantage of you. Now I want you to take this money back and hide it. Don't let anyone know that you have it, okay?"

"If someone finds out, I might get into trouble," she said. "I had to pay that to the court."

"It's your money," I said, shaking my head. "You're not going to get into any trouble. I'm not going to tell anyone. You need this money to live on. Now please take it back."

"Okay," she smiled. "But what will you do about the kids?"

"Don't worry about them," I said. "Everything will work out."

I could see the relief on her face when she took the money back from me. I know I felt a lot better about it.

I managed to pick up some overtime at work. Things started getting a little easier

During the next few months I made some very poor choices when it came to men. Nothing I'm proud of. Then I decided to just work, and when I wasn't I made sure to spend some quality time with my kids. I didn't bother to date any more.

On Kenneth's second birthday Lisa was just four days past her first birthday.

22

I was hoping they would call work off. The snow was getting heavier now. Not too many people showed up.

They decided to shut down every other line and double up the people that they had, so at least some of the lines would run. My line was one of the ones that stayed open. I was happy about that, for it meant I could do my regular job.

Three hours into the shift I was busy doing my job when this feeling came over me that I was being watched. I looked around real quick and noticed a guy staring at me.

I'd never seen him before. *Why is he looking at me?* I asked myself. Well, when you come right down to it, I couldn't take my eyes off him either! Medium built with an athletic physique, he had dark hair and beautiful soft eyes.

He began to walk towards me and I froze. Without hesitation he reached for me and instinctively I melted into his arms. Then he kissed me! I couldn't help myself and kissed him back. It felt like the kiss lasted for five minutes, even though it was only a few seconds.

"Do you believe in love at first sight?" he asked in a gentle voice.

"Not until now," I answered with a shy smile, quite overcome by his smiling eyes.

It was as if I had known him all my life. It must have been a fairy tale that mama had read to me when I was little.

"Are you two people going to do any work?" the boss asked. Everyone around started laughing. I was so embarrassed.

George and I started dating. We really hit it off. He loved my kids. I was on cloud nine. He was the best thing that could ever have happened to me.

George had a little girl from a previous marriage and he brought her to visit me once. What a charming little girl she was, a joy to my heart. She got along great with Kenneth who didn't want her to leave even though she was older than him. They played together so well.

We dated for only a few months before he asked me to marry him. I accepted with great enthusiasm. We set the date for February 14, 1969.

I was finally happy! I couldn't wait to marry him.

Kenneth and Lisa loved him. They would get so excited whenever he came around.

Mama asked me about him and how he was treating me and the kids.

"Oh mama," I beamed. "I could give you all the old clichés, like he loves me and the kids, he's thoughtful and kind, he's good to me and so on and on—but I'm not going to, not because they're not true because they are, everyone of them and more." I smiled and I'm sure my radiance said it all. "What I am going to tell you is something very special to me."

George dedicated a song to me that played on the radio often. One of my favorite singers sang it—Bobby Vinton. The song was *I Love How You Love Me!*

"What makes this song so special to me," I told mama, "is that whenever it plays, George stops whatever he's doing and comes to find me, puts his arms around me and sings the song in my ear." It was true! He could be driving down the road and if that song came on the car radio, he'd pull over onto the side of the road, pull me towards him, hold me and whisper the song in my ear!

"I just love him so much, mama," I said as I was running out the door. I was in a hurry. I had an appointment to have my hair done. I wanted to surprise George. He was coming over later.

Leo and Albert came down to the house to take care of Kenneth and Lisa for me.

While I was gone, Albert passed out cold on the kitchen floor. Leo got scared and ran up the hill to get mama. She ran down the street to the house and found Albert sitting up on the floor. Mama took Kenneth and Lisa up to her house and left a note telling me where to find them. She called the doctor in Sanbornville and he told her to give Albert a couple of aspirin and put him to bed—he probably had the Hong Kong 'flu.

I came home to a note telling me to pick up the kids at mama's and I did. I felt bad for Albert and hoped he would get better soon. George showed up and he loved my hair—I was so pleased. He helped me get the kids ready for bed. That was a fun time for everybody. My cousin showed up about twenty minutes after the kids were in bed. I made orange ice–cream sodas for the three of us and we watched *Get Smart* on TV.

While the show was still on I started getting real sick. *Oh no*, I thought, *I must be coming down with the Hong Kong 'flu that mama told me about*. I kept passing out in between running to the bathroom. It was coming out at both ends!

"I'm not leaving here with you sick like this," said George. "Who will take care of the kids? You're in no shape, honey."

My cousin left after the show was done. I felt bad that I wasn't very good company.

I couldn't believe how sick I was! I couldn't make it to the bathroom any more without the help of George. I would pass out before I got there.

I was sitting on the toilet and thankfully the sink was right beside me. My head was in it, being sick while I sat.

I heard a bang. I looked up and saw George lying on the dining room floor near the bathroom door, less then ten feet away. He had taken his shirt off. He had thrown up all over himself and the floor.

He must have the 'flu too, I thought as I climbed down onto the bathroom floor. I could no longer walk. I crawled on my belly and continued to throw up and pass out on my way to him. I looked at my watch when I climbed to the floor and it was midnight. I finally made it to where he was. It took me thirty minutes to reach him, less than ten feet away.

"George," I said. "Are you all right, honey?" I asked.

He was on his back with my face just above his chest. He lifted his hand and patted me on the back of my head.

"Just put your head down on my chest," he said. His hand never left my head. He pushed it ever so gently to his chest and then patted it again, and said, "Close your eyes… everything will be all right." And so I did.

That was the last thing he said.

Leo came to the house the next day at dinnertime and found us still lying on the floor, unconscious.

When he found us I had turned over on my back and George had turned over onto his chest.

◆   ◆   ◆

"Emelia!" said mama, holding my hand. "Can I get you anything? Are you hungry?"

Why was she holding my hand? I thought.

"How about a nice cold drink?" she asked. "Are you thirsty? Tell me what you would like to drink and I'll get it for you."

"My head hurts," I said, struggling to open my eyes but giving up the effort. "Where am I? I can't move. Why can't I move?"

"Doesn't a cold drink sound good?" said mama. "Tell me what kind of drink you like and I'll get it for you," she said again.

"A glass of ginger ale," I said.

Then Mama started to cry. It was so loud.

"Mama, you're hurting my head more." Why was she crying? I only wanted a glass of ginger ale.

"Can you open your eyes?" a man's voice asked.

They were so heavy. It took a minute but I did it. I could see white sheets all around me. Then I realized that the man was a doctor and the sheets were the closed curtains around my bed. All I could think of is I must have that Hong Kong 'flu pretty bad to be in the hospital. I couldn't move any part of my body and it hurt to breathe. They took me to x–ray and found out that I also had pneumonia.

George's mother was a nurse but I didn't see her there.

"Mama," I said. "Where is George?"

"His mother is taking care of him at home," she said. "He didn't get as sick as you, so he didn't have to come here."

Well, that explains why I didn't see him there, I thought.

"What about Kenneth and Lisa?" I asked. "Do they have the 'flu?"

"They're downstairs in the children's ward," said mama.

"They're sick too?" I asked.

"They're fine," she said. "But they'll be staying there for a while."

I was confused. "If they're fine, then why do they have to stay there?"

"Emelia," said mama, trying to feed me, "you know that Ben and I have to work. There isn't anyone to take care of them right now."

"I feel so weak, mama. I can't even feed myself. It's like I'm paralyzed from the neck down."

"You better get some rest now," said mama. "I'll be back a little later."

I found out why mama was so upset when I asked her for a glass of ginger ale. The doctors told her that I would never come around again. They prepared her for the worst. "It just doesn't look good at this time and we feel that she will stay this way or get worse," they told her. Mama told them that they were wrong! She stayed at my bedside for two days straight, talking to me. That's why I was hearing her asking me all those questions about what I wanted her to get for me. I had no idea that mama had been there that long and I only heard her in the last few minutes before I spoke. I believe with all my heart that it was mama's faith and love and God's will that I did answer her that day.

After a few days I insisted that I see my kids. They didn't want me to, but there was no way they were going to stop me, even if I couldn't move.

They finally got me a wheelchair. It was a job getting me into it. And so they wheeled me to where the kids were.

Kenneth and Lisa were in the same room. They just lay there in the cribs and couldn't move.

The nurse wheeled me up to each of them. Lisa looked at me with big tears in her eyes. I couldn't touch her. My hands wouldn't work. When Kenneth saw me he said, "Mommy"—and his eyes were full of tears too.

"Get me out of here," I whispered to the nurse. I didn't want them to see me cry. I didn't want to frighten them any more than they already were. The nurse and the doctor were right—I shouldn't have gone there, but I *had* to see them. I was so upset. They had to give me a sedative after they got me back into my bed.

Why did mama say they were fine? I asked myself as I fell asleep. When I woke there was a man standing by my bed. He told me his name. I didn't know him.

"I'm with the FBI," he said. "I would like to ask you a few questions."

"FBI?" I was confused. "What do you want?"

"Do you know of any reason why Kenny or anyone else would want to hurt you and your kids?" he asked.

"What? I don't know what you're talking about," I said.

"Would your ex–husband want to kill George? Or you and the kids?"

"Kill George?" I asked.

"Oh, you didn't know?" he frowned. "George is dead."

"*Dead!*" I screamed.

The doctor rushed in. "What are you doing here!" he exclaimed. "I told you that she's not strong enough to answer any of your questions yet. You were not to tell her anything. Get out of here!"

I hadn't been able to move in all the time that I'd been there. I was too weak—but I climbed out of my bed and chased the FBI agent down the hallway. It took three people to hold me down so the doctor could sedate me again.

When I came to, I couldn't move again. Mama was standing by my bed. The doctor had called her so I wouldn't be alone when I woke up.

"Mama!" I said. "George is dead!"

"I know," said mama.

"Why did you lie to me?" I asked.

"I didn't want to, Emelia," said mama. "The doctor told me that it would be too much of a shock to you if you knew the truth. Look what happened when you did find out."

"Mama," I said, "I didn't even get a chance to say goodbye—and now my sweet George is gone!" I cried. "Why wasn't I allowed to go to the funeral? I could have gone in a wheelchair!"

"It was better for you to remember him the way he was," said mama, patiently. "Trust me on this, Emelia—it really was for the best that you stayed here and didn't go."

"But why was the FBI asking me questions about Kenny or someone else that did it—did what? What does all of that have to do with the Hong Kong 'flu?"

"It's not the 'flu," said mama. "It was propane gas poisoning."

"*What!*"

"There was a gas leak," she said. "The house is closed up. They're calling it a crime seen. It's being investigated."

"How will I get the kids clothes—and mine?" I asked.

"They allowed Ben and I to go into the house for about half an hour to get what we could out. They kept an eye on us the whole time. We took the two cribs and most of the baby clothes and a few of the kids' toys, but I never gave it a thought to get any of your clothes out, Emelia." Her voice nearly broke. "I'm sorry," she said.

"It's okay, mama, I don't need any right now, anyway." Then I broke down again. "What will I do without George, mama?" I wailed.

Mama didn't know what to say.

"When you get out of here, you and the kids are going to come and live with us," she said. "I've got everything all set up for the three of you. Now I want you to get some rest."

A couple of days later I went to see the kids again. I was able to feed myself now but I still couldn't walk. I was able to move my arms—that meant that I would be able to touch my kids. I was surprised to see Kenneth standing in his crib. He had to hold on but it was a big improvement from the last time I saw him. He was so happy to see me! Lisa was sitting in her crib. She was still so tiny—over a year old now and she still couldn't walk, and that was before all of this happened. The doctor told me not to worry, she'd walk, but it might take a while.

Lisa gave me a big smile when she saw me. She wouldn't eat for the nurse so I took over and she ate it all.

I went every day at dinnertime and fed Lisa and got to spend some time with Kenneth. I was able to walk now, as long as I wore my back brace that ran down the back of my legs. The doctor said I'd have to wear it for the rest of my life. There's a patch on my back as big as a dinner plate that was frozen by the gas and it runs into the area around the end of the spine.

It seemed like the kids and I had been in the hospital forever. We were going home at last. Well, not home, but to mama's—but we were getting out of there!

It had snowed the day before. The sun was out and it was windy. When mama drove by Lake Wentworth, the wind had blown the snow to make a one–lane road. You couldn't see anything—it was a complete white out. Without warning we had a head on–collision with another car. My head smashed the windshield, Kenneth's tooth went through his lip, and Lisa had a prune on her head as big as an egg! And yet Albert, Leo and mama didn't have a scratch on them. The police came and drove us back to the hospital.

Everything had happened so fast that some of the nurses didn't know that we had even left the hospital!

"I'm a jinx," I said, crestfallen.

Mama slapped my face. "Don't you ever say that again!" she said. "You're not a jinx!"

We were released for the second time from the hospital. We made it all the way home this time. Mama was a nervous wreck by the time we got there. The accident had shaken her up.

The people where I worked took up a collection for me and I was so grateful. I was able to buy some clothes for myself and a few things for the kids, and some of it went to mama for supporting all of us.

It wasn't until six months after the gas accident that they told me I could go back into the house and get the rest of my things. They had found out that the gas connection to the furnace had a leak. Back a few days before Christmas I ran out of gas and it was cold. I had called the gas company in Wolfboro to tell them I had run out and could they please send someone right away? They were very good about sending a truck right over—the only thing was they sent a greenhorn! He knew how to fill the tank but evidently didn't know enough about getting the furnace going. He caused a gas leak at the hook–up in the house. This was told to me by the investigator's findings.

I have since become extremely sensitive to gas fumes. The doctor said I would always be that way.

Mama wanted to come with me but I wanted to be alone.

I had Albert and Leo help me load up step dad's truck with all the furniture—couch, chairs, my bed, stove, my clothes, and everything else that wasn't tied down. I asked them to take it to the dump. I could smell the gas in everything. I had to get rid of it all.

My Christmas tree was as beautiful as the day I put it up. I didn't understand why. It had been up for six months—it should have been all dried up.

I went and got a bucket and cleaning things from mama and I knew I would need a putty knife in order to clean up everything on the floor that had dried up.

"Please let me go and help you clean the house," said mama.

"I need to do this by myself, mama," I said. "Thank you, mama, for being here for me."

"I will always be here for you, Emelia," she said.

"I know," I said softly.

I was in the house for six hours, scrubbing first the toilet, then the sink. I tackled the bathtub. Then I made it to the floors. I got to the spot where I spent my last few minutes with George, remembering him patting me on my head, telling me that everything would be all right. I noticed a half cleaned, faded chalk outline of where George's body had been.

My heart skipped a beat. George!

I proceeded to lie face down inside the chalk line, trying not to let any of my body hang over. I needed so bad to feel his closeness! I lay there, thinking about how I didn't get to see him in the funeral home. I longed for him so badly.

"If only I could have seen you for a minute, darling, I would have whispered in your ear, 'I love how you loved me while you were with me.' Oh George! Why were you taken away from me! I miss you so much!" I cried and cried. "And your little girl—what about her? She won't have her daddy to grow up with and I know you were a good daddy, not like my own..."

I sat up, looked over the chalk line once more, then washed the remaining evidence of what should have been the rest of my life off from the floor.

I thanked God for giving me those last few minutes to be close to what was left of my George. Now he was gone and could only touch me in my memories...

The job was done. Once again the house was clean. It was also empty, just like I was inside—empty.

Every night I prayed to God to take the pain away, with my arms stretched out to the ceiling looking for a hug from Him to comfort me. *Please God, make it stop hurting.*

Sometimes mama would come into my room at night because she could hear me crying.

"Are you okay, Emelia?" she would ask.

"Yes, mama, I'm okay," I would answer.

One night I couldn't stand it. I went into mama's bedroom and sat on the floor next to her. Mama held my hand.

"*Why*, mama?" I cried. "Why did God take George away from me?"

"I don't know, Emelia."

"I needed him, mama."

"I know, Emelia, but I guess God needed him more."

Then I returned to my room, empty and alone, and cried myself to sleep.

On February 14th,1969—St Valentine's Day—my heart felt crushed inside of me. It was to be the day that George and I were to be married! We had decided to save ourselves for each other for this special day.

George died in December of 1968—just twenty–nine years old. The pain was unbearable. I just wanted to die. I felt that I had lived a long life, even though I was only eighteen years old. Nothing good had come to me in my life as a child with daddy; the convent had branded me with a number 64, while most of the nuns were mean; and I'd been married to a man that thought nothing of his children, who was mean, abusive, an alcoholic just like daddy. I had two children, I was divorced, and now I had lost the love of my life. All in eighteen years.

I thank God for my mother who was—and is—my example of strength and love.

23

"**H**ow about going on a date with me?" asked John, Jerry's friend who was home on leave. He was the same friend who had once offered to marry me—when I was pregnant with Kenny's baby.

He and Jerry joined the Navy together but landed up in different places—Jerry on a ship while John went to Germany.

"No thank you," I said as I hurried back to my job. Break was over. Every time he was on leave, the place where we worked would let him come in and work during the time he was home. I didn't see much of him—just when we ran into each other in the cafeteria. He worked on the other side of the building.

"I wonder if mama put him up to this?" I thought. She'd been trying to get me to go out again.

I tried it a couple of times, once with a nice guy at work. Dan had asked me out three or four times before I accepted. That was about six months after George had died. Dan was a little on the chunky side and very quiet. I didn't feel threatened by him, but I didn't want to fall for anyone. I had no idea that Dan would come over as such a great person and I started caring about him.

One night when I was expecting him to pick me up, his roommate came instead, bringing me flowers.

"Where's Dan?" I asked.

"He sent me to tell you that he's awful sorry," said Rick. "Dan and his old girlfriend have gotten back together again."

My heart sank.

"I didn't want to be the one to tell you, Emelia, but his girlfriend wouldn't let him come. Dan asked me if I would explain to you." He smiled apologetically. "He should have told you himself, of course."

"Yes," I said in a small voice. "He should have."

"Can I take you out to get something to eat?" asked Rick.

"No," I said, smiling weakly. "Thank you anyway." Then I became aware that I was still holding the flowers. I felt angry and used. "Oh, would you please give these flowers back to Dan?" I asked. "He can give them to his girlfriend!"

"Dan didn't buy those flowers for you," smiled Rick. "I did."

"Why?" I asked, surprised.

"I like you—and I felt bad that Dan did this to you." He smiled. "Please keep the flowers. I would like you to have them."

"Thank you," I said, and managed another smile. "In that case I'll keep them."

I didn't even know that Dan had had another girlfriend. He certainly didn't act like he did when he was at work, and I'd known him for a long time.

"It won't last long," said Rick, reading my thoughts. "His girlfriend has broken off with him twice before. The only reason she wanted him back was because she found out about *you*."

"Oh, really?" I said, hurt. "Well, as much as I care about Dan, he needn't look me up when his girlfriend dumps him again!"

"I'll tell him," said Rick.

"Please do," I said.

The second time I tried going out, it was with a different guy at work. Sam also seemed like a real nice person.

After dating him for a while, someone told me that he was married. I couldn't believe it. I was furious! I went to see him at break time.

"Sam," I asked him outright, "*Are* you married?"

"Well," Sam hesitated. "I was—I mean, well, I am, sort of, but my wife and I are separated and… and have been for a long time.

"Why didn't you tell me?" I asked.

"Well, I… I didn't think you would go out with me if you…, well, if you knew," he said, clearly searching for the right words. "And…um… I also have two little kids," he added, then smiled sheepishly. "I won't be married much longer, actually… my divorce is almost over with."

"I would like you to be right up front with me, Sam," I said. "And you're right—I never would have gone out with you while you were still married."

"Yes, well… my lawyer says any day now."

The following Sunday Sam brought his two children to see me. They were adorable. He got to have them every Sunday for a few hours.

We had a few more dates but something didn't feel right with me. One Sunday when Sam came to see me with his kids at mama's, he told me he couldn't stay long because of a firemen's meeting he had to attend. Sam was the fire chief.

"I have to get these kids back to their mother," explained Sam. "I need time to get home myself and take a shower, and I have some things to get ready before the meeting."

"Okay," I said, and Sam kissed me goodbye.

I had a bad feeling in the pit of my stomach. I had a good idea where his kids lived by the way he talked once. Mama took care of Kenneth and Lisa for me and I took off in my car and went to Barnstead.

I found it! Sam's car was parked in the yard where the kids lived. I parked in a place where he couldn't see me. I watched to see how long it would take him to leave. I sat there for almost two hours before he came out all cleaned up with a different set of clothes on. I was puzzled. Then a woman came out of the house calling for him.

"Sam honey, you forgot this on the table!" she said. "Don't you need it?"

"What would I do without you!" he replied as he put his arms around her and kissed her the way he had just kissed me only a few hours before.

Again my heart sank.

"I shouldn't be too late," he said.

"I'll wait up for you," she smiled.

"Okay, hon," he yelled out his car window as he drove away from his house—the house where he had been living with his wife and getting along great the whole time.

Why does this keep happening? I asked myself on my long drive home. I was tired of being hurt all the time.

It didn't take me long to end that relationship. I was waiting for him the next day. Sam tried one more time to lie to me but I told him that I knew where he lived and if I ever even saw him with another girl I would give his wife a call.

I don't think I ever would have—but at least it made him sit up and take notice.

It was experiences like these that made me resist Jerry's friend's invitation. It was the second time that John asked me out while being on leave, and again I refused him.

Mama said that she hadn't even seen John, so I guess she didn't put him up to asking me out after all.

One night at work a friend of mine asked me why I didn't go back to school to get my diploma. I couldn't get the thought out of my mind. I thought about it the whole evening.

"Mama," I said. "What do you think about me going back to school?"

"I think that's great!" said mama. "But how are you going to do that? It's the end of October, and school starts the first week of September. You would already be behind all the other kids."

"I don't know yet," I said. "But as soon as I get up in the morning I'll take a ride to Nute High School and find out."

When I got there, they sent me in to see the guidance councilor. He was able to look up my records from when I was in the tenth grade. He told me I would need seven credits to graduate. I had to take two math classes, General Math II and Algebra, and Home Economics, which would be easy for me; also, History, Biology, and I had to have two credits in English—but I only had time to fit one English class in at school. I had to leave school during the last period in order to get to work on time, so I took American Literature by correspondence class that the guidance councilor would keep track of.

I had my hands full. I had no study hall periods. I would study during supper break, from 8:30 p.m. to 9:00 p.m. I also studied and did my homework when I got home from work at 2:00 a.m. until 2:45 or 3:00 a.m. I always tried to make sure that I got at least four hours' sleep. I didn't get to see my kids very much but there were some days that mama couldn't watch them, so I took them to school with me. The teachers loved them and they were well behaved. I took their coloring–in books with me.

"You would never know they were here," said a couple of the teachers.

It always makes you feel good when someone says something nice about your kids. I was glad that it was mama that was taking care of them. I couldn't have left them for such long periods with anyone else.

I remembered what daddy said about it being important to finish school, so I took a ride to Milan—it was just a few miles north of Berlin. Daddy had bought an old run–down farm up there that sat on a large piece of beautiful land. He always had plenty of money. Too bad he never shared it with mama. She worked very hard for him when they were married.

This was the first time I took it upon myself to visit daddy. I couldn't wait to tell him I had gone back to school. I just knew he would be so proud of me! I was finishing my tenth grade, doing the eleventh and the twelfth all in one school year, and I still kept my full–time job with an hour overtime every day and eight hours on Saturday nights—except for that Saturday that I decided to spend with daddy.

Mama said that I didn't have to keep working. I could stay with her rent–free and step dad would support the kids and me while I was in school.

"No mama," I said. "I can't do that to you. I don't pay you enough as it is now. I'm not going to let you and step dad take on such a burden, and I'm not going to get any welfare either. I know how those people can be. I'll support my own kids."

When mama was on A.D.C. in Massachusetts and we had to go to the dentist, he would drill, fill and sometimes pull teeth, then bill A.D.C. for the work done and for the Novocain he used to do it. The only thing was, he never used Novocain. I guess some people think kids are dumb. We were little, not stupid!

Same with the eye doctor. He said I needed glasses, though I wasn't having any trouble seeing. When I moved to N.H. I found out that the glasses he provided were merely fitted with window glass! I was made to stop wearing them. Those people were crooked, but they were not the only ones!

When I was twelve years old, again in Massachusetts, I babysat for a great couple that had three kids. The father of the kids worked as the mayor's chauffeur. It was election year. I found out all about campaigning and I worked hard helping to get this man re–elected. And he won! I was so excited about it—to think I had some small part in his success!

There was a celebration party afterwards. The mayor's chauffeur's family was invited. They brought me along so I could keep an eye on the kids for them. The little boy ran into a room where the mayor and some of his top men had gathered to talk. They never noticed me when I went to get him: if they did, it didn't stop them from saying the things that they did. What they said was so bad that I knew right then and there that I would never help campaign for anyone else ever again. Furthermore, when I was old enough, I would never vote! Those politicians were so crooked! I felt one couldn't trust anybody. What a terrible way to feel at twelve! I wish the public knew how bad those guys were and how much they lied to them.

Wow! I better pay attention to my driving, I thought as I saw a couple of cars off the road. It was getting slippery! I was relieved when I pulled up outside daddy's house.

"Hello," said daddy with a surprised look as he opened the door. "Come in. I never thought I'd see *you* here."

"I thought it was about time I came to visit you," I said.

"Good," he said. "I'm having some soup. Would you like some?"

"No thank you."

"What brings you here?"

"I just thought I'd like to see you." I gave him a smile. "It's been a long time now. I brought some pictures of my kids. I thought you might like to see your grandchildren."

Daddy shuffled through the pictures casually. He had never seen the kids. When Kenneth was born, he actually called the hospital all excited about having his first grandchild, and it was a boy. The nurse told me about it. And yet he never asked one question about any of the pictures. He handed them back to me.

"Oh, by the way, daddy," I said, "I've gone back to school to get my diploma!"

"That's nice," he said as he reached for a beer from the fridge. So his drinking hadn't changed any, I thought.

"I'm glad you're here," said daddy. "There's some things that I want to tell you about your mother."

I couldn't believe it! The last time I saw him I had to listen to him blast Cecile and me out for an hour about quitting school and how important it was to have a diploma if we wanted to get anywhere in life—and now all he could say was 'that's nice!' Was that *it?* I could see just how important it really was to him—no more important than his grandchildren were to him. He only wanted to hear himself talk and maybe play daddy for a few hours. What a disappointment, I thought. Why did I come to see him? I didn't need his approval. He was never there when I was little, so why should I think he would be there for me now?

Oh daddy, I just wanted you to be proud of me, just one time daddy, just once... I thought as I held back the tears.

"Sit here," said daddy. "You know, it wasn't me who deserted you kids, it was your mother. I had nothing to do with it. Your mother used to run around on me."

"I didn't come here to talk about my mother," I said. "I came here to see *you*."

"You need to hear these things," he said gruffly. "Your mother isn't a good person. She ran off with a man."

"Stop, daddy!" I said. "I'm only going to tell you one more time. I don't want to hear anything about mama—not one more word, or I'll leave."

"Okay," he said. "I won't say anything else."

That lasted for about five minutes.

"I treated your mother like a queen," he continued. "I did everything for her, and look what she did to me!"

"Who are you trying to convince, daddy?" I asked. "Me or yourself? I was *there*, daddy. I remember everything you did to mama—I was there!" I yelled.

"Your mother is nothing but a whore!" he screamed back at me.

I got up from my chair without saying another word to him and walked to the door. He reached for me just like he did when I was little.

I'm a little faster now, daddy, I thought as I escaped and walked to my car. It didn't take me long to clean off my windshield. It had stopped snowing, but I knew the roads wouldn't be too good. I had planned on staying the night at daddy's.

"You get back *here!*" screamed daddy. "I'm your father and you're going to listen to me! You hear me, Emelia! *Get back here!*"

I paid no attention to him. *I'm not afraid of you anymore daddy,* I thought. *I would rather drive the hundred miles back to mama's than stay here and listen to your lies.*

Clearly, I meant nothing to him. Daddy wasn't interested in me or my kids. He only wanted to make himself look good to me and make mama look bad. *It won't work daddy!* I cried. That moment of hopeless anguish, as I drove away, will forever be in my mind, just as though it had happened yesterday.

I was happy to get back to my busy life. It helped to stop me from remembering the past as a child and the pain I was still having from feeling empty inside with George gone.

At least school gave me something better to think about. I was determined more than ever to get my diploma and to get it with good marks.

I couldn't have done it without mama's help.

I hated History. Mama would read the chapter, then write down all the important things for me to study. Mathematics was my strong subject—I averaged in the high nineties in both classes. I thought for sure I would win the award, but another senior beat me by one tenth of a percent. I was so disappointed. Then, to my total amazement, I received the award for highest average in English! What a surprise that was!

Jerry's friend John had come home on leave for Christmas. I ran into him and again he asked me out.

"You know, I'm not kidding," he said. "I want us to get together."

"I always thought you were joking around," I said.

"No, I'm not," he said. "I'm serious. How about Christmas night? I'll pick you up at 6:00 sharp."

"Okay," I said. "I'll be ready."

"Great!" he said. "I'll see you then."

I went out and bought a new dress and had my hair done up. It was kind of exciting. I hadn't been out on a date in I don't know how long. It's funny, I'd known this guy for a long time, yet I was still getting butterflies in my stomach.

I was all dressed up and ready to go.

6:00 pm came around but he never arrived!

I was so upset with him for doing that to me! I took a ride to his house to see if his car was in the driveway. It was—along with about ten others. It was 9:00 p.m. and there was a party going on. I saw him come walking out of the house with each arm around a girl. He walked them to their cars, gave them each a quick kiss and went back into the house. I drove back home.

I couldn't believe I went and spent money on a dress and having my hair done! I knew I should have known better!

"Maybe he forgot," said mama.

"Mama, this guy has been asking me out forever!" I said. "I finally say yes and look what he does!" I sighed, exasperated. "I'm going to bed mama," I said.

"Aren't you going to wrap your hair up with tissue?" she asked.

"No, why bother," I said. "Some time in the morning after the kids open up their presents I'll take all the hairpins out and wash it."

I said goodnight and went to my bedroom. The next morning the kids were so excited when they saw that Santa had come. I played with them all day. We all had fun, even mama and step dad.

At 5:00 p.m. the phone rang.

"Don't forget our date tonight!" said John. "I'll be there in an hour to pick you up."

I said nothing, stunned. Had I got the wrong night?

"Hello?" he said. "You forgot, didn't you?"

"Of course not," I said, thinking quickly. "I'll be ready—see you then."

I ran to tell mama. "Mama! The date is *tonight!* Not last night!" I said. "Dumb me! I thought he said Christmas Eve! He must have said Christmas Night!"

"Look at you!" mama laughed. "Your hair's a mess!"

"I *know*," I said. "Mama, please help me take out the hairpins. I'll redo it myself."

I only had one hour to transform myself to the way I looked the night before.

I made it just in time. By the look on his face, I must have turned out all right.

We had a great evening. There were no bands playing anywhere, but we did find a small place that had a jukebox and he played one song after another and we danced all night.

On the way home he stopped at one of his sisters' houses. It was a terrible time to visit, but she didn't mind at all.

We stayed there for some time. In fact, I fell asleep while we visited. I apologized when I woke. Both he and his sister laughed. "It's okay," she said. "My brother told me about your long hours between work and school. You must be tired."

"It still wasn't very nice of me to do that," I said as he was leading me out the door.

We got back to mama's at 2:50 a.m. I realized that I had left my key chain at home. I didn't have the house key to get in and I didn't want to wake anyone, so we sat in the car and talked. I found out in a round-about way that the party at his house the night before was the family Christmas party and the two girls that he walked out of the house with were two of his nieces that he hadn't seen in a long time.

It got to be 5:00 a.m.

"Sara Spa is open," he said. "Do you want to go and have some breakfast?"

"Sounds good!" I said. It was only a short distance away in town, less than a mile away, I thought.

"Great!" he said. "I'm hungry."

We got back to the house at 6:30 a.m.

"Oh no!" I said.

"Now what's wrong?"

"Mama is angry."

"How do you know that?"

"It's only 6:30 in the morning and I can hear the vacuum cleaner running. Mama always works around the house when she's mad about something. I should have left her a note when we were here earlier. She's probably been worried about me."

"Is there anything I can do to help?"

"Yes," I said, brightening. "I have an idea. Just go along with everything I say, okay?"

"I'll do whatever you want," he smiled.

"Mama likes you a lot, so this might put her in a better mood—but don't get nervous. I can fix it later."

Mama didn't say a word to me when we went in. She had that look about her that made you just *know* you had to tread carefully! John took a seat and mama finally stopped the vacuum cleaner.

"Mama, I have good news!" I said.

"You do?" she said in a low tone of voice that gave away her bad mood.

"We're getting married!" I announced.

I thought John was going to fall out of the chair when I said that. I chuckled to myself.

"You are!" exclaimed mama.

"That's right, mother," he said, a little dazed.

The smile on mama's face was such a relief to me.

"We'll have to talk about it later, mama," I said. "He has to drive back to Virginia today."

I walked him out to the car. We were both laughing.

"You could have warned me!" he said

"I kind of enjoyed your reaction," I laughed.

"How are you going to get out of this one?" he asked.

I shrugged. "Oh, I'll wait a couple of weeks, then I'll tell her that we changed our minds. Thank you so much for helping me out!" My smile faded when I noticed the bemused look on his face. "What?" I asked.

"You know," he said thoughtfully, "that doesn't sound like a bad idea."

"What doesn't?" I asked.

"Getting married," he said.

"Don't be silly," I laughed. "I only said that to get out of trouble with mama! Are you crazy?"

"Only about you," he smiled. "Just think about it, okay?" He got into his car, leaving me in a stunned silence. "I'll write you," he said as he drove away.

He can't be serious! I thought.

But he was. The letters started coming in—one right after another. They were written with the most beautiful words I had ever read. It didn't take me long to say yes.

I fell deeply in love with him. Kenneth, now four, and Lisa, three, adored him.

Jerry is going to be so surprised when he finds out that I'll be getting married to his best friend! I thought. *I* certainly was!

I put in for my vacation from work for April and we were married on April 25th, 1970, during my school vacation.

Graduation day arrived. I just wanted to pick up my diploma, but mama had different ideas.

"I've never seen one of my kids graduate," she said. "Please do this for me!"

She had worked so hard to help me out and I thought the least I could do was to let her have her way. So I agreed to attend the graduation ceremony and I'm pleased I did. It was nice seeing my new husband, two children, step dad and mama sitting in the audience. Mama looked so proud when I went to pin her flower on, seeing me as the center of attention. What a great feeling that was!

So I graduated with four A's and three B's!

There was only one thing missing. Daddy didn't come.

But I wasn't going to let that ruin my day—the day mama and I had worked so hard for.

24

Our daughter Cindi was born on May 24th, 1971, thirteen months after we were married.

Twelve years later we were surprised with a son, Shaun, who was born on October 5th, 1983.

My husband had adopted Kenneth and Lisa before they started school. I felt my life had finally come together.

In late 1985 mama told me that Jerry was suffering from headaches. I spoke to Jerry. He said that his doctor told him it looked like it could be an abscess, that's all. Just before Jerry got out of the service he married a girl he met in North Carolina. He took up residence there after his discharge.

Jerry and his wife had three children—a son and two daughters. The youngest daughter had a stroke when she was born, but it was never noticed until she started walking. She went through many surgeries to correct the problem.

Jerry's headaches were better, so he decided to take a trip home to New Hampshire with his family. He did all the driving—his wife didn't know how he managed it at the time.

It was great having him around. It had been a considerable time since I'd seen him.

John and I took Jerry and his wife out to a special dinner that had a well–known guest speaker, an evangelist, that he wanted to hear. Jerry worked full–time as a machinist for a cigarette company in North Carolina, but he was also studying to be a minister—which is why he was so interested in this speaker.

We had finished our dinner when I noticed there was something wrong with Jerry. I asked his wife, but she said he was fine. A few minutes passed before I noticed Jerry was in a dead stare. It looked like he was beginning to drool. I said something to John and we walked Jerry out of the building. We wanted to call an ambulance, but his wife didn't want us to.

John went to get the car. Jerry's wife had now become hysterical, since Jerry wouldn't respond to anything and his balance was off.

I was so scared. I wrapped my arms around my brother and whispered the Lord's Prayer in his ear.

We got him to the hospital that was only a few miles from where we were. The doctor there called Jerry's doctor in North Carolina and found out he didn't have an abscess, but a brain tumor. Without surgery they only gave him six to eight months to live. So—that was why he took an unscheduled trip home, I realized. Clearly he had known, but he didn't tell any of us—and now my Jerry might die! This couldn't be happening, I thought—there must be a mistake!

The doctor told us there was a good chance that Jerry wouldn't make the trip back home. He could die on the way. Also, he said, once the damage was done there was no making it better.

We got Jerry back into the car and started on our way back to mama's house. We were a good hour away from her.

What am I going to tell mama? I asked myself.

I kept talking to Jerry all the way home. Ten minutes before we got there, Jerry started answering my questions. Within the remaining ten minutes he was able to carry a conversation with me—not one hundred percent, but close to it. He remembered nothing of what just happened.

I had everyone stay in the car so I could prepare mama for the change she was about to see in her son.

"I know, Emelia," said mama in a broken voice. "I know that Jerry has a brain tumor. We are going to have to deal with it the best we can. We have to be strong for him." I began to cry and mama put her arms around me. "Now Emelia," she said, "pull yourself together and go bring Jerry into the house."

I led Jerry in by the hand. He looked around, saw mama and gave her a broad smile.

"Hi mommy," he said.

"Hi Jerry," said mama as she put her arms around him, fighting back every tear that was so close to betraying her feelings.

I was so glad that mama hadn't seen him an hour before.

She tried to get Jerry a flight home, but the airline wouldn't take him because of what could happen, and they didn't want the responsibility.

Mama took John and I aside.

"Will you two drive Jerry and his family home in their car, then fly back?" she asked.

"Oh mama!" I said. "I can't! I can't be in the car thinking that my Jerry could die on the way home! I can't deal with that. I don't want to see my brother die! Please mama, don't ask me to do that!" I pleaded.

I forgot that my John was Jerry's best friend.

"I'll drive him home, mom," he said. "Emelia doesn't have to go."

"Thank you," said mama. "Ben will go with you, then the two of you can fly back together."

"I'm sorry, mama," I said.

"It's okay, Emelia," said mama. "I understand. I know you and Jerry are close."

So my husband and step dad left that same night for their nine-hundred–mile trip.

Jerry made it back without any problems on the way. I was so thankful to John for doing that for mama. I was thankful to step dad, too—there isn't anything he wouldn't do for mama. It was a big relief to mama and I when Jerry made it home safely. Three weeks after Jerry was home he went into surgery. Mama and Cecile flew to North Carolina to be there when he woke. I still couldn't bring myself to being there in case he died.

When my vacation came up, I finally went to see Jerry and stayed the week with him. John and I went to chemotherapy with him each time he went during the time we were there.

I prayed that his headaches would get better. *Dear God, please give me the overflow of his pain that is so unbearable for him.*

I found out one thing for sure—God answers prayers! I had an instant headache, but it was nice to see that Jerry wasn't in as much pain as he had been. *Boy, if this is the overflow, I'm glad I didn't ask for the whole thing!* I thought.

What terrible pain he must have been in.

The week went by quickly. It was time for our long ride back to New Hampshire. Jerry came up to the van window.

"I hate to see you leave, sis," he said.

"I know," I said. "I hate leaving."

"I *really* hate to see you leave," said Jerry.

"I know, Jerry," I said. "I don't want to leave—but I have to go back to work."

Jerry shook his head. "You don't understand, Emelia," he said. Then he stuck his head into the window space of the van and kissed me. He whispered in my ear. "You have to be careful for what you pray for," he said. "How's your headache?"

I couldn't say a word. How did he know? I never let on to anyone that I even had a headache, let alone prayed about it.

Jerry looked at me and smiled.

I love you so much, Jerry, I thought as I smiled back at him.

The surgery that Jerry had did nothing for him. The tumor was interwoven into the brain tissue. His chances were still six to eight months at best.

Jerry would never see forty, I thought. He had just turned thirty-nine.

Mama called him every week to see how he was doing. At first she could talk to him, but after a while she had to talk to Jerry's wife.

It was going on eight months and mama wanted all of us to go to North Carolina for thanksgiving dinner. Leo and Albert were already down there. After both of them were married, they all ended up moving to North Carolina. Jerry had been instrumental in getting them each a good job.

Mama was happy that her boys were all together. At least Jerry had his brothers with him, she would say—not that Jerry's wife wasn't taking good care of him, because she was.

We left right after work on a Wednesday night and got there late Thursday. We celebrated thanksgiving on Friday and left Saturday morning and were home late Sunday night. It was an eighteen–hundred–mile trip, but it had been worth every mile.

Jerry didn't know any of us, but it was wonderful being around him one more time. He thought I was his girlfriend and I was not to tell his wife, but I'm not sure who he thought his wife was—he kept changing his mind.

Mama would light up like a Christmas tree every time she managed to get Jerry to sit down long enough so she could try and talk to him. It reminded me of all the times she would tell Jerry that he was the joy of her heart, but I also knew that we all were. Mama had no favorites. We were all the same in her eyes.

We all went back to our busy lives. Mama continued to call to check on Jerry once a week.

A year went by and it was almost two years since they told Jerry of his cancer. He had just celebrated his forty–first birthday. It had been hard on his wife and kids who were with him every day. It was also hard on mama.

I tried not to think about it, though I prayed for God's will for him every day.

"You haven't been asking me about Jerry," said mama. "He's not doing good."

"I know, mama," I said. "Someday I'm going to be able to talk to him."

"Emelia," said mama. "Jerry is too far gone for you to be able to talk to him. He doesn't understand anything."

"Mama," I said, "In my heart I know that I will talk to him again. I can't explain it. It's like a promise from God. I know it will happen and I also know that He will let me know when that time comes."

Another year passed. Jerry would turn forty–two in three days. Every night after work I stopped at mama's to pick up Shaun on my way home. Mama took care of him—he was five years old then. I was so used to stopping that I automatically stopped on Saturdays after work.

Shaun usually hung out with his father until I got home shortly after noon.

I sat down to have a chat with mama and jumped right back up on my feet.

"What's the matter?" asked mama.

"I have to go!" I said.

"Go? You just got here," said mama.

"I know, mama, but I *have* to go right now!"

"Why?" She looked at me, confused.

"I have to go and call up Jerry."

"Oh, Emelia, don't put yourself through that," pleaded mama. "I called him yesterday for his birthday and he couldn't even come to the phone to hear me say it. Please, Emelia, don't do this to yourself."

"It will be okay, mama," I said. "But I must go. It's time! I've waited three years for this! I'll call you later." Then I rushed out the door.

What usually took thirty minutes to drive only took twenty–two. *Good,* I thought, *no one is home right now—it will be quiet to call Jerry.*

I dialed his number. I was so excited. It felt like my heart was trying to get out.

"Hello," the voice said.

"Jerry?" I asked.

"Yes," he said. "It's me. How are you?"

"I'm okay," I said. "Do you know who this is?"

"Of course I do," he laughed. "It's *sheote!*"

How I hated that name, but it sure sounded good this time. *He can call me an outhouse any old time he wants to!* I thought.

"Do you think I would forget my baby sister?" he asked.

Not only could Jerry talk—he understood everything we were talking about.

"Where is everybody?" I asked.

"The kids have gone out and my wife dozed off on the couch."

Jerry and I talked just under two hours and he did most of the talking, recalling times from when we were kids growing up to telling me not to worry about him. He was going back into surgery the following week. The doctors were going to try and relieve the pressure the tumor was putting on one of his eyes. It was causing it to go blind and his headaches had increased.

"Emelia," said Jerry. "I'll be going home soon."

"I know, Jerry," I said, trying to hold back the tears.

"Don't cry, Emelia," said Jerry. "Be happy for me. I'll be with my father in heaven."

"I know, Jerry," I cried. There was no holding it back anymore. The tears flowed as we said our goodbyes.

Just like I knew in my heart that I would talk to Jerry someday, I also knew that would be the last time I would ever hear his voice again.

Thank you God for keeping your promise to me, I cried as I sat quietly in the living room chair.

Jerry went in for his surgery like he said.

Mama and step dad drove to North Carolina to see him in the hospital. Mama sat down on Jerry's bed and took his hand into hers. It had been two days now and Jerry hadn't come to yet.

"Jerry," said mama. "Jerry, it's mommy."

Jerry turned his head to mama's voice and opened his good eye. "Mommy," he said, then he closed his eye and turned his head back to where it was before.

Mama would find out later on from Jerry's wife that that word—Mommy—was the last word Jerry ever said.

The doctors didn't know how long Jerry would live. Mama and step dad traveled back to New Hampshire. Jerry's wife agreed to call mama if there were any changes.

I hadn't heard anything yet. It had been two weeks going on three since Jerry's surgery.

Thursday night I started to feel fidgety. By Friday I was ready to pull my hair out. Friday afternoon I realized what was wrong.

Jerry was going to die that weekend—I was sure of it.

People started asking me what my problem was.

I told them that I had to get everything done, that I wouldn't be there on Monday. They asked me why and I told them. They thought I was crazy. It didn't matter what they thought—I knew that it would come to pass.

I went into work on Saturday morning to finish putting a cement machine together and got it running. I made sure my boss knew I would be out for a few days for what was about to happen.

"I'll see you Monday," he said as he left the building.

I know you won't see me Monday, I thought as I finally left.

I was late getting home. It was after 1 p.m. I took a shower, then packed a suitcase for John, Shaun and myself. I wasn't dressed yet when John came home. I had forgotten to gas the car up, so I asked him to.

"You can gas up the car tomorrow," he said. "You're not going anywhere today, are you?"

"Please go fill the car up," I said. "We have to be ready."

He finally said he would and left.

"Check the oil too," I said as he went out the door.

When he got home, I asked him to put the suitcase in the car.

"Aren't you kind of overdoing it?" he asked.

"Please, John," I said.

"Emelia!" he protested.

"Never mind," I said. "I'll do it myself."

"Okay, okay!" he said. "I'll do it, but I'm only going to have to take it out again later."

My girlfriend lived three or four houses down the road from me. She was in her yard. John motioned for her to come over and she did.

"What's wrong?" she asked me.

"I'm waiting for a phone call," I said. "Jerry is dying."

"Emelia," she said, "you know he doesn't have much more time to live. Why are you flipping out on everyone today?"

I sat down with her at the table for a few minutes, then stood up.

"Now what's wrong?" she asked.

"I have to call the hospital right now," I said. "I have to find out how Jerry's doing."

I went to the phone, dialed the number, then hung up the phone.

An overwhelming peace came over me. I sat back down.

"I thought you were going to call the hospital?" my friend asked.

"I was," I said.

"Why didn't you?" she asked.

"Jerry just died," I said.

"You can't be serious!" she said.

"Yes, I am."

"What are you going to do now?"

"I'm going to wait half an hour to give them enough time to tell Jerry's wife and kids, then I'll call the hospital."

Thirty minutes went by and I called. They hooked me up with the nurse's station near Jerry's room.

"Hi, this is Emelia calling from New Hampshire. I'm calling to find out how Jerry Dion is doing."

"Are you a relative of his?" she asked.

"Yes, I am," I said. "Jerry is my brother."

"We haven't been able to reach his wife yet." She paused. "I'm so sorry—your brother died half an hour ago."

I hung up the phone.

"What did they say?" asked my girlfriend.

"Jerry died half an hour ago," I said.

Now I knew why this happened the way it did. *Thank you God*, I said. *I didn't have to hear that my Jerry died through mama's tears, and mama doesn't have to hear that her son died from nine hundred miles away. This way I'm the one that has to tell her. I can be with her to comfort her. She won't be alone.*

John, Shaun and I got into the car and headed for mama's. A few hours went by before we could leave. Mama had to pack and we waited for Leo who had moved back to New Hampshire the year before, and for Cecile.

There were four drivers in mama's car—Cecile, Leo, step dad and mama.

John, who felt bad about things that happened earlier, Shaun and myself went in my car. It would have been too crowded to all go in one car.

I had been so wound up for two days that I did all the driving in my car. My husband had been up most of the night pumping out water in someone's cellar and he couldn't keep his eyes open. Mama wanted Leo to relieve me for a while, but I couldn't rest, so I went right back to driving.

Daddy showed up the day of the funeral. He walked up to mama. "My condolences on the death of your son," he said.

Mama just looked at him with tears filling her eyes and didn't say a word.

Oh daddy, how could you be so cruel to mama, I thought. *When Jerry was alive you could never tell mama to her face that he was your son, even though you knew he was. You had to play your little games at someone else's expense. Now, with Jerry's death, you're too proud to say OUR son!*

I feel deep down inside of me that you, Jerry's own daddy, are the one that brought this on to him. There were all those times you grabbed him by the hair of his head and banged his head over and over again against the wall!

Yes, in my heart I knew that Jerry's tumor started a long time ago—when he was just a little boy.

Jerry celebrated his forty–second birthday on January 31st, 1988, and died nineteen days later on February 19th, 1989.

I thank God that Jerry died with the same grace that he lived by.

25

In September of 1989 I received a phone call telling me that daddy died. A heart attack, I was told.

I'd been to four other funerals in Berlin, N.H., in the seven months since I went to North Carolina for Jerry's. Two of them were for my uncles and two for my aunts, different families but all on daddy's side.

One of them was uncle Al—he was my favorite. Jerry stayed with him when all us kids were separated.

I still can't believe that he and daddy were brothers. They seemed to be complete opposites. I adored uncle Al and aunt L. She passed away later on. I wonder if they knew how much I cared for them? I guess I should have made it a point to tell them.

I called mama to tell her about daddy.

"Are you sure?" asked mama.

"Yes," I said.

"I'll get hold of Leo and Albert," said mama. "What about Cecile?"

"I'm sure she got the same phone call that I did," I said. "But I'll make sure. Will you be going to the funeral, mama?"

"No," she replied. "But do me a favor?" she asked. "Will you make sure it's him?"

"Oh mama!" I said.

I remember when mommie died a few years ago. I wasn't the only one that mommie treated badly. She hated mama and wasn't very nice to her. She never wanted daddy to marry her in the first place and she made that pretty clear every time we were around her. Poppie, on the other hand, loved mama and treated her real nice. When mommie died, mama went to the funeral. I think she wanted to see poppie again, for it had been many years since she had seen him. When I asked her mama confirmed that she did want to see poppie again.

"Yes," she said, "You're right, I wanted to see poppie again," and then she added: "But I can't tell a lie—I also wanted to make sure that bitch was dead!"

"Mama!" I said.

"You want me to be honest, don't you?" she asked.

"Yes," I said. "It's okay, mama, I feel the same way. They were two of the same kind, her and daddy."

When I went to mommie's house after the funeral, I tried to make myself go up to the third floor, but all I could do was stare at the door that led to it. I thought if I went up there that I could make the nightmares go away.

I tried again when poppie died and I still couldn't make myself do it. Now it's too late—the house is sold.

"Okay mama," I said this time. "I'll make sure it's him."

I ordered the flowers at a local flower shop, then picked them up on my way to Berlin.

Albert and Cecile came with me in my car. My husband John would join us in a few hours and Leo would meet us there later that evening. We split up in two motel rooms.

Later that night, Leo, Albert, Cecile and John all had a few drinks. Cecile managed to contact some of our cousins that mommie had disowned years earlier.

Maybe this is what it took for daddy to be proud of us: we had a party—in his honor, of course!

I'm not sure what time the party ended, but it was after midnight when John and I went to bed.

I couldn't help but feel how daddy looked so harmless lying there in his casket. I looked at him and the questions ran through my mind.

Look at you now, daddy! What did you gain from all your abuse?
Why did you always hurt mama, daddy? She never hurt you.
Why couldn't you have been there for us, daddy? We were there
for you.
Why didn't you love us daddy? We loved you.
Why did you have to be so cruel, daddy?
Why Daddy, Why?

Now it was too late for daddy to make amends, for he was gone.
Jerry's death started the year off—and his ended it.

Daddy always told us that when he died all of us would get plenty of
money. That was the way he put it, and he did have plenty. I guess it
wasn't meant to be, though—someone else got it all. His children got
nothing. Mama never even got the two thousand dollars that he owed
her, though she never really expected it anyway. None of us did. His
life was a disappointment to his family, so why should his death be any
different? It wasn't so much that we didn't get anything—it was the
fact that again daddy had lied to us. If he really wanted us to have
something, then he could have protected our inheritance. Instead, he
chose not to, and someone else got it all. The sad part about it was that
that 'someone else' could have done the right thing, but so far has cho-
sen not to. But who knows, maybe some day she might have a change
of heart—after all, it's only been twelve years since daddy died!

Mama stopped by where I worked. It must be important, I thought,
for she never bothered me at work. The company didn't mind—I'd
been with them for fifteen years, and that would eventually stretch into
twenty–five before they closed their doors for good. I had worked my
way up to the position of foreman. I remember how pleased I was and
told daddy about it, and he told me I should be a secretary—they make
more money! I realized that it didn't matter what I became, it would

never be good enough for daddy. My husband was proud of me and that's all that mattered.

"What's up, mama," I asked.

"I want to tell you about a phone call that I got," she said breathlessly. "I'll explain after."

We went to a quiet place. "Who called you, mama?" I asked.

"Well, the phone rang and I answered it…"

◆   ◆   ◆

"Hello," mama said.

"Hi," a man's voice answered. "Is this Irene?"

"Yes, it is."

"Someone gave me your name. They told me that you might be able to help me out."

"Help you out?" asked mama.

"They thought you might have some information that could help me find my parents."

Mama's heart missed a beat. Could this be Paul?

"To whom am I speaking?" she asked. She could hardly wait for the answer and held her breath.

"Oh, I'm sorry, this is Stephen. I live in California."

Mama's heart sank. "I don't know how I can be of any help to you," she said.

"They told me that you worked at the orphanage in Manchester, N.H., back in 1945?"

"Yes, I did work there during that time."

"You did? Well, I was born in 1945. All I could find out was that my father wouldn't let my mother take me home and I was adopted when I was a year old. Do you remember anything like that?"

Mama went quiet on the other end.

"Hello?" he said. "Are you still there?"

"Yes," said mama. "I'm still here."

"Oh, and by the way, my birth mother named me Paul."

"Paul!"

"Yes. Do you have any idea where I can go from here?"

"Yes, I do!" said mama, her heart racing. "*I'm* your mother! I can't believe it—you *found* me! You have no idea how much I have prayed for this day!"

◆　　　◆　　　◆

"Paul?" I said.

"Yes!" smiled mama.

"Mama, I remember that name growing up!"

"You do?"

"Yes. Jerry and I used to ask each other who Paul was. Daddy kept asking you who his father was."

"That's right! But your father asked me who the father was of all you kids!"

"I know, I remember." It felt like the floor was dissolving under my feet. "So I have *another* brother?"

"Yes! Your father gave him away to be adopted. He said that he wasn't the father—but he *was!* Your father had a sick mind."

"You don't have to tell me, mama," I smiled sadly. "I was there living his sick mind."

Mama and step dad went and picked up Paul and his wife at the Portsmouth N.H. bus station on January 8th, 1990.

Mama got us all together at her house to meet him and his wife. It was a wonderful reunion. I wished Jerry could have been there. I think he would have appreciated the fact that he had an older brother.

How do you like that, daddy? I asked myself. *Paul is back! And there's nothing you can do about it.*

It was nice seeing mama smile again. The loss of Jerry took a lot out of her. I pray to God that I never have to bury one of my children the way she had to. That has to be the hardest thing a parent could ever do. It's just not natural.

John and I were having problems after almost twenty–two years of marriage.

Even though I loved him as much as I did the day I married him, we were divorced.

We had a lot of good times and we had bad times too. The bad started to outweigh the good.

Everyone thought that he and I would be together forever, and so did I—but things don't always happen the way you want them to.

Many things took place that hurt too much to talk about. Maybe someday I'll be able to face it head on, the way I'm facing the rest of my past. Who knows?

The good thing that happened was I was remarried to a wonderful man almost six years later. Bob is fourteen years my senior but you wouldn't know it. He is about to celebrate his sixty–fifth birthday and is still not doing too bad for having had open–heart surgery and just recently suffering a stroke during another surgery. Bob is very limited now in what he can do, but he does try to do as much as he can. I really do appreciate him.

Shaun is eighteen and is a senior in high school. He still lives at home with us in Dover, N.H.

Cindi is married to a real nice guy. They have three children and live in North Carolina.

Lisa also lives in North Carolina with her two daughters. Kenneth is married to a wonderful girl and they live in California. They are still hoping for children.

John, my ex–husband, is doing fine, and I wish him all the best in the world.

My first husband, Kenny, died a few years ago from throat cancer.

Paul and his wife moved to Farmington, N.H., where Leo and his wife live with their children.

Albert resides in Concord, N.H. He's not married anymore but he does have three great kids, and his ex–wife is my best friend and has been for a good number of years.

Cecile has two grown daughters and she and her husband live in Sanbornville, N.H.

Mama and step dad live in Rochester, N.H. They have been married for thirty–nine years now.

Step dad is the greatest dad that anyone could ever have. Daddy was angry with me a long time ago when he heard me call him dad.

"*I'm* your dad!" he said. "You don't call anyone else dad but me. I fathered you, not Ben!"

"Nice time to want to be a father to me!" I said. "As far as I'm concerned, Ben has been more of a dad to me than you ever thought of being." Then I added: "You know something, daddy? Any man can father a child, but it takes someone very special to be a dad—and that's Ben. He has earned that respect and he deserves that honor."

Daddy never mentioned it again. The only reason he said something in the first place was because he had remarried and wanted me to call his new wife mom. I have nothing against her—it's just that only my mama has that honor.

My mama didn't just give birth to me—she cherished me and protected me.

Even though we all live in different towns and cities in New Hampshire, mama and I are still only twenty miles from each other. At least once, maybe twice a year, mama has a cookout at her house and brings us all together, and what a good time we have!

Mama showed me how to be strong, to go on with life no matter what. Now when I come to that park bench where the Columbia Hotel stood before it burnt down, I don't have to be sad anymore. The grass under my feet and the cool breeze on my face are welcome reminders that the bad old days are gone.

I visit George's grave every year, and have done so for the past thirty–two years. I still miss him. I always will.

I spend every thanksgiving and Christmas with mama. She is my favorite person in the whole world.

I have forgiven daddy. I go to the cemetery every year to see him, to put flowers on his grave and to tell him that I love him.

Best of all, I have come to realize that God has been with me every step of the way—and I know that He will be with me until the end.

THE END

0-595-21498-3